China's New Public Health Insurance

Especially since the 2003 SARS crisis, China's healthcare system has become a growing source of concern, both for citizens and the Chinese government. China's once praised public health services have deteriorated into a system driven by economic constraints, in which poor people often fail to get access, and middle-income households risk to be dragged into poverty by the rising costs of care. The New Rural Co-operative Medical System (NRCMS) was introduced to counter these tendencies and constitutes the main system of public health insurance in China today. This book outlines the nature of the system, traces the processes of its enactment and implementation, and discusses its strengths and weaknesses. It argues that the contested nature of the fields of health policy and social security has long been overlooked, and reinterprets the NRCMS as a compromise between opposing political interests. Furthermore, it argues that structural institutional misfits facilitate fiscal imbalances and a culture of non-compliance in local health policy, which distort the outcomes of the implementation and limit the effectiveness of insurance. These dynamics also raise fundamental questions regarding the effectiveness of other areas of the comprehensive New Health Reform, which China has initiated to overhaul its healthcare system.

Armin Müller is a Postdoctoral Fellow at Georg-August-University in Göttingen, Germany.

China Policy Series

Series Editor: Zheng Yongnian, East Asian Institute, National University of Singapore

China's New Public Health Insurance

Insurance

Challenges to Health Reforms and the
New Rural Co-operative Medical System

Armin Müller

Routledge
Taylor & Francis Group

LONDON AND NEW YORK

First published 2017
by Routledge

2 Park Square, Milton Park, Abingdon, Oxfordshire OX14 4RN
711 Third Avenue, New York, NY 10017

Routledge is an imprint of the Taylor & Francis Group, an informa business

First issued in paperback 2018

Copyright © 2017 Armin Müller

The right of Armin Müller to be identified as author of this work has been asserted by him/her in accordance with sections 77 and 78 of the Copyright, Designs and Patents Act 1988.

All rights reserved. No part of this book may be reprinted or reproduced or utilised in any form or by any electronic, mechanical, or other means, now known or hereafter invented, including photocopying and recording, or in any information storage or retrieval system, without permission in writing from the publishers.

Notice:
Product or corporate names may be trademarks or registered trademarks, and are used only for identification and explanation
without intent to infringe.

British Library Cataloguing in Publication Data
A catalogue record for this book is available from the British Library

Library of Congress Cataloging in Publication Data
Names: Müller, Armin, 1981- author.
Title: China's new public health insurance : challenges to health reforms and
    the new rural co-operative medical system / Armin Müller.
Other titles: China policy series ; 47.
Description: Abingdon, Oxon ; New York, NY : Routledge, 2017. | Series:
    China policy series ; 47 | Includes bibliographical references and index.
Identifiers: LCCN 2016022167| ISBN 9781138639065 (hardback) | ISBN
    9781315624792 (eBook)
Subjects: | MESH: National Health Programs | Health Care Reform | China
Classification: LCC HG9399.C62 | NLM WA 540 JC6 | DDC 368.4/
    200951–dc23
LC record available at https://lccn.loc.gov/2016022167

ISBN: 978-1-138-63906-5 (hbk)
ISBN: 978-0-367-02680-6 (pbk)

Typeset in Times New Roman
by Taylor & Francis Books

Contents

List of illustrations

Figures

Tables

Acknowledgement

I am very grateful for the support of various people and organizations, which was indispensable for writing this book. First, I would like to thank the German Research Foundation (DFG), whose sponsorship of the research training group 1613 "Risk and East Asia" at the University of Duisburg-Essen provided me with the financial means and organizational framework to pursue my doctoral research. I remain deeply indebted to my supervisors Thomas Heberer and Gunter Schubert, whose support and guidance have accompanied me through most of my university career. My special gratitude goes to Yu Xianyang, WJY, Yan Shuangwu, YBR and ZH, who helped me organize my fieldwork in rural China, and to Karen Shire and Flemming Christiansen, whose advice and support has always been of considerable value. Furthermore, I would like to thank my interview partners, whom I have assured confidentiality, and the diligent students of Renmin University, Shandong University and Wuhan University, who accompanied me to the field and transcribed most of my interviews. Last but not least, I would like to thank Zheng Yongnian for considering this book for the *China Policy Series*, and the anonymous reviewer for the constructive and conscientious comments which helped to improve the manuscript.

List of Abbreviations

Abbreviation	English—*Pinyin*
ADB	Asian Development Bank
CHFP	Commission of Health and Family Planning—*Weisheng Jihua Shengyu Weiyuanhui*
CIRC	China Insurance Regulatory Commission—*Zhongguo Baoxian Jiandu Guanli Weiyuanhui*
CMS	Cooperative Medical System—*Hezuo yiliao*
CPC	Communist Party of China—*Zhongguo Gongchandang*
DRC	Development and Reform Commission—*Fazhan Gaige Weiyuanhui*
DRG	Diagnosis-Related Groups
FDA	Food and Drug Administration (former State Drug Administration)—*Shipin Yaopin Jianduju*
MoA	Ministry of Agriculture—*Nongyebu*
MoCA	Ministry of Civil Affairs—*Minzhengbu*
MoF	Ministry of Finance—*Caizhengbu*
MoH	Ministry of Health (CHFP since 2013)—*Weishengbu*
MoHRSS	Ministry of Human Resources and Social Security—*Renli Ziyuan he Shehui Baozhangbu*
MoLSS	Ministry of Labor and Social Security (MoHRSS since 2008)—*Laodong he Shehui Baozhangbu*
MSA	Medical savings account—*Jiating zhanghu*
NPFPC	National Population and Family Planning Commission (CHFP since 2013)—*Renkou he Jihua Shengyu Weiyuanhui*
NRCMS	New Rural Cooperative Medical System—*Xinxing nongcun hezuo yiliao*
PBoC	People's Bank of China—*Zhongguo Renmin Yinhang*
PEG	NRCMS Pilot Evaluation Group—*Xinxing Nongcun Hezuo Yiliao Shidian Gongzuo Pingguzu*
PICC	People's Insurance Company of China—*Zhongguo Renmin Baoxian Gongsi*
PRC	People's Republic of China—*Zhonghua Renmin Gongheguo*
PSU	Public service unit—*Shiye danwei*

SARS	Severe acute respiratory syndrome—*Yanzhong jixing huxi zonghezheng*
TCM	Traditional Chinese medicine—*Zhongyi*
THC	Township health center—*Xiangzhen weishengyuan*
UEBMI	Urban Employees' Basic Medical Insurance—*Chengzhen zhigong jiben yiliao baoxian*
URBMI	Urban Residents' Basic Medical Insurance—*Chengzhen jumin jiben yiliao baoxian*
WHO	World Health Organization
WTO	World Trade Organization

1 Introduction

The People's Republic of China was once praised as a model for other developing countries for its healthcare system and the rapid and comprehensive progress it achieved with very limited resources, most notably in the rural areas. At the time, the collective economy and support from leaders of the Communist Party of China (CPC) provided the foundation for these successes, which are largely associated with the barefoot doctors, public health campaigns and cooperative medical care. Barefoot doctors were agricultural workers who received a few months of training to enable them to provide preventive and primary care. Public health campaigns relied on mass mobilization for proper garbage disposal and vermin extermination. Cooperative medical systems (CMSs) used a share of the collective economic resources to finance basic health services in the communes and brigades. These three policy tools strongly depended on collective agriculture as an institutional foundation, either directly or indirectly.

In the course of the 1980s, collective farming was replaced by the household responsibility system—that is, a return to household farming. Among the far-reaching socio-economic consequences of this move was the loss of feasibility or effectiveness of the crucial policy tools of collective rural healthcare. The CMS and the former barefoot doctors were closely associated with the Cultural Revolution, and this image contributed to a lack of political support at the central level. The CMS had been a pet project of Mao Zedong, but it had too few stakeholders in health administration and in the bureaucratic leadership core of the party-state in the early 1980s. With the central government unable or unwilling to provide functional equivalents for the vanishing institutional basis, the rural healthcare system by and large collapsed. The CMSs ceased to operate, campaigns failed to mobilize the rural population—now in control of and depending on its own labor—and village clinics were largely privatized. In the cities, this change was much more gradual in nature and less comprehensive. Nevertheless, in urban and rural China the responsibility to finance the healthcare system and the financial risks of healthcare were shifted to households (Duckett 2011; Heberer 2001).

Between 1980 and 2000, the government's share in healthcare financing had decreased from 36.2 to 15.5 percent, the share of various forms of societal financing such as health insurance and collective economic resources decreased from 42.6 to 25.6 percent, and the share of individual out-of-pocket payments increased from 21.2 to 59 percent (CHFP 2014). State funding displayed a strong urban and public sector bias, with the largest share spent on state cadres' health insurance and large urban hospitals (Huang 2013: 67). The rural healthcare system has been relying almost entirely on out-of-pocket payments from a section of the population often characterized by a chronic scarcity of financial resources. Health service providers were seriously underfunded, and economic constraints and the need to maximize profit therefore came to dominate their interactions with patients. Patients increasingly had to rely on household savings and credit from networks of friendship and kin to pay for ever more expensive hospital bills. People started avoiding visits to the doctor in the event of illness. When they finally went, the illness had often developed to a level of seriousness that was beyond the capacity of the still comparatively cheap township health centers (THCs). Families lacking the financial resources for the urban hospitals often faced extremely tough choices of allocating resources between generations and sexes. Some studies report a concentration of health spending and access to healthcare on the income-generating parts of the family, at the expense of children, the elderly and women (Cailliez 1998; Gu 2005).

The early 2000s were formative years for today's health policy and reforms in China. Illness and accidents had become the most potent poverty generator in the rural areas, and in the urban areas it was catching up fast (MoH 2004). This therefore became a direct threat to the social status of the new middle-income strata in both the urban and rural areas: the illness of a family member could drag an entire household into poverty for a period of time or indefinitely (Liu et al. 2003). The phenomenon of illness-induced poverty was captured in the phrase "descending or re-descending into poverty" (*yinbing zhipin, yinbing fanpin*). Furthermore, the severe acute respiratory syndrome (SARS) crisis in 2003 not only remorselessly exposed the insufficiencies of China's healthcare, disease monitoring and prevention systems, but also illustrated the potentially catastrophic impact of epidemics on economic development (Wong and Zheng 2004). Today, the SARS crisis is regarded as the starting point of a political discussion on the nature of China's health system, which ultimately led to comprehensive health reform in 2009. This New Health Reform (*xin yigai*), scheduled to be completed by 2020, aims to strengthen the role of the state and restore the public-welfare orientation and public-service nature of China's healthcare system, the commercialization of which was officially deemed a failure by important bureaucratic actors in the central government. The period of the Hu and Wen administration has laid the crucial policy foundations for the development of China's health system in the 2010s and beyond (Huang 2013).

The government's self-description with regard to health policy reflects the ideological trends that dominate in the leadership core of the party-state. Experts distinguish between four major phases: before 1978, communist ideology was paramount; between 1978 and 2002, market orientation largely dominated; between 2002 and 2012, a more government-oriented thinking aimed at expanding the role of the state; and under Xi Jinping, there is a renewed emphasis on the market (Yip and Hsiao 2015). Since 2003, bureaucratic actors and public intellectuals have represented pro-government and pro-market attitudes with an unprecedented degree of publicity, thereby somewhat narrowing the gap between governmental self-description and ideology on the one hand and actual politics on the other (Huang 2013).

Throughout this time, health costs have seen an unceasing rise, and violent attacks against doctors and nurses seem to have become a daily phenomenon (Tang et al. 2012). These trends raise serious doubts about the Chinese government's ability to effectively turn around the logics of action in the health sector. The central government has produced numerous decisions and policies. The results of these interventions are, however, often ambiguous. On the program level, they tend to alter specific elements of the health system in the desired way: the introduction of a rural health insurance leads to the reimbursement of health costs, and the abolition of profits for drug sales leads to lower unit prices for drugs. However, on the system level, health costs as an aggregate continue to rise and the financial burden of health costs on rural households continues to increase. Although these phenomena have some "natural" causes, such as the demographic transition, the institutional structures that govern the health system tend to intensify these developments rather than balance them out.

In recent years, academic researchers have increasingly come to acknowledge the complexity of health systems as a challenge to governance and steering. Conceiving of health systems as comprised of actors and functions, they find counterintuitive and non-linear effects as the results of policy interventions (Savigny and Adam 2009; Xiao et al. 2013; Zhang et al. 2014). Others have argued that a governance perspective can shed new light on the problems of Chinese health reforms by analyzing the relationships between government, providers and users, and the incentive structures shaping their preferences (Ramesh et al. 2014). This book relies on a conceptual approach that is new to this field of study and synthesizes the advantages of both these lines of inquiry. It focuses on the strategic interactions of government actors and healthcare providers in the context of the systemic interdependence between the institutional structures of the multi-level state on the one hand and the healthcare system on the other hand. Actors' preferences are strongly conditioned by the context of institutional structures, particularly on the lower administrative levels. Many of the counterintuitive effects of Chinese health policies are rooted in institutional misfits within the public finance system, and between public finances and health sector regulation. To the extent that health sector regulation remains infeasible or unsustainable in practical operations, these institutional misfits breed informal practices, undermine effective policy implementation and contribute to rising health costs.

The production of health policy decisions in the Chinese political system and their implementation in the context of interdependent yet misfit institutional structures are central issues of this study. It focuses on organizational actors in a national and local context. At the center of the inquiry is the case of the New Rural Cooperative Medical System (NRCMS—*xinxing nongcun hezuo yiliao*), a rural health insurance system that has been implemented since 2003. The process of reaching an agreement on the NRCMS in national politics, and its implementation in a local context, illuminates the limitations of decision-making, steering and governance in Chinese health policy. Furthermore, it casts new light on the feasibility and sustainability of the policies under the umbrella of the New Health Reform since 2009, and how structural reforms of public finances, the transformation and formalization of governmental functions, and a more independent legal system can help to decrease the institutional misfits and enhance the Chinese government's capacity to govern and steer the health sector.

Even though the NRCMS is officially part of the New Health Reform, it was largely implemented before 2009. Numerous Chinese and Western studies exist on this topic, which broadens the larger basis of data on which this book can draw. It therefore constitutes the perfect case study to explore the fundamental issues and problems of China's larger health reform agenda, and how prevalent dynamics of political decision-making and the allocation of public finances constrain health reforms.

The New Rural Cooperative Medical System: A Health Insurance for the Rural Areas

Health insurance is an important pillar of China's emerging new welfare regime. Its extension towards universal coverage has been a central part of the 2009 New Health Reform. The basis for this extension had mainly been laid in the decade preceding the New Health Reform, when a new form of mainly tax-funded health insurance was developed and implemented in rural and urban China. In rural China, the NRCMS was implemented between 2003 and 2008. It is China's largest health insurance system, with around 736 million insured as of 2014. The Urban Residents' Basic Medical Insurance (URBMI—*chengzhen jumin jiben yiliao baoxian*) was modeled on the NRCMS; it was enacted in 2007 and covered around 315 million insured by 2014. The two systems complement the Urban Employees Basic Medical Insurance (UEBMI—*chengzhen zhigong jiben yiliao baoxian*) established in 1998 on the basis of the former, *danwei*-based system of worker insurance. As of 2014, it covered 283 million insured (CHFP 2013).

Health insurance in China is fragmented along the lines of formalized employment and the urban–rural divide: the UEBMI mainly covers urban employees with a formal labor contract; the URBMI mainly covers citizens with a non-agricultural household registration and without UEBMI coverage; and the NRCMS primarily covers citizens with an agricultural household registration (Müller 2016). The formal level of funding in the UEBMI covers between 60 and 70 percent of average per capita urban health costs, while overall cost coverage of the NRCMS and the URBMI remains below 30 percent (CHFP 2014). Despite an almost universal coverage of the population, China's fragmented health insurance system is highly unequal in terms of benefits and social protection.

The NRCMS constitutes an adapted form of the old Cooperative Medical System (CMS—*hezuo yiliao*), which had survived in modified form in some pockets of rural China. In the second half of the 1980s and throughout the 1990s, rural health insurance was not a priority issue on the political agenda of the central government. The share of Chinese villages retaining a CMS system usually oscillated between 5 and 10 percent, and rose above 10 percent only temporarily during two policy initiatives in 1991 and 1997. Between 2000 and 2002, the issue was upgraded on the political agenda, and the leadership core clearly began to prefer a rural health insurance system operated and financially supported by the government. In the context of China's social policy, rural health insurance was promoted as a measure of poverty alleviation rather than social insurance. The CMS and the NRCMS were seen as solutions to the problem of illness-induced poverty that was classically associated with expensive inpatient care. However, in the course of the demographic transition and with the rising prevalence of chronic diseases, outpatient and drug expenditure came to play an increasingly important role.

The 2002 reform was followed by a swift extension of the NRCMS: within six years it officially covered all county-level jurisdictions in rural China and more than 90 percent of rural residents. By 2008, the NRCMS spent RMB 66 billion to insure 815 million people—the more established UEBMI spent RMB 208 billion to insure 200 million (MoH 2009b). By 2010, NRCMS spending rose to RMB 119 billion to insure 836 million (MoH 2011). But despite the swift progress in the rural areas, a large urban–rural gap remained.

The NRCMS has two principal sources of financing: premiums from the rural households and contributions from different levels of government. Governmental contributions—the most important source—are organized as a system of matching funds conditional on the previous payment of premiums. In 2011, 14.7 percent of the overall NRCMS funding came from household premiums, 37.7 percent from central transfers and 46.7 percent from the local governments. Among the local transfers, 55.2 percent came from the provinces and 31.9 percent from the counties. In Eastern China, the subnational levels of government shouldered most of the financial burden, whereas in Central and Western China, about half of the funding came from the center. Administrative documents furthermore mention collective support as a source of funding, although its overall impact is marginal (Chen and Zhang 2013: 61–4).

The introduction and extension of the NRCMS was part of the increased political attention given to the rural areas and their population in the first decade of the twenty-first century. Under the heading of the Three Rural Problems (*san nong wenti*) and the Construction of a New Socialist Countryside (*shehui zhuyi xin nongcun jianshe*), an array of development projects was initiated in the rural areas, which received an unprecedented level of financial aid (Schubert and Ahlers 2012). The first decade of the twenty-first century also saw the reintroduction of other public systems of social security in rural China, such as the Minimum Livelihood Guarantee (*zuidi shenghuo baozhang*) and the New Rural Social Pension Insurance (*xinxing nongcun shehui yanglao baoxian*). These programs were part of the new social and developmental policies in the rural areas, but their financial structure went beyond time-limited projects. They established the administrative foundations of a state-organized, largely tax-financed social security system sustained by permanent streams of transfer payments to the rural areas. Furthermore, they constituted part of a governmental strategy of relegitimation through social stability and security (Heberer 2009).

Given their effective consolidation and progressive development, these programs can potentially protect the rural population from social risks related to health, old age, unemployment or poverty. They may also substantially decrease rural households' reliance on savings and credit for coping with social risks and facilitate domestic demand and economic development. However, by creating growing financial burdens on the local governments, there is also the risk of financially overburdening them and rendering them unable to fulfill the center's promises. As this study will show, the effectiveness of China's rural social policy is crucially affected by the dynamics of governing in the local state and by institutional misfits.

The Conceptual Approach and Rationale of this Book

Previous research on the NRCMS has been largely concentrated in the fields of health economics, social-scientific health studies and China studies. Research in the first of these two fields is dominated by quantitative methodology, as well as (often) a strict adherence to methodological individualism and the idea of identifying optimal policy options (see, for example: Babiarz et al. 2010; Ma et al. 2012; Wagstaff et al. 2009; Wagstaff and Lindelow 2008; Wang et al. 2008; Zhang et al. 2010). These analytical and methodological choices narrow the scope of research questions. They leave a substantial gap in research, most notably regarding inter-organizational processes and phenomena difficult to measure and analyze quantitatively for methodological or practical reasons. Furthermore, there is often an implicit notion of the (central or local) government as a solitary decision-maker constrained primarily by practical constraints, such as scarce resources and state capacity. Finally, in particular those studies following a classic principal-agent approach suffer from the lack of sensitivity to structural contextual factors that is inherent in this approach (Kiser 1999).

In China studies, qualitative research is more prevalent, but the number of studies on the NRCMS is much smaller. In terms of content, this book fills a gap between two previous volumes on Chinese health policy: one analyzing the politics of state retrenchment in the early reform period (Duckett 2011) and another comparing health governance in the Mao era and reform era, with a particular emphasis on the New Health Reform (Huang 2013). In terms of the analytical approach, it fills a gap with its dual focus on both national and local politics, and its emphasis on the interaction of bureaucratic actors. Furthermore, it challenges central paradigms in the previous research on the NRCMS. For example, one study has interpreted the NRCMS as a new, market-based mechanism of governance based on voluntary enrollment (Klotzbücher and Laessig 2009). Another influential study analyzed the policy process from the analytical perspective of advocacy coalitions, high-lighting the role of researchers as advisors of the government and the prac-tical constraints of fiscal capacity in the policy process (Wang 2009). Both implicitly assume the central government to be an integrated actor with a coherent set of preferences. They subsequently focus on how this actor can be convinced of a specific policy option and/or how this option can be best rea-lized in a context of low state capacity and potentially devious local govern-ment agents. This study instead highlights internal divisions and bureaucratic conflicts as shaping political decision-making at the central level. Policy decisions are thus interpreted as compromises between opposing interests, which are often vague and contradictory.

This book aims to provide a new perspective on the NRCMS, which is systematically contextualized in the multi-level state's institutional structures and the recent political history of the People's Republic of China (PRC). It seeks to deepen the understanding of how genuinely political issues shaped and determined Chinese social and health policy in the course of the past decades. Furthermore, it aims at providing a contextualized view on China's health sector, identifying corridors of feasible political action in the context of the prevalent constellations of opposing political interests at the central and subnational levels, and the dominant modes of decision-making.

In order to do so, it chooses actor-centered institutionalism as a conceptual framework—an augmented rational choice approach typically using game-theoretical constellations as a heuristic to reconstruct political decision-making and processes of steering and governance. It assigns analytical prior-ity to the organizational level and composite actors, and rationalist explana-tions following the principle of decreasing abstraction, while allowing a systematic contextualization of strategic interactions in complex institutional contexts characterized by systemic interdependence (Lindenberg 1992; Mayntz 2009; Scharpf 1997).

Systemic interdependence (Mayntz 2009) is based on the structural com-plexity of modern societies and states with regard to their internal differ-entiation into functional contexts of action and multi-level hierarchies of administration. Structural complexity facilitates parametric links between institutions, which can mutually influence each other's determining factors. Institutional structures can have either beneficial or corruptive effects on other institutions or social processes. The systemic interdependence between the public finance system and health sector regulation is of particular import for this study. The public finance system in itself is dysfunctional, as it cen-tralizes fiscal revenues and decentralizes fiscal expenditures without effective redistribution mechanisms to guarantee sufficient state capacity at the local level (Wong 2009). Health sector regulation, on the other hand, implicitly relies on a functional public finance system to support the social functions of healthcare providers, most notably accomplishing public health tasks and providing cheap basic curative care in accordance with the pricing system. The institutional rules of the public finance system and health sector regulation thus partly neutralize each other at the local level and breed an array of informal practices that characterize virtually every field of health policy.

The bureaucratic structure of the Chinese state and public sector is rather complex. In the vertical dimension, it is differentiated into five official administrative levels—the center, the province, the city, the county and the township level—and the realm of local self-administration below. Each level usually only interacts directly with the next level above or next level below. In the horizontal dimension, there are numerous differentiated branches of administrative bodies and public service units (PSUs). They display complex patterns regarding the partition of labor and regulatory authority, and political and administrative processes unfold across the horizontal and vertical cleavages. These particularities of the political system of the PRC are captured in the approaches of fragmented authoritarianism and de facto federalism (Lieberthal and Lampton 1992; Zheng 2007). This study analytically distinguishes two types of multi-level arenas in order to reduce this complexity: one national policy arena that includes the central and provincial levels; and the local policy arenas, which are centered on the county level, but also include the city level above and the township and village levels below. Decisions in the national arena are usually of direct or indirect import for the entire country, which includes provincial approaches to health policy. Decisions in the local arenas are primarily relevant in a local context, but also influence the national policy processes and create aggregate effects on the national level.

In the national arena, actor-centered institutionalism helps to focus this study on issues of political contestation between two camps of bureaucratic actors. Their policy preferences are strongly determined by their organizational self-interest, and they form issue-related coalitions based on the compatibility of their preferences. Such coalitions of ministries and other bureaucratic actors operate in the shadow of hierarchy under the leadership core of the party-state (Heberer 2008: 73f.; Scharpf 1997). Coalition-building requires active coordination across the administrative levels and hierarchies, and between bureaucratic actors on the same level. The growing entanglement between the central and provincial levels (Heilmann 2004: 109f.) both requires and facilitates such coalition-building. The coalitions are dependent on high-ranking patrons in the leading government and party organs for coordination and representation of their interest in the strategic decision-making bodies. Furthermore, the political climate and balance of power is decisive for the relative strength and the feasible courses of action of the coalitions. "Experimentation under hierarchy" (Heilmann 2008) constitutes a tool for developing policy options in line with the coalitions' preferences, as the example of the insurance industry's involvement with the NRCMS in this study illustrates.

In the local arenas, this study will focus on the interaction of local governments and healthcare providers. Actors in the local arenas are more strongly constrained by the institutions devised in the national arena. County governments and administrations, and their subordinates on the township level, are treated as integrated actors, whose cohesion is facilitated by the pressures of the leading cadre evaluation system and contradictory institutional structures (Heberer and Schubert 2012).[1] The PSUs in the three-tier healthcare system on the other hand are not integrated, but form an actor aggregate due to the similarity of their interests and preferences. These actors are agents of the higher levels, but—as this study will show—they are constantly confronted with contradictory and infeasible requirements.

Actor-centered institutionalism typically uses game-like constellations to reconstruct policy processes and determine the dynamics of interaction between the actors on an abstract level.[2] Actors' preferences are determined empirically and put in an ordinal hierarchy. The mode of interaction is decisive for the outcome in any given actor constellation and depends on the institutional setting in which the constellation is embedded. Scharpf distinguishes four settings: anarchic fields or minimal institutions, networks, associations and organizations. He furthermore distinguishes four modes of interaction: unilateral action, negotiated agreements, majority votes and hierarchical direction. The institutional settings differ in the number of modes of interaction they can support, and the modes of interaction are affected by the institutional setting into which they are embedded (Scharpf 1997).

In the national arena, pro-government and pro-market actors face each other in a prisoner's dilemma played in an organizational context in the shadow of hierarchy. Until 2001, the institutional setting resembled an anarchic field due to the low political priority of rural health insurance and the resulting weakness of the institutional regime in the policy field. Beginning in 2001, the political priority of rural health insurance rose, and the leadership core began to expect cooperation. In the shadow of hierarchy, the opponents began to negotiate compromises. Subsequently, a cooperative policy regime was institutionalized, which by 2005 finally covered all the former opponents.

In the local arenas, this study analyzes two types of recurrent decision-making processes: local policy design, and budgetary funding and regulatory enforcement of the NRCMS. Both usually take the form of negotiations between the local government on the one hand and the healthcare providers on the other. Local policy design decisions take the form of a prisoner's dilemma, in which the insurance system and its adaptations are designed in a way that suits the interests and preferences of the negotiating parties. There is, however, some local variation connected to the rural population as a third actor interfering indirectly with the process and altering the hierarchy of preferences of the government. Budgetary funding and regulatory enforcement is strongly affected by the institutional misfits described above, and tends to take the form of a deadlock constellation. Neither the local governments nor the healthcare providers are willing and able to fully conform to their institutional roles. Rather, they tend to collude and comply selectively in accordance with their own interests and preferences.

Methodology, Data and Fieldwork

This study relies on different types of data, which were triangulated in order to increase the reliability of the findings. The principal sources of data are (1) fieldwork and expert interviews, (2) Chinese administrative documents, decrees and laws, (3) newspaper articles, policy reports and academic studies from the PRC, and (4) Chinese statistical data. The conditions of data production on the Chinese mainland have been considered in the process of analysis. The author expects his interview partners to adapt their accounts in accordance with their own interests and in a way that presents them in a favorable light. The interviewees' position in the political and social system and their access to information have been considered in the analysis. Chinese statistical data are interpreted as biased and too optimistic, but generally reflecting changes in certain indicators over time. Administrative documents are cited throughout the text by their abbreviation, provided it is stated on the source document. The abbreviation usually indicates the issuing administrative organ, the internal department in charge and/or the nature and priority of the content.

Due to the analytical approach of this study, the fieldwork data is not presented in the form of case studies. Rather, it is used along with other sources to reconstruct the general dynamics of decision-making in the context of institutional misfits. This approach sacrifices some of the thickness of highly grounded case studies in order to generate more generalizable hypotheses about the policy processes. This allows the author to connect phenomena such as informal practices to the institutional structures affecting the healthcare system and the actors within it.

Semi-structured interviews were conducted in the course of several field trips to different jurisdictions in local China in 2010 and 2011. Contacts with the local health administrations were established either directly or through the intermediation of academics. Table 1.1 lists the county-level jurisdictions visited during the field trips. In A County and C District, fieldwork was conducted only on the county, township and village levels, and there were no direct visits to the city-level administrative organs. Contacts were established with the county-level bureaus of health. In Beilun, no previous contacts were established, and interviewing was only possible at the township level. In Inner Mongolia and Shandong, fieldwork began at the city-level bureau of health and proceeded down the administrative hierarchy.

In 2010, fieldwork began with a focus on C and Z City, which belong to the least economically developed parts of Shandong Province and were comparatively representative of rural China in terms of reported rural income

Table 1.1 Overview of the Field Sites

County/ District	A County	B County	D District	C District	E District	F County	G County	Beilun District
City	Y City		T City	H City	C City		Z City	Ningbo City
Province	Jiangsu	Inner Mongolia		Hubei		Shandong Province		Zhe-jiang
Year	2010, 2011	2011	2011	2011	2010	2010	2010	2011

levels. In 2011, return visits to Shandong were no longer possible. In one of the two cities, the concurrent arrival of a central inspection team complicated the author's fieldwork, and a major corruption scandal involving the health system erupted soon after. One of the three counties had furthermore announced a major reform initiative for 2011, the implementation of which was not, however, reported in the news or on the website of the local bureau of health in the course of that year.

In 2011, the focus of fieldwork therefore shifted to A County, B County and C District, which were above-average localities in the national context. Beilun District was visited mainly to catch up on the development of its NRCMS, which was one of the few in China to be run by a commercial insurance company on a for-profit basis. By 2011, this model had already been abandoned for several years. In T City, the NRCMS administration and funds had been centralized at the city level by 2011, and the NRCMS administrators at the city level were responsible for the NRCMS in B County and D District. B County first implemented a county-level NRCMS in 2006, which was centralized at the city level in 2009. A County, B County and C District constitute an above-average sample, based on a comparison with the average annual per capita income figures used for the classification of counties in the National Health Service Survey.[3]

Overview of the Chapters

The six main chapters can be grouped into pairs regarding their analytical focus. Chapters 2 and 7 analyze the health system as a whole, and focus on systemic interdependence and the institutional structures governing the health sector. Chapters 3 to 6 analyze the rural healthcare system, the CMS and the NRCMS. Chapters 3 and 4 focus on the national arena, analyzing the policy process connected to the introduction of rural health insurance. Chapters 5 and 6 focus on the implementation processes of the NRCMS in the local arenas. Chapter 2 provides a background for this book, analyzing the development between the planned economy era and 2009. Chapter 7 focuses on the regulatory changes in the course of the New Health Reform, providing an outlook on the future development of China's health system. Chapter 3 focuses on the CMS initiatives up to 2000, and Chapter 4 on the NRCMS initiative. Chapter 5 provides background on the local dynamics of implementation and an analysis of the policy design decisions. Chapter 6 focuses on the effects of systemically interdependent yet misfit institutions on the governing and operations of the NRCMS.

Chapter two provides an overview of the institutional changes in the health sector during the transition from economic planning to reform and opening policies. Before the reforms, China was characterized by a relatively coherent set of institutional structures, which strongly contributed to its successes in healthcare. Public healthcare facilities provided health services that were kept artificially cheap by the pricing system. Public hospitals were compensated for the low prices by substantial support from state budgets—most notably for staff salaries. Other facilities were largely integrated into and supported by the collective economy. Furthermore, user fees and insurance funds were an important source of financing, and profits on drug sales were introduced to cross-subsidize service provision when public support no longer appropriately compensated for the state's pricing policies. The urban healthcare system and the state hospitals benefitted from fiscal equalization, and urban health insurance systems provided comprehensive social security. The rural healthcare system was organized on the basis of subsistence and thus financed by local resources, and rural cooperative health insurance only provided basic social security.

The first two decades of the reform period were primarily characterized by the decline of public support for healthcare providers, who came to rely increasingly on user fees to finance themselves. Overall, change was gradual in the urban areas, and swift and comprehensive in the rural areas. The collective economy in the rural areas ended in the 1980s, and under the reformist leadership no functional equivalent was provided as a basis for rural healthcare. Village clinics were largely privatized, and, like the THCs, came to rely primarily on user fees when public support and the cooperative medical system disappeared. Without the protective functions of social pooling and the collective economy, households had to finance all healthcare expenditures themselves. The pricing system was not appropriately adapted to the institutional environment, and thus distorted the incentives of healthcare facilities and doctors. Financial shock due to catastrophic health costs and illness-induced poverty became a common phenomenon in the rural areas as a result. The changes were more gradual in the urban areas due to the continued existence of effective health insurance, state-owned enterprises and other carrier institutions for healthcare providers. Nevertheless, by the early 2000s illness-induced poverty was rising fast in urban China as well.

Chapter 3 analyzes the policy process connected to the introduction of a new rural health insurance system in the 1980s and 1990s, with a comparative perspective on the policy process in rural pensions. Both health and pension insurance were part of the endeavor to establish a public social security system in the rural areas after the collapse of the collective economy. The process began in 1985 with a call for local policy experimentation, and was to achieve universal health coverage by 2000. However, it took until after 2000 for the central government to choose a framework for rural health insurance and gather the political support necessary for its effective implementation, and in pensions a similar program only followed in 2009. This chapter also provides important new insights for the existing research on rural tax reforms and rural pensions in the 1990s, and points to the synergies of a comparative analysis of the different fields of policy (Bernstein and Lü 2000; Göbel 2010; Shi 2006).

The policy process was determined by the contradiction between pro-government and pro-market forces. They were coalitions of bureaucratic actors supported by politicians in the leadership core of the party-state. The pro-government side was headed by the Ministry of Health (MoH), which had a direct interest in mobilizing resources for the healthcare system, and the Ministry of Civil Affairs (MoCA), which was in charge of public social security in the rural areas. Both had direct stakes in strengthening public commitment to social security. The main actor on the pro-market side was the Chinese insurance industry, most notably the People's Insurance Company of China (PICC), which had a vital interest in the development of markets for social security in the vast rural areas. The fiscally conservative Ministry of Finance (MoF) was a natural ally, as it sought to limit budgetary commitments of the state. For most of the 1980s and 1990s, rural social security was determined by a political status quo in which both sides guarded their core interests and none could fully realize its visions.

The political priority of rural social security was rather low, and the policy process was therefore heavily affected by developments in other policy fields and national politics in general. The 1980s were characterized by a status quo between the two sides which displayed a slight dominance of the market reformers. After the events of 1989, the pro-government side gained influence and pushed through a CMS initiative supported by subsidies from the central and provincial levels, thus doing away with local subsistence as part of the status quo. After the market reformers regained strength in 1992, they accused the formally voluntary CMS of being informally coercive and constituting a financial burden for the villagers. The subsidies were suspended and CMS coverage decreased again. The MoH then launched a second CMS initiative more in line with the status quo, which was integrated with the national health reform in late 1996. However, after the rise of Zhu Rongji to Premier, the CMS was again attacked as an involuntary system and a burden. Coverage declined, and the newly reformed insurance industry used the opportunity to expand into the rural markets.

Chapter 4 analyzes the processes of policy formulation and implementation for the NRCMS. While commercial insurance was quickly expanding in the rural areas, the preferences of the leadership core of the party-state shifted towards a greater role of the state in rural health insurance. A change in Jiang Zemin's orientation was pivotal to this process, which led to a new, state-subsidized CMS program. In 2001, various provinces began to prepare the implementation, and the program was enacted before the Sixteenth Party Congress in 2002, which initiated the leadership transition to the Hu Jintao and Wen Jiabao administration. The new policy assigned commercial insurance the status of complementary insurance, but allowed for cooperative projects with local governments in wealthy areas. Nevertheless, the NRCMS was a blow to the insurance industry.

The NRCMS program was piloted between 2003 and 2005, before being extended to all of rural China between 2006 and 2008. The pilot stage remained strongly affected by the contradiction between pro-market and pro-government actors. The market coalition had been weakened as its major ministries, the MoF and the Ministry of Agriculture (MoA), were now integrated into a cooperative decision-making regime that supported NRCMS implementation. In the course of the SARS crisis, however, the minister of health was sacked and replaced by Wu Yi, a market reformer. The MoH leadership was now divided between a pro-market minister and a pro-government party secretary.

Between 2003 and 2005, accusations about the NRCMS not being implemented on a voluntary basis came up again. The MoH halted the extension of piloting in 2004 to investigate such accusations, and delayed the implementation process. At the local level, insurance companies acted as delegate agencies for NRCMS management in various localities, although not all localities and models were initially accepted for entering the subsidized framework of the NRCMS. The conflict lasted until 2005, when the status of the insurance industry in the NRCMS policy was formally guaranteed by integrating the China Insurance Regulatory Commission (CIRC) in the central decision-making body and drafting central policy guidelines about the role of insurance companies. Wu Yi resigned as minister of health in the same year, accusations about involuntary enrollment gradually stopped, and problems regarding enrollment were subsequently addressed in a different political vocabulary. The MoH-led official evaluation of the NRCMS concluded that some deviations from voluntary enrollment were unavoidable and should be tolerated.

Chapter 5 analyzes the local decision-making processes regarding the NRCMS policy design, which is an interactive process between local governments and healthcare providers, most notably county hospitals and THCs. It begins with an analysis of the interests and preferences of local governments and healthcare providers in the context of the misfit institutions of the state and the healthcare sector described in Chapter 2. Furthermore, it analyzes the procedural context of the implementation process, in which counties with better administrative and fiscal capacity, experience in health reforms and populations more ready to join the NRCMS were selected for the first cohorts. These first cohorts were more thoroughly analyzed and represent an above-average sample of NRCMS counties. The vast majority of later counties had to deal with worse conditions, but could largely copy the institutional structures generated by the pilots.

The high share of counties deciding to cover outpatient services, most notably via medical savings accounts (MSAs—*jiating zhanghu*), is puzzling. Local governments should be interested in minimizing their budgetary expenditures, but outpatient reimbursement adds numerous small-scale transactions which, especially in the case of MSAs, may have little or no protective effect. At the same time, they weaken the capacity of the NRCMS to protect against catastrophic expenditures, most notably for inpatient services. The dominance of this model becomes rational when viewed as the outcome of negotiations between local governments and healthcare facilities, which are indirectly influenced by the preferences of the rural population. Local governments seek to decrease their administrative expenditures for the NRCMS, in particular for reimbursement processes and premium collection. Therefore, they want to delegate administrative tasks to the healthcare providers, most notably to the THCs. In order to compensate the THCs, which provided relatively few inpatient services during the early years of the NRCMS, outpatient services needed to be integrated into the NRCMS reimbursement plans. Furthermore, the rural population was often reluctant to join the NRCMS, and coercive enrollment strategies were risky in the early years, when the central dispute between pro-government and pro-market actors was not yet settled. Especially poorer social strata sought direct and visible benefits from the NRCMS, which outpatient reimbursement could offer them. Many were opposed to the idea of social pooling, and MSAs could directly allocate their contributions back to them. Informally, MSAs and outpatient funds could be directly used to pay for the premiums and thus spare local cadres much of the expensive, risky and tiring premium-collection process. Ultimately, considering the villagers' preferences and integrating the THCs into the administration decreased the pooling capacity of the NRCMS, and in some areas converted it into a fully government-funded service.

Chapter 6 analyzes the effect of the institutional misfits in central–local relations and health sector regulation on the operations of the NRCMS in a local context. Being part of a more general governance problem, the institutional misfits constitute remote causes that negatively affect the budgetary financing and regulatory enforcement in the health sector. Local governments lack the capacity and incentives to appropriately finance the healthcare providers, which in turn neglect their formal institutional role. Lacking public support to provide subsidized health services and focus on public health work, they overcharge and induce demand to make ends meet economically. Local governments, on the other hand, have little incentive to strictly supervise or sanction this behavior. This pattern of interactions is conceptualized as a deadlock constellation. It provides an explanatory model for a large share of the informal practices in the local health sector, and of the unintended, non-linear and counterintuitive effects of interventions in virtually all areas of health policy.

The deadlock affects the NRCMS in various ways. The administrative funding and county-level contributions to the NRCMS funds are under substantial threat of budgetary shortfalls, and decrease the effectiveness of the NRCMS both financially and administratively. The healthcare providers systematically induce demand in order to appropriate NRCMS funding, which compensates to some extent for the lack of public financial support and increases overall health costs. Supervision and sanctions remain largely ineffective, as the NRCMS administrative organs lack sufficient capacity, jurisdiction and political mandate. The NRCMS funds thus come to replace local budgetary expenditures and contribute to the rising costs of healthcare.

The various cost-containment policies of the NRCMS also suffer directly from this dynamic of interactions. Positive lists for drugs and services decrease the scope of reimbursement and the transparency of the NRCMS, but this may to some extent be compensated via collusion between doctors and patients. The regime of bulk purchases and bidding introduced in the early 2000s significantly decreases the purchasing prices for drugs. Local governments and providers, however, tend to collude and informally enhance the profit margins for drugs, rather than decrease sales prices. The reforms thus fail to lower health costs. Finally, alternative provider-payment mechanisms have some potential to change providers' incentives and decrease costs. Their applicability is, however, limited by problems of administrative capacity, and they are potentially affected by the deadlock's dynamics of interaction.

Chapter 7 analyzes the main reform initiatives of the New Health Reform and their potential to reverse the dynamics described in Chapter 6. While overseeing an expansion of the existing health insurance programs, the New Health Reform focuses on the areas of service provision and market regulation. It aims at fundamental structural changes that, given effective implementation, have the potential to transform the problematic dynamics that characterize the Chinese health sector. However, they will not function effectively without sufficient budgetary support from the public finance system and improved mechanisms of accountability.

In market regulation, its main initiatives are the Essential Medicines program and the reforms of service pricing. The core of the former is a reorganized and drastically shortened list of 497 Essential Medicines, which is amended by the provincial governments. Supply with Essential Medicines is organized via bidding and bulk purchasing on the provincial level in connection with provincial distribution systems. For THCs, Essential Medicines are to constitute 100 percent of the pharmaceutical portfolio, and the profit margin for these drugs was abolished. This eliminated the main source of profits for THCs. Furthermore, the New Health Reform promotes various initiatives to reform service prices. By increasing the cost-recovery rates of medical services, it seeks to adapt the pricing system to the capacities of the local state and adapt the distorted incentives of health providers, which should ultimately enhance cost control.

In service provision, the New Health Reform aims at a comprehensive reorganization of the operations of China's health providers. For THCs, the focus defined with the Essential Medicines reform was clearly on state provision. A high reliance on local budgetary support, however, raises questions regarding the fiscal sustainability of the reform. Public hospital reform aimed at reanimating their public welfare orientation and gained particular attention. A first cohort of pilots has not achieved a breakthrough, however. In 2012, a separate reform for public county hospitals with more specific guidelines was put into operation. Local governments are given the choice either to appropriately finance their hospitals or to privatize them. Private ownership of county hospitals was linked to the right of market pricing—that is, private or semi-private facilities can arguably set healthcare prices themselves and thus increase the cost-recovery rates for medical services.

The Conclusion summarizes the findings of this book, contextualizes them in the existing research on health policy and the NRCMS, and outlines their implications for the ongoing process of health reforms. A feasible blueprint for the reform of the healthcare system needs to strengthen the institutional fit between health sector regulation on the one hand and the multi-level state on the other hand. Political contestation and systemic interdependence substantially narrow the scope of feasible policy options the central government can pursue in the ongoing reforms. The dysfunctional public finance system limits the role that local governments can play in the health sector. At the same time, such a blueprint would need to gain political majorities in a contested policy field with a prevalence of consensual modes of decision-making. The corridor for feasible policy solutions is therefore quite narrow, and deviating from it is likely to produce more institutional misfits and informal practices, rather than the desired results.

Notes

1 In this respect, the analytical perspective of this study differs from other governance approaches to health policy, which emphasize bureaucratic fragmentation at the sub-national levels of government (Ramesh et al. 2014). These differences are connected to the interpretation of the role of the CPC and its function in coordinating the fragmented government apparatus. There is no doubt that local bureaucratic fragmentation constitutes a problem on the operational level for processes such as monitoring, and that local governments often have only incomplete knowledge about their healthcare providers. This study puts greater weight on the role of the CPC, and local leading party cadres in particular, in withdrawing the political mandate for effectively sanctioning healthcare providers from the administrative organs in charge. Effective sanctions and monitoring could easily contradict sensitive interests of local political elites.
2 It is important to emphasize that games serve as a heuristic to reconstruct policy processes in this context, rather than for the development of formal, game-theoretical models.
3 The MoH distinguishes between four types of counties, with type-one counties being the wealthiest and type-four counties being poverty counties. Type-three counties are most representative of rural China. A County was a type-one county in 2003 and a type-two county in 2008. B County was a type-two county in 2003 and 2008, even though it was classified as a national poverty county. C District was a type-one county in 2003 and a type-two county in 2008. According to the MoH

survey, type-three counties are most representative of rural China. Income statistics in China have to be interpreted carefully, as they tend to be inflated. Overall, the average conditions for the implementation and operations of the NRCMS in rural China were arguably worse than in the field counties. A County was a less developed locality in Jiangsu Province with about 1 million inhabitants. C District was part of a large and prosperous urban area in Hubei Province, but also incorporated a substantial share of rural areas. A County and C District had comparable volumes of gross domestic product and fiscal revenue, while A County had a larger population and thus lower per capita values. B County was a national poverty county in Inner Mongolia, and its primary sector contributed the smallest share to the local gross domestic product. According to official statistics, the gap between local fiscal revenues and expenditures was considerably smaller in B County than in A County and C District. However, local administrators and health staff pointed out that, as a poverty county, B County received substantial financial transfers from the higher levels of government, which arguably played an important role in healthcare financing (Hubei Bureau of Statistics 2004, 2008; Inner Mongolia Bureau of Statistics 2004, 2008; Jiangsu Bureau of Statistics 2004, 2008; MoH 1999: 14; MoH 2009a: 7).

Bibliography

Babiarz, K. S. *et al.* 2010, New Evidence on the Impact of China's New Rural Cooperative Medical Scheme and its Implications for Rural Primary Healthcare: Multivariate Difference-in-Difference Analysis, in: *BMJ*, 341, c5617.

Bernstein, Thomas P. and Xiaobo Lü 2000, Taxation without Representation: Peasants, the Central and the Local States in Reform China, in: *The China Quarterly*, 163, 742–763.

Cailliez, Charlotte 1998, *The Collapse of the Rural Health System*, online: www.cefc. com.hk/article/the-collapse-of-the-rural-health-system (accessed July 18, 2012).

Chen, Zhu and Mao Zhang (eds) 2013, *Zhongguo xinxing nongcun hezuo yiliao fazhan baogao 2002–2012 nian (The NRCMS Development Report 2002–2012)*, Beijing: Renmin Weisheng Chubanshe (People's Health Press).

CHFP 2013, *Zhongguo weisheng he jihua shengyu tongji nianjian (China Statistical Yearbook of Health and Family Planning)*, Beijing: Zhongguo Xiehe Yike Daxue Chubanshe (China Harmony and Medicine University Press).

CHFP 2014, *Zhongguo weisheng he jihua shengyu tongji nianjian (China Statistical Yearbook of Health and Family Planning)*, Beijing: Zhongguo Xiehe Yike Daxue Chubanshe (China Harmony and Medicine University Press).

Duckett, Jane 2011, *The Chinese State's Retreat from Health: Policy and the Politics of Retrenchment*, London: Routledge.

Göbel, Christian 2010, *The Politics of Rural Reform in China, State Policy and Village Predicament in the Early 2000s*, Abingdon: Routledge.

Gu, Xin, Mengtao Gao and Yang, Yao 2005, *Zhenduan yu chufang: Zhimian Zhongguo yiliao tizhi gaige (China's Health Carle Reforms: A Pathological Analysis)*, Beijing: Shehui Kexue Wenxian Chubanshe (Social Sciences Academic Press).

Heberer, Thomas 2001, China: Der Markt sprengt das alte Sozialsystem (The Market Blows Up the Old Social System), in: *Der Überblick*, 1, 54–59.

Heberer, Thomas 2008, Das politische System der VR China im Prozess des Wandels. In *Einführung in die politischen Systeme Ostasiens*, eds Thomas Heberer and Claudia Derichs, 21–177, Wiesbaden: VS Verlag für Sozialwissenschaften.

Heberer, Thomas 2009, Relegitimation through New Patterns of Social Security: Neighbourhood Communities as Legitimating Institutions, in: *The China Review*, 9, 2, 99–128.

Heberer, Thomas and Gunter Schubert 2012, County and Township Cadres as a Strategic Group. A New Approach to Political Agency in China's Local State, in: *Journal of Chinese Political Science*, 17, 3, 221–249.

Heilmann, Sebastian 2004, *Das politische System der Volksrepublik China, 2. aktualisierte Auflage*, Wiesbaden: VS Verlag für Sozialwissenschaften.

Heilmann, Sebastian 2008, Policy Experimentation in China's Economic Rise, in: *Studies in Comparative International Development*, 43, 1, 1–26.

Huang, Yanzhong 2013, *Governing Health in Contemporary China*, New York: Routledge.

Hubei Bureau of Statistics (ed.) 2004, *Hubei tongji nianjian (Statistical Yearbook of Hubei)*, Beijing: Zhongguo Tongji Chubanshe (China Statistics Press).

Hubei Bureau of Statistics (ed.) 2008, *Hubei tongji nianjian (Statistical Yearbook of Hubei)*, Beijing: Zhongguo Tongji Chubanshe (China Statistics Press).

Inner Mongolia Bureau of Statistics (ed.) 2004, *Neimenggu tongji nianjian (Statistical Yearbook of Inner Mongolia)*, Beijing: Zhongguo Tongji Chubanshe (China Statistics Press).

Inner Mongolia Bureau of Statistics (ed.) 2008, *Neimenggu tongji nianjian (Statistical Yearbook of Inner Mongolia)*, Beijing: Zhongguo Tongji Chubanshe (China Statistics Press).

Jiangsu Bureau of Statistics (ed.) 2004, *Jiangsu tongji nianjian (Statistical Yearbook of Jiangsu)*, Beijing: Zhongguo Tongji Chubanshe (China Statistics Press).

Jiangsu Bureau of Statistics (ed.) 2008, *Jiangsu tongji nianjian (Statistical Yearbook of Jiangsu)*, Beijing: Zhongguo Tongji Chubanshe (China Statistics Press).

Kiser, Edgar 1999, Comparing Varieties of Agency Theory in Economics, Political Science, and Sociology: An Illustration from State Policy Implementation, in: *Sociological Theory*, 17, 2, 146–170.

Klotzbücher, Sascha and Peter Laessig 2009, Transformative State Capacity in Post-Collective China: The Introduction of the New Rural Cooperative Medical Scheme in Two Counties of Western China, 2006–2008, in: *European Journal of East Asian Studies*, 8, 1, 61–89.

Lieberthal, Kenneth G. and David M. Lampton (eds) 1992, *Bureaucracy, Politics, and Decision Making in Post-Mao China*, Berkeley, CA: University of California Press.

Lindenberg, Siegwart 1992, The Method of Decreasing Abstraction. In *Rational Choice Theory. Advocacy and Critique*, eds James S. Coleman and Thomas J. Fararo, pp. 3–20, London: Sage Publications.

Liu, Yuanli, Keqin Rao and William C. Hsiao 2003, Medical Expenditure and Rural Impoverishment in China, in: *Journal of Health, Population and Nutrition*, 21, 3, 216–222.

Ma, Yuqin, Lulu Zhang and Qian Chen 2012, China's New Cooperative Medical Scheme for Rural Residents: Popularity of Broad Coverage Poses Challenges for Costs, in: *Health Affairs*, 31, 5, 1058–1064.

Mayntz, Renate 2009, *Sozialwissenschaftliches Erklären, Probleme der Theoriebildung und Methodologie* (Social-Scientific Explaining, Problems of Theory-Building and Methodology), Frankfurt am Main: Campus Verlag GmbH.

MoH 1999, *Guojia weisheng fuwu yanjiu—1998 nian di er ci guojia weisheng fuwu diaocha fenxi baogao (Research on National Health Services—An Analysis Report of the Second National Health Service Survey in 1998)*, online: www.nhfpc.gov.cn/cmsresources/mohwsbwstjxxzx/cmsrsdocument/doc9907.pdf (accessed July 18, 2016).

MoH 2004, *Di san ci weisheng fuwu diaocha fenxi baogao (The Third National Health Service Survey Analysis Report)*, online: www.nhfpc.gov.cn/cmsresources/mohwsbwstjxxzx/cmsrsdocument/doc9908.pdf (accessed July 18, 2016).

MoH 2009a, *2008 Zhongguo weisheng fuwu diaocha—di si ci jiating jiankang xunwen diaocha fenxi baogao (The 2008 National Health Service Survey—The Fourth Household Health Survey Analysis Report)*, online: www.nhfpc.gov.cn/cmsresources/mohwsbwstjxxzx/cmsrsdocument/doc9911.pdf (accessed July 18, 2016).

MoH 2009b, *Zhongguo weisheng tongji nianjian (China Statistical Yearbook of Health)*, Beijing: Zhongguo Xiehe Yike Daxue Chubanshe (China Harmony and Medicine University Press).

MoH 2011, *Zhongguo weisheng tongji nianjian (China Statistical Yearbook of Health)*, Beijing: Zhongguo Xiehe Yike Daxue Chubanshe (China Harmony and Medicine University Press).

Müller, Armin 2016, Hukou and Health Insurance Coverage for Migrant Workers, in: *Journal of Current Chinese Affairs*, 45, 2, 53–82.

Ramesh, M., Xun Wu and Alex J. He 2014, Health Governance and Healthcare Reforms in China, in: *Health Policy and Planning*, 29, 6, 663–672.

Savigny, Don de and Taghreed Adam (eds) 2009, *Systems Thinking for Health Systems Strengthening*, Geneva: Alliance for Health Policy and Systems Research; World Health Organization.

Scharpf, Fritz W. 1997, *Games Real Actors Play, Actor-Centered Institutionalism in Policy Research*, Boulder, CO: Westview Press.

Schubert, Gunter and Anna Ahlers 2012, County and Township Cadres as a Strategic Group: "Building a New Socialist Countryside" in Three Provinces, in: *The China Journal*, 67, 67–86.

Shi, Shih-jiunn 2006, Left to Market and Family—Again? Ideas and the Development of the Rural Pension Policy in China, in: *Social Policy and Administration*, 40, 7, 791–806.

Tang, Shenglan, Jingjing Tao and Henk Bekedam 2012, Controlling Cost Escalation of Healthcare: Making Universal Health Coverage Sustainable in China, in: *BMC Public Health*, 12, S1.

Wagstaff, Adam *et al.* 2009, Extending Health Insurance to the Rural Population: An Impact Evaluation of China's New Cooperative Medical Scheme, in: *Journal of Health Economics*, 28, 1, 1–19.

Wagstaff, Adam and Magnus Lindelow 2008, Can Insurance Increase Financial Risk? The Curious Case of Health Insurance in China, in: *Journal of Health Economics*, 27, 4, 990–1005.

Wang, Hongman, Danan Gu and Matthew E. Dupre 2008, Factors Associated with Enrollment, Satisfaction, and Sustainability of the New Cooperative Medical Scheme Program in Six Study Areas in Rural Beijing, in: *Health Policy*, 85, 1, 32–44.

Wang, Shaoguang 2009, Adapting by Learning, The Evolution of China's Rural Health Care Financing, in: *Modern China*, 35, 4, 370–404.

Wong, Christine 2009, Rebuilding Government for the 21st Century: Can China Incrementally Reform the Public Sector?, in: *The China Quarterly*, 200, 929–952.

Wong, John and Yongnian Zheng (eds) 2004, *The SARS Epidemic, Challenges to China's Crisis Management*, Singapore: World Scientific.

Xiao, Yue *et al.* 2013, Essential Drugs Policy in Three Rural Counties in China: What Does a Complexity Lens Add?, in: *Social Science and Medicine*, 93, 220–228.

Yip, Winnie and William Hsiao 2015, What Drove the Cycles of Chinese Health System Reforms?, in: *Health Systems and Reform*, 1, 1, 52–61.

Zhang, Luying *et al.* 2010, How Effectively Can the New Cooperative Medical Scheme Reduce Catastrophic Health Expenditure for the Poor and Non-Poor in Rural China?, in: *Tropical Medicine & International Health*, 15, 4, 468–475.

Zhang, Xiulan *et al.* 2014, Advancing the Application of Systems Thinking in Health: Managing Rural China Health System Development in Complex and Dynamic Contexts, in: *Health Research Policy and Systems*, 12, 44.

Zheng, Yongnian 2007, *De Facto Federalism in China, Reforms and Dynamics of Central-Local Relations*, Singapore: World Scientific.

2 Systemic Interdependence and Institutional Change in the Health System of Post-Mao China

In the course of the Reform and Opening period (since 1979), the regulatory institutions that govern China's healthcare system changed. This institutional change turned a public service, which once achieved health outcomes in the rural areas that made China the *avant-garde* of health policy among developing countries, into a partly dysfunctional set of organizations driven primarily by economic constraints. One major cause of this development has been the fiscal crisis that hit China during the transition, and to which the government reacted with reforms that created a largely dysfunctional public finance system: centralizing revenue mandates, keeping expenditure mandates decentralized and failing to install an effective system of fiscal redistribution. The results of this development were twofold. On the one hand, many local governments henceforth suffered from heavy fiscal imbalances—that is, they lacked the financial resources to live up to their formal responsibilities in public service provision and other areas. On the other hand, local governments in general had strong incentives to concentrate their financial resources on economically and politically lucrative projects, by informal means if necessary. Even in wealthy areas, urbanization and economic development had priority over financing public service provision and healthcare (Wong 2009; World Bank 2007a).

The regulatory institutions governing the healthcare system were, however, not systematically adapted to the changes in the public finance system and local fiscal state capacity. On the one hand, healthcare providers were comprehensively commercialized, but, on the other hand, they were continuously expected to perform social functions without separate financing, such as the provision of cheap basic healthcare services and public health work. At the same time, the coverage of health insurance decreased and shifted the growing financial burden of supporting the commercialized health sector to households. Commercialization and the decrease of insurance coverage were more gradual processes in the urban areas, whereas they were swift and comprehensive in the rural areas where the collective economy had been the primary financial foundation of the healthcare system.

Due to the systemic interdependence of health sector regulation and public finances, many of the processes and operations in China's healthcare system were pushed into informality. On the one hand, healthcare providers at the township level and above largely remained public or semi-public in terms of ownership status and were formally designated non-profit providers. At the grassroots level, non-public provision was more common, with private practitioners and clinics. On the other hand, there were far-reaching formal mandates focusing on public health tasks and formal requirements to adhere to the pricing system. The public finance system determines the level of fiscal capacity available for funding the health sector at the local levels, and health sector regulation determines the level of public funding that the healthcare facilities need for their daily operations and the fulfillment of their social functions. Based on fieldwork in rural Guangxi in the late 1990s, Cailliez summarizes how these institutional misfits transform the health system as a functional context of interaction between healthcare providers and patients: "The health system no longer functions as a public service: it is entirely subject to economic constraints" (Cailliez 1998). Chapters 5 and 6 will analyze in greater detail how the institutional misfits influence policy implementation and the interaction of local governments and healthcare providers.

This chapter primarily focuses on the institutional change in China's health system during the reform period, up to the enactment of the New Health Reform, which will be discussed separately in Chapter 7. The first part will analyze the institutional structures that governed the healthcare system in the planned economy period, and the second part will analyze the institutional structures of the reform period. Both will analyze separately the fields of service providers, risk protection and health insurance, and market regulation. The third part will briefly summarize the social effects of the institutional change, which became a driving force for the introduction of the new rural health insurance system which will be analyzed in the following chapters. This chapter also provides an important basis for Chapter 6, which analyzes the local implementation and maintenance of the NRCMS in a context of interdependent but misfit institutions. Chapter 7 will build upon this chapter and provide a summary, which analyzes the most recent reform initiatives under the New Health Reform and their effects on the institutional misfits.

The Planned Economy Period

Service Providers

The formative years of the Chinese healthcare system were strongly characterized by the institutions of the planned economy in the rural and urban areas, and by the Marxist ideology of the government. Following the model of the Soviet Union, the PRC established a public system of health service provision supported by the state and the planned economy. A basic three-tier structure for the provision of primary, secondary and tertiary health services emerged, which continues to the present day with slight modifications and is illustrated in Table 2.1. City, district and county hospitals were mainly state-owned

Table 2.1 The Three-Tier Healthcare System in Urban and Rural China

	Urban areas	Rural areas
Tertiary care	City hospital	County hospital
Secondary care	District hospital	Township health center (commune health center)
Primary care	Street clinics	Village clinics (brigade clinics)

Source: Liu and Yi 2004: 6.

PSUs focusing on curative care. They were connected to the administrative hierarchy of state actors—most notably the line administration of the ministry of health—and accompanied by other functionally differentiated networks of PSUs, as, for example, anti-epidemic stations or maternal and childcare hospitals. The street- and village-level organs, as well as the commune health centers, were more generalist providers in charge of curative care and services in public health. The substantial successes in improving the health status of the rural population during the planned economy era were sustained by a clear focus on public health, campaign-style public health measures and a massive transfer of human resources from the cities to the rural areas (Liu and Yi 2004: 6f.).

Financially, the system was strongly backed by public funding. The state-owned hospitals and other PSUs were part of the civil service: doctors usually had an established post (*bianzhi*), which guaranteed them lifetime employment and a salary from public budgets. The *bianzhi* system was and remains a key structural element in Chinese personnel administration (Brødsgaard 2002). The budgeting process for public hospitals went through different stages. During the 1950s, all hospital revenues were transferred to the government's treasury department, and the government covered all hospital expenditures (*quan'e guanli, cha'e buzhu*). During the 1960s and 1970s, the mode of financing shifted to gap budgeting: budgetary funding from the government covered at least the salary costs of the hospitals, which could usually retain revenues from services; surpluses were transferred to the government, and deficits were covered by the government (*quan'e guanli, ding'e buzhu, jieyu shangjiao*). Public health organs were financed via full-range budgeting from the 1950s to the 1970s: budgetary funding would cover salaries and operational costs, and revenues were transferred to the government (Bloom and Tang 2004: 23f.; Liu and Yi 2004: 7; Zhou 2008: 124f.).

Large government departments, the army and state-owned enterprises often operated their own healthcare facilities for primary and secondary care. In the rural areas, the collective economy was a crucial institutional carrier of the healthcare providers. The health centers of the People's Communes were largely financed via resources from the collective economy, and the barefoot doctors and midwifes in the production brigades were usually farmers with basic medical training. At the grassroots level, the collective organization of the economy guaranteed policy implementation and the provision of services (Liu and Yi 2004: 7).

Risk Protection and Health Insurance

Risk protection for the population was organized via various socialized health financing schemes. The Government Health Insurance Scheme (*gongfei yiliao*) was organized by each level of government and covered the employees and retirees of party and state organs (*jiguan danwei*) and PSUs, as well as disabled veterans and university students. It was fully tax-funded and provided free healthcare, although it excluded some types of services and drugs. The Labor Health Insurance Scheme (*laodong yiliao baoxian*) was organized by larger state-owned enterprises to cover employees and their dependants, as well as retirees. For employees, treatment was free, and they received a certain share of their salary during the time of absence. For dependants, 50 percent of health costs were covered (Bloom and Tang 2004: 24–7; Zhang 2005: 57–62).

Healthcare financing and risk protection in the rural areas was more strongly based on subsistence. Risk protection was organized via the CMS, which was mainly funded by contributions of the rural population. The CMS funds could be organized and pooled on the level of the commune or the brigade. Brigade funds were the dominant mode and characterized by substantial instability due to the small size of the risk pool. The benefit packages differed considerably: they usually included free services and/or free or subsidized drugs at the village clinic, and sometimes covered a certain share of the costs of inpatient or outpatient treatment at the commune health center for patients with a referral. According to estimates, the CMS covered 50 to 70 percent of the total medical expenditure of its beneficiaries (Klotzbücher 2006: 111–6; Liu and Yi 2004: 8).

Market Regulation

Chinese health markets under the planned economy were organized on a fee-for-service basis, and healthcare financing relied on user fees, social pooling and state and collective funding. User fees were regulated by the public pricing system, which constituted a crucial tool of social policy. Setting low prices for services and drugs was important for granting the poorer strata of the population access to medical services. Prices were adapted to the mode of gap budgeting: as public budgets covered the hospitals' salary expenditures, healthcare prices did not include the costs of salaries (*buhan gongzi de jiage*). In 1958, 1960 and 1972, the government substantially decreased prices for health services, but it was either unable or unwilling to sufficiently compensate the costs from governmental budgets. In order to compensate the hospitals for their financial losses, the government introduced a 15 percent profit margin on drugs sold by the hospitals' own pharmacies, which the hospitals could retain. This created a mode of cross-subsidizing underpriced medical services with profits from drug sales, which came to dominate hospital financing in the reform period (Bloom and Tang 2004: 23f; Li 2008: 145; Zhou 2008: 125).

Drugs were produced in accordance with government plans and distributed via a government-organized network, in which drug distributors or companies acted as middlemen between healthcare providers and factories (Dong et al. 1999a). The public pricing system regulated all stages of the production and distribution process, setting price levels and legitimate price differentials for ex-factory prices (*chuchangjia*), wholesale prices (*pifajia*) and retail prices (*lingshoujia*). Ex-factory prices included the costs of production plus a 5 percent profit margin, wholesale prices were based on the ex-factory prices plus a 5 percent profit margin, and retail prices added another 15 percent profit on the basis of the wholesale price. This basic regulatory structure remained in place through most of the reform period, even though there were substantial alterations (Zhou 2008: 120f.).

The Market Reforms of the 1980s and 1990s

Service Providers

After the death of Mao and Deng's rise to power, the Cultural Revolution was discredited and the central government adopted a more market-oriented ideology. The health sector was one of the earliest targets of commercialization in the reform era. Core initiatives such as the administrative reforms of the hospital sector or the reintroduction of private practitioners were initiated in 1979 and 1980 respectively by the MoH (MoH 1980; MoH, MoF and National Head Office of Labor 1979). At the same time, the minister of health, Qian Xinzhong, drafted new regulations for the rural CMS program and defended it despite its Cultural Revolution image (People's Daily, February 7, 1979; People's Daily, December 24, 1979). The motivation of these reforms was pragmatic rather than ideological: the MoH perceived the health system to be underfunded, but was too weak to lobby successfully for more funding (Duckett 2011: 36). On the one hand, the reforms abolished the monopoly of the public sector in health service provision and legalized private practitioners, which had emerged since 1978. On the other hand, they introduced performance-based incentives to public hospitals, which were perceived as overstaffed, ineffective and difficult to access at the time (People's Daily, October 11, 2006).

In 1979, the MoH initiated experimentation with a new administrative model for public hospitals, which was confirmed, specified and extended to public health organs in 1985 and 1989. The reforms introduced performance-based incentives to the operations of hospitals on an experimental basis. Local governments would continue to regulate hospitals' operations by defining their tasks (*ding renwu*) and fixing the number of beds (*ding chuang-wei*), the number of civil servant positions (*ding bianzhi*), professional and technical standards (*ding yewu jishu zhibiao*), and subsidies for their expenditures (*ding jingfei buzhu*). Budgetary funding for public hospitals was to shift away from paying salaries for the contracted workers towards more input-based, lump-sum budgets oriented towards the number of beds. Local governments furthermore retained a financial responsibility for building construction and renovation, purchasing technological equipment and paying pensions for the retired staff. As compensation for declining financial support from the government, hospitals were allowed to retain the profits of their operations and distribute them among the health staff in the form of social benefits and bonuses. More productive individuals were to be rewarded (MoH, MoF and National Head Office of Labor 1979).

The economic risks and opportunities of health service provision were to a large extent shifted to the hospitals. Input-based budgeting was a problematic and inflexible tool: it gave local governments few options to prioritize their spending or budget cuts, and the latter often needed to be made across the board (World Bank 2002: 83–8, 120–3). Internally, hospital managers used bonus payments to establish powerful incentives for employees and departments to maximize profits, rather than prioritizing quality care. Over the years, this has negatively affected the professional ethics of the medical profession and its reputation in the PRC (Hsiao 2008).

Public hospital reform was further extended and institutionalized in the course of the 1980s. A document of the State Council in 1985 specified that public hospitals were allowed to take on additional staff beyond the *bianzhi* limitations on a contract basis and encouraged the use of contract responsibility systems in personnel management. Outpatient departments were to prolong their opening hours and the usage rates of equipment were to be raised. In 1989, the State Council officially allowed for the creation of special, high-end service centers in public hospitals that exclusively catered for wealthy patients, linked the service income of hospitals to the level of their technological equipment, and allowed for hospital staff to work overtime and provide services in their free time (Guofa 1985: 62; Guowuyuan 1989).

Grassroots healthcare providers in the rural areas were hit hard by economic reforms. The institutions of the collective economy—communes and brigades—that had been their carrier units vanished with the introduction of the household responsibility system. The village committees and township governments that replaced the brigades and communes had far less control over local economic resources and were less able to provide financial support. By the mid-1980s, a substantial share of the village clinics were already privately operated by one (*geti ban*) or several (*lianhe ban*) doctors. However, even the clinics officially operated by the village committee received hardly any support other than a location and building, and in practice it is often hard to tell the difference between private and village-operated clinics. Although the share of formally public clinics increased between 1990 and 2010, this does not necessarily indicate a corresponding increase in public financial input (Interview 111013).

Governmental budgetary funding for hospitals declined substantially during the 1980s and 1990s, which is closely connected to the reforms of the public finance system. The share of government funding in health costs remained relatively stable between 35 and 40 percent during the period 1980–1985, before declining steeply in the second half of the 1980s and remaining low throughout the 1990s (CHFP 2013). The reforms of the public finance system had largely been a response to the fiscal crisis that hit China—like many post-planned economies—in the course of transition. In 1988, the central government replaced the old, redistributive system of fiscal transfers by a fiscal contracting system, thus decoupling fiscal revenue from expenditure (Bird and Wong 2005: 29). In the 1994 tax reform, fiscal revenues were centralized, but the central government failed to establish an effective system of intergovernmental transfers to compensate local governments for their losses. The 1994 reform left subnational public finance regulations to the discretion of the provinces, and indirectly sparked a trend of resource concentration at the provincial level (World Bank 2002: 25). The public finance system began to exacerbate fiscal imbalances and intensified the fiscal crisis at the county and township levels (Lam 2010: 149, 166). Local governments were increasingly unable and unwilling to finance hospitals, which is reflected in the changing structure of governmental health expenditure: "until 2003 ... 80 percent of the government's healthcare budget was used to provide healthcare coverage to China's 8.5 million state cadres" (Huang 2013: 67).

According to the political guidelines of the Fourteenth National Party Congress in 1992, healthcare facilities should finance their running costs via operational revenues and depend on the state for capital investment, most notably for construction (*jianshe kao guojia, chifan kao ziji*) (Han 2013). But local governments often failed to live up to this responsibility, especially in the rural areas and in Central and Western China. The Three-Items Construction program (*sanxiang jianshe*) was the main governmental construction program in rural health in the eighth and ninth five-year plan periods. It was almost exclusively financed from the resources of local governments and the healthcare facilities. Eligibility for intergovernmental support depended on initial investments of the local government, which contributed to the low take-up of program funds in poor regions (Klotzbücher 2006: 150–3). The share of healthcare facilities' copayments could vary between 20 and 80 percent of the overall costs of a project (Cao 2001; Cui 1995; Fang 2003). The program spent about RMB 6.8 billion on capital investment between 1991 and 1994 (Guowuyuan 1996). During the entire eighth five-year plan period, 2.7 percent of the overall spending came from the center, 28.5 percent from the provincial, prefecture and county levels combined, 20.9 percent from the townships and 40.9 percent from the health facilities (World Bank 2002: 124). Local governments' average capital investment expenditure in 2002 amounted to RMB 4.01 million in type-one counties, RMB 2.46 and RMB 2.31 million in type-two and type-three counties, and only RMB 70,000 in type-four counties (MoH 2004: 142). Governmental programs and initiatives only accounted for a part of the capital investment activities, and the framework of governmental programs left substantial copayments to local governments and the healthcare facilities.

In general organizational terms, China's healthcare providers can be distinguished according to three administrative characteristics: registered ownership (*dengji zhuce leibie*), organizing unit (*zhuban danwei*) and mode of management (*guanli leibie*). In terms of ownership, they can be either public (*gongli*, about 56 percent of all facilities in 2012) or non-public (*fei gongli*, 44 percent); public providers further subdivide into state-owned (*guoyou*, 12.9 percent) and collective (*jiti*, 43.6 percent) units, and non-public providers further subdivide into mixed ownership (*lianying*, 2.9 percent) and privately owned (*siying*, 40.6 percent). The organizing units subdivide into government units (*zhengfu ban*, 15.1 percent), societal units (*shehui ban*, 50.5 percent) and individuals (*geti ban*, 34.5 percent). The health administration is the most common organizing unit for healthcare facilities among the government units (14.6 percent). The vast majority were classified as non-profit providers; only 27.6 percent of the hospitals and 23.9 percent of the grassroots providers were registered as for-profit facilities. This complex system of classifications allows for a substantial variation in terms of regulatory standards and policy exposure (CHFP 2013).

The organizing unit and mode of management are of particular importance for a provider's status regarding financial regulations. As a document of the State Council clarified in 2000, non-profit providers are expected to perform a social function that includes adhering to the state pricing system for medical services. For-profit facilities, on the other hand, can set their service prices autonomously. Government-operated (*zhengfu ban*) non-profit units are entitled to financial support from the government, and the service prices should cover their operational costs after deducting governmental support and drug revenues. Other non-profit units were not entitled to such governmental support, and their service prices would—in theory—have to allow for more flexibility to compensate for that (Guobanfa 2000: 16).

The organizational characteristics of health providers also have an impact on their personnel administration, in which the system of "established posts" (*bianzhi*) is a key organizational element. "Bianzhi refers to the authorized number of personnel (the number of established posts) in a party or government administrative organ (*jiguan*), a service organization (*shiye danwei*) or a working unit (*qiye*)" (Brødsgaard 2002: 364). *Bianzhi* generally characterizes both state-financed organs and their employees. The administrative *bianzhi* (*xingzheng bianzhi*) characterizes governmental and party units, and it is under central authority.[1] Healthcare providers would usually be covered by the *shiye bianzhi* or the *qiye bianzhi*, if they are covered by the *bianzhi* system at all. Many formally public non-profit facilities remain outside the *bianzhi* system, most notably many THCs and village clinics (Brødsgaard 2002: 364).

The public service bianzhi refers to PSUs (*shiye danwei*)—including state-owned, government-operated hospitals—and their formal employees.

Responsibility for the PSU *bianzhi* system is decentralized: every level has jurisdiction over its own facilities. Formally, the salaries and social security benefits in PSUs are similar to those of cadres. The budgetary allocations to which PSUs are entitled, however, depend on the type of facility. Fully funded PSUs (*quan'e danwei*) are entitled to full budgetary financing, whereas partly funded PSUs (*cha'e danwei*) are merely entitled to a certain percentage of the salaries to be covered by the local budget. Public hospitals usually belong to the latter category. Self-financed PSUs (*zishou zizhi danwei*) are still included in the *bianzhi* system of personnel administration, but are not entitled to budgetary support (cf. World Bank 2002: 122).

The decision-making power for hiring personnel lies not with the PSU itself, but is scattered across different administrative organs: the *bianzhi* bureau, the personnel bureau, the bureau of finance and the respective line administration. The *bianzhi* bureau has jurisdiction over the authorized number of personnel, whereas the personnel bureau is responsible for the details of recruitment and remuneration. Formal employees entitle the PSU to budgetary payments, given its status of being either fully or partly funded. The autonomy of PSUs with regard to personnel is limited by life-long employment, but PSUs can also have a second category of "self-financed employees" (*zishou zizhi renyuan*) which need no authorized posts. They are entirely financed by the PSUs' own revenues and allow for some flexibility in staffing.

> The formal distinction between the two categories is that the services provided by self-financed staff might be considered commercial in nature, rather than of a 'public benefit' nature. In practice, this category is often used to take on extra staff, sometimes at the request of local governments, because the PSU has sufficient self-raised funds to pay for them … [U]ntil recently, the vast majority had *de facto* life-long contracts and received the same pay as the formal employees.
>
> (World Bank 2007b: 42)

Since 2002, the central government has been promoting a more temporary employment system (*pinyongzhi*) in order to improve the flexibility in PSUs' personnel management (World Bank 2007b: 41ff.).

The PSU *bianzhi* system is at the heart of many problems facing public hospitals. Its static nature inhibits flexible adaptation of the personnel structure to a changing environment. It is connected to a largely input-based system of budgeting, which does not allow for prioritized spending or budget cuts on the side of local government. This is especially problematic under the conditions of substantial fiscal imbalances, which do not allow the local governments to fulfill all their budgetary responsibilities or to react flexibly to budgetary shortfalls. At the same time, however, local governments' jurisdiction over the PSU *bianzhi* allows them to use PSUs as employers of last resort—and, for example, pressure them to hire local graduates. This leads to the paradox of

PSUs which are at the same time underfunded and overstaffed, often with unqualified personnel (Burns 2003; World Bank 2002: 120–3, 148).

The most crucial problem, however, is that the *bianzhi* system is by and large financially void: even though the *bianzhi* staff is officially part of the civil service, this does not mean that the state will live up to the financial claims connected to this status. Local governments under fiscal stress often cut their expenditures on local PSUs, and salary payments are usually affected by this. The *bianzhi* system manifests the contradiction of a public service that is largely privately financed: the government retains formal jurisdiction over personnel affairs, but hospitals largely need to generate the funding for salaries themselves, despite their formal claim to budgetary financing. Capital investment for construction and equipment is characterized by similar contradictions.

This contradiction is even more severe for grassroots providers that are not part of the *bianzhi* system. Even though there is no formal claim to public salary payments, they are classified as non-profit facilities and expected to adhere to the pricing system. Formally, budgetary input for such providers would arguably be calculated on bed capacity rather than number of staff (World Bank 2002: 122ff.). China's grassroots healthcare facilities numbered 912,620 in 2012; among them, 653,419 were village clinics, and 692,158 were classified as non-profit (CHFP 2013). Although THCs and Shequ health service centers are at least partly covered by the *bianzhi* system, this is arguably a rare exception for village clinics. Nevertheless, these facilities are expected to function as a public service, focusing on public health and delivering cheap services in curative care (Weiguicaifa 2006: 340).

Risk Protection and Health Insurance

With regard to risk protection, the first two decades of the reform era were largely characterized by retrenchment and a continuous shifting of social risks to households. In the rural areas, the CMS systems by and large imploded when the institutions of the collective economy were dismantled. The CMS lost its institutional foundation and vanished in the absence of new political, regulatory or financial support (Duckett 2011). The social risks of health were almost entirely shifted to households during the 1980s, although the CMS and other diverse forms of insurance continued to be experimented with in some pockets of rural China.

In urban China, retrenchment was more gradual and piecemeal. Labor Insurance formally remained in place until 1998, but its effective coverage was gradually undermined. It covered an increasingly smaller share of the urban population due to urbanization, rising unemployment and the rising inflow of migrant workers into the cities. The share of health costs covered by labor and government insurance decreased due to increasing financial problems of local governments and state-owned enterprises (Bloom and Tang 2004: 24–7, 31f.; Duckett 2011: 73–95).

In 1998, Labor Insurance was replaced by the new UEBMI (Guofa 1998: 44). The reform had been systematically prepared by strategic local experimentation and the formation of a leading group at the ministerial level. The UEBMI was controlled by management organs in the line administration of the newly established Ministry of Labor and Social Security (MoLSS), which now had jurisdiction over urban health insurance. It was financed by contributions of employers and employees. It continued to cover employees and retirees, but coverage for their dependants was dropped. Regarding the types of services, coverage was limited by an essential drug list that included about 1,400 Western and 500 manufactured Chinese medicines, as well as different local regulations (cf. Bloom and Tang 2004: 33; Tian et al. 2012). The coverage of costs was decreased by the introduction of copayments and deductibles. The insurance funds consisted of individual MSAs and risk-pooling funds at the city level. Individual contributions are usually deposited into the MSAs, and employer contributions into the pooling funds. As a rule of thumb, the MSAs cover outpatient expenditures, while inpatient expenditures are eligible for reimbursement from the pooling funds within the limitations of copayments and deductibles. There is substantial local variation of these basic rules (Bloom and Tang 2004: 31–7).

Figure 2.1 illustrates the coverage of different health insurance schemes in the Chinese population in 1993, 1998 and 2003. The share of people not covered by any insurance in those years was 69.9 percent, 76.4 percent and 70.3 percent respectively, and the vast majority of them were rural citizens. By 2003, UEBMI, the CMS and commercial insurance emerged as the main insurance systems. Together, they arguably covered about 25 percent of the Chinese population. As noted above, the share of services and costs covered by these insurance systems could be severely restricted (MoH 2004: 16).

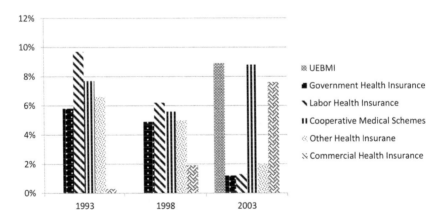

Figure 2.1 Insurance Coverage of the Population in the Early Reform Period
Source: MoH 2004: 16.

With the retrenchment of public social security, the Chinese population increasingly turned to alternative forms of social security. China's emerging markets provided alternative sources of medical care and social security: apart from the growth of commercial insurance, people increasingly relied on the pharmacy system for self-treatment. The proportion of the sick who resorted to self-medication while forgoing professional treatment rose from around 20.8 percent in 1993 to 28.5 percent in 1998, and to 35.7 percent in 2003 (MoH 1994: 30; MoH 1999: 52; MoH 2004: 33). Especially in the rural areas, the importance of informal social security provided by community, friends or family and kin increased dramatically. The main sources of rural social security were family solidarity (*jiating baozhang*) and the rights to collective land (*tudi baozhang*) (Zhang 2005). The vacuum of social security that the collective institutions left behind was filled by diverse actors and practices. Informal credit arrangements in family and friendship networks became an important strategy of coping with financial shock (Gu 2005). The difficulties in accessing and financing healthcare, along with the more open political climate of the reform period, facilitated a revival of traditional healers and shamanistic practices (Heberer 2001). Furthermore, spiritual and religious organizations such as Qi Gong groups or Pentecostal churches benefitted from the new social insecurity, which created a fertile ground for the traditional notions of health and sickness that were part of their moral agenda (Kupfer 2008; Oblau 2011). Informal social security, however, is not only less effective than formal health insurance and services, but also provides a fertile ground for political mobilization, as the Falun Gong incidents illustrate.

Market Regulation

After 1979, the Chinese government began to relax its control of the processes of commodity production and distribution. A dual system emerged on a fee-for-service basis, in which the prices for some goods and services were set or regulated by the government, whereas others were set by the interplay of supply and demand. Three pricing mechanisms operated in this dual system: first, fixed prices set by the government (*guojia dingjia*); second, leading prices (*guojia zhidao jia*), which allowed for a fluctuation of the actual price within a defined scope; and, third, market prices (*shichang tiaojie jia*). Setting ex-factory, wholesale and retail prices continued to be applied to certain commodities, organizations or a certain share of the production. For medical drugs, the line between market and government prices was largely drawn according to the type of drug. For medical services, on the other hand, the distinction between for-profit and non-profit healthcare providers became crucial.

The reforms in 2000 created the systems of service and drug pricing that dominated the following decade, until the New Health Reform began to alter them. The Development and Reform Commission (DRC) emerged as a super-ministry with comprehensive jurisdiction in product and service pricing. Its main policy tools were fixed prices (*dingjia*) for drugs and leading prices (*zhidao jia*) for services. Furthermore, the Essential Medicines list, positive lists for the different insurance systems, classification lists for health services and so on were important tools for market regulation and health planning. Service prices are normally determined at the provincial level in negotiations with the hospitals (Liu et al. 2000: 158). The system for drug prices covers the provincial and central level; it is more opaque and complicated, and targeted by systematic lobbying of the pharmaceutical industry and the protectionism of provincial governments (Duckett 2011: 18; Yang 2009).

Service Prices

Medical services remained integrated into the larger system of price regulation in the reform period. For basic medical services, prices were often set below the costs of production, so that hospitals incurred losses from their regular operations. Starting in the mid-1980s, higher prices with a profit margin were set for new types of medical services—most notably services involving high-tech equipment. Along with the 15 percent profit margin for drug sales, such services could cross-subsidize the provision of basic health services.

For non-profit healthcare providers, low service prices made cross-subsidizing a necessity, as a study of Liu and colleagues indicates:

> We estimated costs of 130 service items. … A comparison of estimated costs of those services with their regulated fees … indicated that about 6% of the services had a cost-recovery rate of less than 10%; 12% had a recovery rate between 10 and 20%; about half had a recovery rate between 21 and 50%. In terms of service types, the recovery rate for hospital registration procedure was only 16%; the rate for hospital bed and board was only 25%; the recovery rate for surgical operations was about 30%; for general examinations and treatments, it was 40%. In only 4% of services (especially high-tech services) were fees set higher than their costs.
>
> (Liu et al. 2000: 158)

The dysfunctionality of this system can be demonstrated by a hypothetical example of a small THC, with no lucrative high-tech services and little to no government support. If it provided RMB 300 worth of basic medical services to a patient, the net loss would be RMB 150 at a cost-recovery rate of 50 percent. In order to compensate for this loss via drug sales, the THC would need to sell the patient RMB 1,000 worth of drugs with a profit margin of 15 percent. This would formally uphold pricing regulations, but at the same time seriously violate medical ethics and contradict the interests of the patient (see also Dong et al. 1999b).

During the 1980s and 1990s, the State Planning Commission was responsible for pricing policies, while the local price bureaus—in cooperation with the health authorities—were in charge of defining service items and setting fixed prices for services. As a result, every province had its own classification system and pricing standards, which contained many loopholes and allowed for overcharging. One common strategy was "unbundling": systematically increasing health costs by disaggregating services into smaller items and charging them separately. A task force organized by the health economics institute of the MoH in 1998 criticized the decentralized denomination system as chaotic and allowing too many loopholes and opportunities for manipulation by the hospitals (Li 2008: 145ff.; Liu et al. 2000: 159f.; Zhou 2008: 127–30).

These criticisms were addressed in the reform of health service pricing in 2000, which introduced a national catalog of service items mandatory for for-profit as well as non-profit facilities. Service pricing came under the jurisdiction of the Reform and Development Commissions (*Fagaiwei*) and the health bureaucracy at the central, provincial and prefectural level. The central level defined a national index of service items, which became the mandatory frame of reference for all healthcare providers. The central level also specified the calculation methods for production costs and defined the general principles and specific policies of service pricing. The province sets and adapts leading prices and may delegate some of these responsibilities to the prefectural level. Fixed prices for health services were generally abolished, so leading and market prices remained the only pricing mechanisms for health services. State leading prices were mandatory for non-profit healthcare facilities, while for-profit facilities were allowed to set their own (market-based) prices. The health and price bureaucracies were made responsible for controlling prices and production costs of services, with the national index of health service items setting a standard for the denotation and content of health service items that is mandatory for non-profit as well as for-profit health providers. After consultations with the provinces, the first index appeared in 2001 and has been adapted several times since then (Jijiage 2000: 1751; Jijiage 2001: 1560; Li 2008: 148f.).

The reform arguably achieved a certain progress towards unifying national standards; it was also characterized by certain imperfections and was ineffective in various ways. Many provinces strategically delayed the implementation, in some cases for several years, and health service expenditures arguably did not decrease after the implementation (Li 2008: 148f.). It arguably failed to enforce the national index of service items as a basis for accounting: in a 2012 document on problems related to service pricing, the DRC felt the need to re-emphasize that newly created service items were the mandatory basis of accounting for all non-profit providers and that unbundling was acceptable under no circumstances whatsoever; furthermore, when service items were merged, provincial pricing authorities were to closely monitor the process to avoid additional financial burdens for the patients (Fagaijiage 2012). Furthermore, service prices under this new system did not differentiate the price level according to the level of the facility. They thus created incentives for patients to visit hospitals on higher administrative levels, where they would get the same service items at the same price, but apparently with better quality (*China Economic Times* 2015).

As Professor Yu Baorong argues, despite its attempt to include service costs in the pricing methods, the 2000 reform failed to rationalize China's health pricing structures. Hospitals' commonly used accounting systems do not reflect the prices of particular services very well, and the costs of labor inherent in the prices can only be calculated indirectly. Most pricing departments continue to use the incremental base number method to calculate prices. In order to properly implement the 2000 reform and include the costs of production, new methods of price calculation are required. Finally, there needs to be a link-up between service pricing and governmental support and subsidies for hospitals. If the government compensates most operational expenditures, its dominant role in pricing is justified. If it compensates only a part of those expenditures, it can set leading prices to cover the remaining costs. If the government gives no support to hospitals, the latter should set the prices themselves. Even after the 2000 reform, health service prices thus largely failed to accurately reflect the costs of production and the balance of supply and demand (Yu et al. 2012: 27f.).

Drug Prices and Pharmaceutical Sector Regulation

Service pricing, drug pricing and drug distribution mechanisms are highly interdependent issues, as those regulatory systems provide a joint structure of incentives for healthcare providers. Regulations for drug pricing and distribution saw a substantial liberalization during the 1980s, which was subsequently reduced again when liberalization did not achieve the desired outcomes. With regard to pricing, in 1984 the central government issued a catalog of 374 medicines for which ex-factory and retail prices were set by a central organ, while jurisdiction over the rest was left to the provinces. In 1986 and 1988, central policies released control of pharmaceutical pricing and greatly extended the scope of market-based pricing. In a parallel move, the static drug distribution system was liberalized: drug wholesale stations were allowed to trade with providers across administrative levels and jurisdictions, drug factories were allowed to trade with hospitals directly, and private salespersons and drug collectors emerged. The latter often operated without a license: they purchased old drugs from households and resold them via retailers—for example, to village clinics. The new pharmaceutical regulation was characterized by substantial liberalization (Dong et al. 1999a; Zhou 2008: 132f.).

The market dynamics did not, however, develop as intended, which was to some extent rooted in the structures of the pharmaceutical sector. By the middle of the 1990s, only 10 percent of more than 5,000 pharmaceutical producers qualified as middle-sized or large enterprises. Small- and medium-sized businesses are difficult to monitor and often have close relations to the government. The intense pressure for competition and asymmetric information and monitoring difficulties facilitated problematic business strategies that involved decreasing drug quality and securing sales via kickbacks. Health providers continued to charge a 15 percent profit margin based on the wholesale price; neither hospitals nor pharmaceutical companies were thus interested in low price levels. There was a general trend towards high drug prices and high kickbacks, and drug expenditures rose quickly in the late 1980s and early 1990s. The quality of drugs was also often substandard due to problematic production and circulation processes. Among the effects of marketization were rising costs and drug safety issues (Dong et al. 1999a; Liu 2011: 229–54; Zhou 2008: 132ff.).

The central government reacted by tightening control over the pharmaceutical sector again during the 1990s. In 1996, a new system for drug pricing returned to setting leading and fixed prices, most notably for drugs with a monopoly status, certain preventive and curative medicines of extensive clinical application, and other special types of drugs. The National Price Bureau (*Wujiaju*), later incorporated into the DRC, and its provincial counterparts were assigned the responsibility to set prices. They were in charge of the drugs in the national and local drug catalogs respectively. The health and drug administrations on all levels, as well as the price bureaus below the provincial level, were prohibited from setting prices. For drugs not listed in the catalogs, the manufacturing enterprises could, in principle, set the prices themselves. The pricing mechanisms and positive lists were adapted various times through the 1990s and 2000s. Ex-factory prices were to cover production costs and allow for a profit of up to 20 percent. Sales prices were to promote a rational distribution of drugs and allow for a profit. As a rule of thumb, there are markups of 15 percent at the wholesale and retail stages respectively (Jijiaguan 1996: 1590; Zhou 2008: 135–53).

Beyond this basic outline, there are more complex regulations in the pricing system. A 1997 amendment added more detailed rules for price calculation and assigned higher profit margins to enterprises with "good manufacturing practices," a regulation that was subsequently used by provincial governments for protectionism and support of their own affiliated industries, which undermined the reliability of good manufacturing practices as a quality indicator (Jijiaguan 1997: 199; Zhou 2008: 146–50). Unlike regular health services, the prices for self-manufactured medicines of the providers were allowed to "include the costs of labor" and thus yielded a larger profit margin, which contributed to healthcare facilities' medically dubious preferences for intravenous treatment instead of oral treatment (World Bank 1997: 43).

In 2000, the Planning Commission adapted the pricing system for drugs again. Its focus was to shift away from production and wholesale prices to retail prices, for which maximum levels were to be defined via the tool of fixed prices. Maximum retail prices were to be fixed either by the government or by the manufacturing company, and the manufacturing companies were encouraged to print those prices on the box to prevent fraudulent behavior. The scope of state pricing included the medicines in the new UEBMI catalog, and a number of medicines with a "monopoly-character," including psychotropic drugs, anesthesia, vaccines for immunization, and drugs for family planning. The National Planning Commission was in charge of pricing class-A drugs on the UEBMI list and drugs with a monopoly character; the provincial planning commissions were in charge of class-B drugs on the UEBMI list. In the 2000s, government pricing covered only a small share of the types of medicines, but a large share of the volume of pharmaceutical sales: by 2009, "approximately 10 percent of drugs (accounting for 40 percent of revenues) are subject to price regulation" (Wagstaff et al. 2009: 117). Despite frequent governmental price reductions in the 2000s, the costs of healthcare and hospitalization kept growing. As Meng and colleagues indicate, there were numerous strategies hospitals and local governments could use to protect their revenues (Meng 2005). Much like the 2000 service pricing reform, the drug pricing reform changed the institutional framework of pricing but did not alter the dynamics of cost development (Jijiage 2000: 961).

Purchasing and Circulation

In the course of the 1980s and 1990s, the rigidity of economic planning in the pharmaceutical sector was relaxed and the channels of trade were liberalized. The pharmaceutical sector grew comparatively fast from the 1980s. Due to large numbers of small-scale producers and traders, it is generally characterized by over-competition and over-capacity. By the middle of the 1990s, only 10 percent of more than 5,000 pharmaceutical producers qualified as middle-sized or large enterprises. Over-competition pressured producers and wholesale companies to supply at low prices—often by compromising quality—and to share part of their profit margin with the hospitals they sold to. "Kickbacks" (*huikou*) are a prominent mechanism of such profit-sharing. The incentives of healthcare facilities were usually determined by under-financing and the pricing system: minimizing the purchasing price and increasing the "15 percent" profit margin, which tended to be calculated on the basis of the formal leading price, rather than the actual purchasing price.[2] During the 1990s, problems of drug security became more visible at the grassroots level, most notably at village clinics and small clinics (*zhensuo*), and with hospitals' self-manufactured drugs. The general configuration of interest, consolidated by over-competition in the pharmaceutical markets and the informal privatization of healthcare facilities, has persisted through different regimes so far (Gong et al. 2010; Liu 2011: 229–32; Zhou 2008: 132ff.).

During the 1990s, drugs salespersons and retailers entered the circulation system as new actors, making it more complicated and competitive. Sales could be facilitated across administrative levels, jurisdictional boundaries and directly between producing companies and healthcare facilities. For THCs and village clinics, the county wholesale stations remained important sources, but markets and bazaars in urban centers also played an important role. The liberalized system was effective in fulfilling demand, but was more difficult to regulate and control, with illegal drug collectors buying left-over medicine from households and reselling it. Many wholesale companies operated without a license and withdrawn from public control, while low-quality, fake or illegal merchandise were common phenomena (Dong et al. 1999a; Liu 2011: 231).

Around 2000, the Food and Drug Administration (FDA)[3] began to promote bulk purchasing and auctions moderated by the government, which should facilitate quality controls and lower purchasing prices, and thus allow for cheaper merchandise and higher quality for patients. The new system was based on urban bottom-up initiatives[4] of the 1990s and was complemented by major reforms targeting the pharmaceutical sector, such as the centralization of drug registration and the mandatory extension of regulatory standards for good manufacturing and sales practices (Guobanfa 2001: 17; Liu 2011: 229–54). The central reform explicitly prohibited local governments from interfering directly with the purchasing, with the main carriers to be the hospitals or independent organs, which were to be licensed and monitored by the provincial health administrations and FDAs (Guobanfa 2000: 16; Guoyaoguanshi 2000: 306; Weiguicaifa 2000: 232). However, the direct interference of local governments was widespread in rural and urban China (Weiguicaifa 2000: 148).

Neither hospitals nor pharmaceutical companies were genuinely interested in lowering retail prices and passing the benefits to the patients. To many local governments, the reform provided a new source of extra-budgetary revenues. Rather than actually lowering retail prices, the price reductions would benefit local governments and hospitals: localities such as A County merely lowered the wholesale prices, but raised their own profit margin by retaining the retail prices of the governmental pricing system (Interview 111124).[5] Although the 2000 regime arguably enhanced drug security to some extent, the impact of competitive purchasing mechanisms was severely restricted by the failure of the FDA's regulatory reforms and the lingering lack of a nationally integrated, transparent and reliable system of quality indicators. The multitude of different products produced by the fragmented pharmaceutical sector and the lack of reliable and transparent quality standards undermined the local purchasers' ability to compare and assess the quality of different products. Instead, they ultimately depended on the experience-based knowledge of the local doctors, and decision-making often focused primarily on price. Much like the pricing reforms, bidding reforms had a hard time achieving sustainable decreases in health costs (Gong et al. 2010; Yang 2009).

Rising Health Costs and Illness-Induced Poverty in the Reform Period

This chapter has discussed the systemic interdependence and gradual institutional change in China's health sector regulation in the context of the larger transition of the state and the public sector in the reform period. The findings can be summarized as follows. First, the Chinese public finance system in itself has become dysfunctional in the course of the reform era. The transition towards a more market-based economy sparked a fiscal crisis to which the government reacted by centralizing fiscal revenues, while fiscal expenditure mandates remained largely unchanged. Second, health sector regulation has not been thoroughly adapted to this development, which led to an over-stretching of the state in the health system. Hospitals and grassroots health providers continue to be expected to perform social functions—that is, to provide basic health services priced below the costs of production—and public health services such as disease prevention and mother-and-child care. The systemic interdependence between public finances and health sector regulation here manifests itself in the form of massive institutional misfits.

The effects of the institutional misfits on the steering and governance of the health sector in a local context will be discussed in greater detail in Chapter 7. At this point, it is important to note that the mode of financing of healthcare facilities shifted towards a dominant reliance on user fees and the profits for drug sales and diagnostic tests that the pricing system allowed for. Healthcare facilities came to be driven by economic constraints rather than medical constraints, and doctors also acted as sales personnel for drugs and diagnostics tests. As a result, unnecessary medical expenditures increased considerably and the former efficiency of the Chinese healthcare system was largely sacrificed.

Figure 2.2 illustrates the structural changes that occurred in the composition of healthcare financing between 1978 and 2012, which were a direct effect of the institutional changes described above. The category of government expenditures includes funding for health services, contributions to health protection, administrative costs for healthcare protection and birth-planning expenditures. Societal expenditures include the resources from social and commercial insurance, as well as the funding of societal operators of health providers, donations and philanthropy, and revenue from administrative services. Individual expenditures mean the out-of-pocket payments of the patients, which they finance through their income, savings or credit from friends and relatives. Overall, individual financing grew continuously during the reform period from about 20 percent of total health expenditures in 1978 to about 60 percent in 2001. After that, the relative share of government and societal expenditures increased again gradually, and individual expenditures decreased to 34 percent in 2012 (CHFP 2014).

Change in the institutional structures described above facilitated the structural changes in healthcare financing. It also facilitated the rapid growth of overall health costs, with annual rates of 17 percent in the 1990s and 2000s. The distortion in pricing regulations and treatment behavior manifests itself in the high share of drug costs in overall health costs during this time: 40 percent, compared with a 15 percent average in OECD countries. An estimated 30 percent of hospitalizations in China are not medically necessary, and this largely reflects induced demand with little or no productive effects on overall health status. Not only did state retrenchment increase the share of

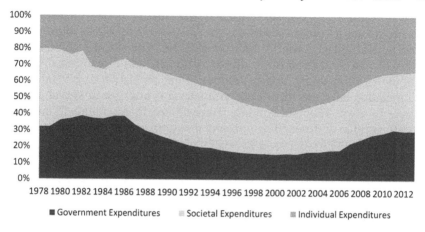

Figure 2.2 Healthcare Financing in the PRC by Sources of Funding
Source: CHFP 2014.

out-of-pocket payments in healthcare financing, but the misfit institutional structures—most notably of the pricing system—further amplify the financial burden on patients by incentivizing and pressuring doctors and healthcare facilities to induce demand (Chen et al. 2010; Tang et al. 2012).

The National Health Service Survey, which has been conducted every five years since 1993, illustrates major trends in the health system. In its sample, which claims to be representative of the Chinese population, the share of those falling sick and not visiting a doctor rose from 36.4 percent in 1993 to 48.8 percent in 2003, and dropped again to 37.6 percent in 2008. The share of those resorting to self-treatment instead of seeing a doctor rose from 20.8 percent in 1993 to 35.7 percent in 2003, and fell again to 27.1 percent in 2008. Among the poor within the samples, the share of those impoverished by accidents and illness rose from 15.2 percent in 1998 to 30 percent in 2003 and to 34.5 percent in 2008. In rural China, the respective figures were 21.6, 33.4 and 37.8 percent. At the time of writing, a comprehensive report about the 2013 survey was not yet publicly available. Access to health services worsened until around 2003 and then improved again. Health reforms arguably contributed to this trend, although official statistics suggest a greater impact of rising rural incomes. Income statistics, however, often paint too optimistic a picture. Illness and accidents, on the other hand, have become the most important generators of poverty in both urban and rural China (MoH 1994, 1999, 2004, 2009).

Illness-induced poverty had been recognized as a local problem since the 1980s, and it became a national policy concern during the 1990s. With the withering or collapse of public social security in the urban and rural areas, households were directly exposed to the risk of high healthcare costs, which are often connected to inpatient treatment and chronic and infectious diseases. The situation of the healthcare system became perceived as a source of social destabilization, as it was threatening the status of the newly ascended rural middle income groups. Furthermore, the SARS incident in 2003 illustrates that epidemics also have a considerable potential for economic destabilization.

Finally, the lack of access to proper healthcare and formal social security, and the direct exposure of large sections of the population to existential risks of livelihood have provided fertile ground for various religious and spiritual groups to grow. They are typically characterized by a traditional, moralistic and/or spiritual understanding of health and disease, and the promise of good health to their followers occupies a central position in their teachings. Health issues are, for example, a driving force behind the spread of Pentecostal Christian groups or Falun Gong. From the perspective of the political system, the healthcare system has the potential not just for social but also for political destabilization (Kupfer 2008; Oblau 2011).

List of Interviews

Interview 111013: Interview with a THC director in C District, October 13, 2011.
Interview 111124: Interview with a local cadre in A County, November 24, 2011.

Notes

1　The administrative *bianzhi* refers to state, government and party organs as well as certain social organizations (*guojia jiguan, zhengdang jiguan* and *shehui tuanti*) and their formal employees. Authority over the administrative *bianzhi* is centralized and ultimately rests with the State Commission of Public Sector Reform (*Zhongyang Jigou Bianzhi Weiyuanhui*). It sets the overall number of authorized civil servant posts for the entire public sector and the different provincial jurisdictions. Provincial governments have jurisdiction over the distribution of their own civil service posts and over the prefectural level. Furthermore, the number of administrative organs is restricted, and establishing new administrative units requires the examination and approval of the next higher level of government. The administrative *bianzhi* regulates the salaries and privileges of cadres whose remuneration is composed of a basic salary and various complementary payments, the standards for which are set by the local government. (See: Shah and Shen 2007; Website of the State Commission of Public Sector Reform: www.scopsr.gov.cn, accessed: September 8, 2015.)
2　Theoretically, this was prohibited in 2001, when the center promoted a new regime of bulk purchases and auctions. This restriction was widely ignored, however, which is why the decreases in purchasing prices hardly ever resulted in lower costs for the patients (Gong et al. 2010; Guobanfa 2001: 17).
3　Market-oriented forces in the central government tried to install a strong regulatory agency—the FDA—to monitor the pharmaceutical sector. The FDA, established under Zhu Rongji's leadership, can to some extent be seen as a market-oriented antipode to the planning bureaucracy that became the DRC. Founded as the State Drug Administration in 1998, its competences were extended in 2003 to include food safety as well. One of its core projects was to integrate pharmaceutical market regulation at the central level and to establish a national system of quality indicators for drugs. Drug registration and approval were centralized, but the FDA was unable to install

nationally comparable quality indicators for drugs—the GMP standard—against the resistance of the provinces. Its effectiveness as a regulatory agency was constrained by a lack of personnel and financial capacity, and massive corruption within the department, which ultimately led to the execution of its commissioner Zheng Xiaoyu and to the integration of the FDA into the MoH (Yang 2009).
4 The initiatives of centralized bidding and purchasing date back to the public auctions of the First People's Hospital of Pingdingshan City in Henan in 1994. Three larger types of approaches were developed in the 1990s: first, single hospitals or groups of hospitals would determine the most suitable company themselves by bidding or consultations; second, the local government would take a leading role in organizing a platform for the bidding process and act as a supervisor and gatekeeper for companies by controlling access to the platform; third, the government would conduct the purchases itself. Local experiments resulted in a number of different models, in which the leading administrative role was usually played either by the local governmental purchasing department (*caigou bumen*) or by the health bureaucracy. Where the local government restricted itself to merely playing a regulatory role, the conduct of bidding and purchasing could be delegated to intermediary organizations, or special markets could be created (Xie and Zhang 1999; Yu 2001; Zhang and Hu 2000).
5 Bulk purchasing and auctions were profitable for local governments, as they could charge a part of the price differential, which already indicates that drugs were not sold at purchasing cost. Local administrators in A County acknowledged that, before the 2009 reforms, the profit margin would be widened considerably by decreasing the wholesale prices through bulk purchasing and selling at official retail prices (Interview 111124; Klotzbücher 2006: 260f.).

Bibliography

Bird, Richard M. and Christine Wong 2005, China's Fiscal System: A Work in Progress, Rotman School of Management Working Paper no. 07-11, online: http://papers.ssrn.com/sol3/papers.cfm?abstract_id=875416 (accessed October 20, 2012).

Bloom, Gerald and Shenglan Tang (eds) 2004, *Health Care Transition in Urban China*, Aldershot: Ashgate.

Brødsgaard, Kjeld E. 2002, Institutional Reform and the Bianzhi System in China, in: *The China Quarterly*, 170, 361–386.

Burns, John P. 2003, "Downsizing" the Chinese State: Government Retrenchment in the 1990s, in: *The China Quarterly*, 175, 776–802.

Cailliez, Charlotte 1998, *The Collapse of the Rural Health System*, online: www.cefc.com.hk/article/the-collapse-of-the-rural-health-system (accessed July 18,2012).

Cao, Xiaoqing 2001, Nongcun weisheng sanxiang jianshe de shijian yu tihui (Practice and Lessons of the Three-Items Construction Program in Rural Healthcare), in: *Weisheng Jingji Yanjiu (Health Economics Research)*, 7, 22.

Chen, Wen et al. 2010, Availability and Use of Essential Medicines in China: Manufacturing, Supply, and Prescribing in Shandong and Gansu Provinces, in: *BMC Health Services Research*, 10, 1, 211.

CHFP 2013, *Zhongguo weisheng he jihua shengyu tongji nianjian (China Statistical Yearbook of Health and Family Planning)*, Beijing: Zhongguo Xiehe Yike Daxue Chubanshe (China Harmony and Medicine University Press).

CHFP 2014, *Zhongguo weisheng he jihua shengyu tongji nianjian (China Statistical Yearbook of Health and Family Planning)*, Beijing: Zhongguo Xiehe Yike Daxue Chubanshe (China Harmony and Medicine University Press).

China Economic Times 2015, Chongqing yigai fengbo jingshi yiliao fuwu jiage gaige (Reforming Health Service Prices: Warnings and Inspirations from the Disturbance of Chongqing's Health Reforms), online: www.hkcd.com/content/2015-04/09/con tent_921692.html (accessed June 24, 2015).

Cui, Shaoqing 1995, Nongcun weisheng sanxiang jianshe de shijian yu tihui (Practice and Lessons from the Three Items Construction Project in Rural China), in: *Zhongguo Nongcun Yixue (China Rural Medicine)*, 23, 11, 2–3.

Dong, Hengjin *et al.* 1999a, Drug Policy in China: Pharmaceutical Distribution in Rural Areas, in: *Social Science and Medicine*, 48, 777–786.

Dong, Hengjin *et al.* 1999b, Health Financing Policies—Providers' Opinions and Pre-scribing Behavior in Rural China, in: *International Journal of Technology Assess-ment in Health Care*, 15, 4, 686–698.

Duckett, Jane 2011, *The Chinese State's Retreat from Health: Policy and the Politics of Retrenchment*, London: Routledge.

Fagaijiage 2012, San bumen guanyu guifan yiliao fuwu jiage guanli ji youguan wenti tongzhi (Notification from Three Ministries about the Regulation of Health Service Price Management and Problems Connected to It).

Fang, Zheng 2003, Nongcun weisheng "Sanxiang jianshe" de shijian yu tihui (Practice and Lessons of the "Three Items Construction" Program), in: *Zhongguo Weisheng Jingji (China Health Economics)*, 22, 4, 14–15.

Gong, Sen, Wei Wang and Liejun Wang 2010, Gaige yu wanshan woguo yaopin jiz-hong caigou zhidu de zhengce yanjiu (Policy Study of the Reform and Improvement of the Centralized Bidding and Purchasing System for Medicines). In *Shipin yaopin anquan jianguan zhengce yanjiu baogao 2010 (The 2010 Research Report on Reg-ulatory Policy in Food and Drug Safety)*. Shipin yaopin lanpishu (Blue Book of Food and Drug Security), ed. Minhao Tang, 262–279, Beijing: Shehui Kexue Wen-xian Chubanshe (Social Sciences Academic Press).

Gu, Xin, Mengtao Gao and Yang, Yao 2005, *Zhenduan yu chufang: Zhimian Zhong-guo yiliao tizhi gaige (China's Health Care Reforms: A Pathological Analysis)*, Beijing: Shehui Kexue Wenxian Chubanshe (Social Sciences Academic Press).

Guobanfa 2000, 16, Guowuyuan Bangongting zhuanfa Guowuyuan Tigaiban deng bumen guanyu chengzhen yiyao weisheng gaige de zhidao yijian de tongzhi (Noti-fication from the General Office of the State Council about the Leading Opinion of the State Commission for Restructuring and other Departments on Urban Health Reform).

Guobanfa 2001, 17, Guowuyuan Bangongting zhuanfa Guowuyuan Tigaiban deng bumen guanyu zhengdun he guifan yaopin shichang yijian de tongzhi (Notification from the General Office of the State Council about the Opinion of the State Com-mission for Restructuring on Reorganizing and Standardizing the Drug Market).

Guofa 1985, 62, Guowuyuan pizhuan Weishengbu guanyu weisheng gongzuo gaige ruogan zhengce wenti de baogao de tongzhi (Notification from the State Council about the Report of the MoH about Several Problems in Health Policy).

Guofa 1998, 44, Guowuyuan guanyu jianli chengzhen zhigong jiben yiliao baoxian zhidu de jueding (Decision of the State Council about Establishing the Urban Employees' Basic Medical Insurance).

Guowuyuan 1989, Guanyu kuoda yiliao weisheng fuwu youguan wenti de yijian (Opinion about Problems Regarding the Extension of Health Services).

Guowuyuan 1996, Guowuyuan Bangongting zhuanfa Weishengbu, Guojia Jiwei, Caizhengbu guanyu nongcun weisheng "sanxiang jianshe" "ba wu" jinzhang qingkuang he "jiu wu" gongzuo yijian baogao de tongzhi (Notification from the General Office of the State Council about the Report of the MoH, the State Planning Commission, and the MoF about the "Three Items Construction" Program, its Progress in the 8th Five-Year Plan Period and its Opinion on Work in the 9th Five-Year Plan Period).

Guoyaoguanshi 2000, 306, Guanyu yinfa yaopin zhaobiao daili jigou zige rending ji jiandu guanli banfa de tongzhi (Notification about the Decree on the Necessary Qualifications and the Administrative Supervision of Medicines Bidding Agencies).

Han, Ronglian 2013, Xin Yigai xingshi xia gongli yiyuan de dingxing jiqi gaige moshi tantao (Discussion of the Nature and Reform Models of Public Hospitals under the New Health Reform), in: *Shanxi Yiyao Zazhi (Shanxi Medical Journal)*, 42, 12, 1436f.

Heberer, Thomas 2001, China: Der Markt sprengt das alte Sozialsystem (The Market Blows Up the Old Social System), in: *Der Überblick*, 1, 54–59.

Hsiao, William C. 2008, When Incentives and Professionalism Collide, in: *Health Affairs*, 27, 4, 949–951.

Huang, Yanzhong 2013, *Governing Health in Contemporary China*, New York: Routledge.

Jijiage 2000, 1751, Guanyu yinfa quanguo yiliao fuwu jiage xiangmu guifan—shixing—de tongzhi (Notification about the National Regulation of Health Service Items—Trial Version).

Jijiage 2000, 961, Guojia Jiwei yinfa guanyu gaige yaopin jiage guanli de yijian de tongzhi (Notification from the State Planning Commission about the Opinion on the Reform of Drug Price Management).

Jijiage 2001, 1560, Guojia Jiwei, Weishengbu guanyu yinfa "Yiliao fuwu xiangmu chengben fentan cesuan banfa—shixing" de tongzhi (Notification from the State Planning Commission and the MoH about the "Experimental Measures Regarding the Calculation and Sharing of Health Service Item Costs").

Jijiaguan 1996, 1590, Yaopin jiage guanli zanxing banfa (Preliminary Regulation of Medicine Price Controls).

Jijiaguan 1997, 199, Yaopin jiage guanli zanxing banfa de buchong guiding (Amendment to the Preliminary Regulation of Medicine Price Controls).

Klotzbücher, Sascha 2006, *Das ländliche Gesundheitswesen der VR China: Strukturen, Akteure, Dynamik (The Rural Health Sector of the People's Republic of China: Actors, Structures, Dynamic)*, Frankfurt: Peter Lang.

Kupfer, Kristin 2008, Soziale Sicherung in der Volksrepublik China und die Rolle spirituell-religiöser Gruppen (Social Security in the PRC and the Role of Spiritual and Religious Groups). In: *Ost- und Südostasien zwischen Wohlfahrtsstaat und Eigeninitiative: Aktuelle Entwicklungstendenzen von Armut, Alterung und sozialer Unsicherheit (East and Southeast Asia between the Welfare State and Individual Initiative: Current Development Trends of Poverty, Ageing, and Social Insecurity)*, eds Karl Husa, Rolf Jordan and Helmut Wohlschlägl, 201–215. Vienna: Universität Wien Institut für Geographie und Regionalforschung.

Lam, Tao C. 2010, The County System and County Governance. In *China's Local Administration: Traditions and Changes in the Sub-National Hierarchy*, eds Jae H. Chung and Tao C. Lam, 149–173. London: Routledge.

Li, Li 2008, *Woguo yiliao fuwu jiage guize de lilun yu shizheng fenxi (Theoretical and Empirical Analysis of the Regulation of Health Service Prices in China)*, Beijing: Jingji Kexue Chubanshe (Economic Science Press).

Liu, Peng 2011, *Zhuanxing zhong de jianguan xing guojia jianshe: jiyu dui Zhongguo yaopin guanli tizhi bianqian—1949–2008—de anli yanjiu (Building the Regulatory State in Transition: A Case-Based Study on the Change of China's System of Drug Administration—1949–2008)*, Bejing: Zhongguo Shehui Kexue Chubanshe (China Social Science Press).

Liu, Xingzhu, Yuanli Liu and Ningshan Chen 2000, The Chinese Experience of Hospital Price Regulation, in: *Health Policy and Planning*, 15, 2, 157–163.

Liu, Xingzhu and Yunni Yi 2004, The Health Sector in China—Policy and Institutional Review, Background Paper of the World Bank Rural Health Study.

Meng, Qingyue 2005, Review of Health Care Provider Payment Reforms in China, Background Paper for the World Bank Rural Health Report, Washington, DC: World Bank.

MoH 1980, Guanyu yunxu geti kaiye xingyi wenti de qingshi baogao (Report and Instructions about Allowing Individual Healthcare Practitioners to Start a Business).

MoH 1994, *Guojia weisheng fuwu yanjiu—1993 nian guojia weisheng fuwu zong diaocha fenxi baogao (Research on National Health Services—An Analysis Report of the National Health Service Survey)*, online: www.moh.gov.cn/publicfiles/business/htmlfiles/mohwsbwstjxxzx/s8560/201009/49159.htm (accessed June 7, 2012).

MoH 1999, *Guojia weisheng fuwu yanjiu—1998 nian di er ci guojia weisheng fuwu diaocha fenxi baogao (Research on National Health Services—An Analysis Report of the Second National Health Service Survey in 1998)*, online: www.nhfpc.gov.cn/cmsresources/mohwsbwstjxxzx/cmsrsdocument/doc9907.pdf (accessed July 18, 2016).

MoH 2004, *Di san ci weisheng fuwu diaocha fenxi baogao (The Third National Health Service Survey Analysis Report)*, online: www.nhfpc.gov.cn/cmsresources/mohwsbwstjxxzx/cmsrsdocument/doc9908.pdf (accessed July 18, 2016).

MoH 2009, *2008 Zhongguo weisheng fuwu diaocha—di si ci jiating jiankang xunwen diaocha fenxi baogao (The 2008 National Health Service Survey—The Fourth Household Health Survey Analysis Report)*, online: www.nhfpc.gov.cn/cmsresources/mohwsbwstjxxzx/cmsrsdocument/doc9911.pdf (accessed July 18, 2016).

MoH, MoF and National Head Office of Labor 1979, Guanyu jiaqiang yiyuan jingji guanli shidian gongzuo de yijian (Opinion about Strengthening the Economic Administration of Hospitals).

Oblau, Gotthard 2011, Divine Healing and the Growth of Practical Christianity in China. In *Global Pentecostal and Charismatic Healing*, ed. Candy G. Brown, pp. 307–327. New York: Oxford University Press.

People's Daily 1979, Guanyu nongcun hezuo yiliao, chijiao yisheng de jige wenti (On Problems Regarding CMS and the Barefoot Doctors). February 7.

People's Daily 1979, Weishengbu deng wuge danwei lianhe fabu "nongcun hezuo yiliao zhangcheng—Shixing cao'an" jinyibu gonggu wanshan nongcun hezuo yiliao zhidu (The MoH and Four Other Units Jointly Issue the "Trial Draft of CMS Regulations" in Order to Consolidate and Improve the Rural CMS System). December 24.

People's Daily 2006, 1979: Chushi tisheng de yiyuan gaige (1979: The First Sounds of Hospital Reform), October 11, 2006, online: http://finance.people.com.cn/GB/8215/71080/4907018.html (accessed June 22, 2016).

Shah, Anwar and Chunli Shen 2007, Fine-Tuning the Intergovernmental Transfer System to Create a Harmonious Society and a Level Playing Field for Regional Development. In *Public Finance in China. Reform and Growth for a Harmonious*

Society, eds Jiwei Lou und Shuilin Wang, pp. 129–154. Washington, DC: World Bank.

Tang, Shenglan, Jingjing Tao and Henk Bekedam 2012, Controlling Cost Escalation of Healthcare: Making Universal Health Coverage Sustainable in China, in: *BMC Public Health*, 12, 58.

Tian, Xin, Yaran Song and Xinping Zhang 2012, National Essential Medicines List and Policy Practice: A Case Study of China's Health Care Reform, in: *BMC Health Services Research*, 12, 1, 401.

Wagstaff, Adam *et al.* 2009, *Reforming China's Rural Health System*, Washington, DC: World Bank.

Weiguicaifa 2000, 232, Guanyu yinfa yiliao jigou yaopin jizhong zhaobiao caigou shidian gongzuo ruogan guiding de tongzhi (Notification about Several Regulations Regarding the Piloting of the Concentrated Bidding and Purchasing of Drugs for Healthcare Facilities).

Weiguicaifa 2000, 148, Weishengbu guanyu jiaqiang yiliao jigou yaopin jizhong zhaobiao caigou shidian guanli gongzuo de tongzhi (Notification from the MoH about Strengthening the Administration of Bidding and Purchasing Pilots for Health Facilities' Medicines).

Weiguicaifa 2006, 340, Guanyu yinfa "Nongcun weisheng fuwu tixi jianshe yu fazhan guihua" de tongzhi (Notification about the "Plan for the Construction and Development of the Rural Healthcare System").

Wong, Christine 2009, Rebuilding Government for the 21st Century: Can China Incrementally Reform the Public Sector?, in: *The China Quarterly*, 200, 929–952.

World Bank 1997, *Financing Health Care, Issues and Options for China*, Washington, DC: World Bank.

World Bank 2002, *China—National Development and Sub-National Finance*, online: www.worldbank.org/research/2002/04/1768217/china-national-development-sub-na tional-finance-review-provincial-expenditures (accessed February 8, 2012).

World Bank 2007a, *China: Improving Rural Public Finance for the Harmonious Society*, Report No. 41579-CN, online: www-wds.worldbank.org/external/default/ WDSContentServer/WDSP/IB/2007/12/21/000020953_20071221113708/Rendered/P DF/415790CN.pdf (accessed April 25, 2012).

World Bank 2007b, *China: Public Services for Building the New Socialist Countryside*, Report No. 40221-CN, online: www-wds.worldbank.org/external/default/WDSCon tentServer/WDSP/IB/2008/01/16/000020953_20080116091210/Rendered/PDF/40221 0CN.pdf (accessed November 10, 2012).

Xie, Hongli and Xiuhua Zhang 1999, Qianyi yaopin jizhong zhaobiao caigou (Discussing Centralized Bidding Purchases of Drugs), in: *Zhongguo Weisheng Jingji (China Health Economics)*, 18, 12, 29–30.

Yang, Dali 2009, *Regulatory Learning and its Discontents in China: Promise and Tragedy at the State Food and Drug Administration*, online: https://daliyang.files.wordp ress.com/2013/09/sfda.pdf (accessed June 22, 2016).

Yu, Baorong 2001, Jiushi niandai woguo yiliao jigou yaopin caigou fangshi gaige shijian huigu (A Review of Chinese Hospitals' Drug Purchasing Reforms in the Nineties), in: *Zhongguo Weisheng Jingji (China Health Economics)*, 20, 2, 24–25.

Yu, Baorong *et al.* 2012, *Yiliao fuwu chengben ji jiage tixi yanjiu (An Empirical Study on Health Care Costs and Pricing in China)*, Jinan: Shandong Daxue Chubanshe (Shandong University Press).

Zhang, Renwei and Shanlian Hu 2000, Woguo dangqian shishi yaopin jizhong zhao-
    biao caigou de gaikuang (The Current Situation of Centralized Bidding and Pur-
    chasing of Medicines in China), in: *Zhongguo Weisheng Jingji (China Health
    Economics)*, 19, 11, 21–24.
Zhang, Wei 2005, *Sozialwesen in China (Social Security in China)*, Hamburg: Dr.
    Kovac.
Zhou, Xuerong 2008, *Zhongguo yiliao jiage de zhengfu guanzhi yanjiu (Government
    Control of Medical Prices in China)*, Beijing: Shehui Kexue Chubanshe (Social
    Science Press).

3   Contested Policy

The Two Attempts to Rebuild the CMS

The institutional changes described in Chapter 2 have been the outcome of political processes and the balance of power between pro-government and pro-market actors in the national arena. They have been the target of constant contestation and political conflict, as this chapter will show using the example of the CMS in the 1980s and 1990s. By the mid-1980s, the central government had decided to establish a public rural social security system until the year 2000, which was to guarantee, among other things, universal access to healthcare. On the one hand, the social problems caused by the fallback on family as the primary guarantee of social security already had become visible by the mid-1980s (Hsiao and Du 1985). On the other, the one-child policy would ultimately render the model of family-based social security unsustainable. As noted in Chapter 2, the overburdening of families' financial capacity by illness-related burdens and financial shocks increasingly caused temporary or permanent impoverishment in the rural areas. Against this background, the central government decided to explore new options for the rural welfare regime. The problem of illness-induced poverty was to become pivotal in the process of agenda-setting for a rural public health insurance system.

The main choice was between state-provided healthcare and a more market-oriented approach. A market-oriented approach meant the primary responsibility of the PICC for local insurance programs and individual insurance contracts. The MoH and the MoCA were the main ministerial stakeholders of state-provided social security, and they were not ready to leave social security in the rural areas to the PICC alone. The second half of the 1980s was thus characterized by strategic local experimentation with various risk-pooling programs in health and pensions. The 1990s saw two initiatives to rebuild the CMS in the rural areas, one enacted in 1991 and the other in 1996/97. Both of the programs failed to attain nationwide coverage at the implementation stage. By 2000, insurance companies were expanding quickly in the rural areas.

This chapter will analyze the policy process around the establishment of a rural social security system between 1985 and 2000, focusing on health insurance and the CMS. The first part will introduce the main actors in the national arena and the political status quo between the pro-government and pro-market actors during this time. The second part will focus on the competing experiments in the 1980s. The third and fourth part will analyze the first and second initiative to rebuild the CMS in the rural areas. Chapter 4 will continue with the policy process of the NRCMS.

Bureaucratic Actors and the Dynamics of Politics in the National Policy Arena

Policy Options, Actors and Preferences

In the national arena, issue-related coalitions and aggregates of corporate actors play a dominant role. Chinese health policy is characterized by the opposition of pro-government and pro-market actors (Yip and Hsiao 2015). Bureaucratic actors and elite networks align in changing coalitions in order to promote their interests and political visions. The preferences of some bureaucratic actors were clearly dominated by institutional self-interest, whereas the preferences of others depended strongly on the political allegiance of the ministry's leadership. Furthermore, the political balance in the leadership core had an important effect on the mode of interaction between the actors of both sides. Among the most crucial personalities were the Premiers Li Peng and Zhu Rongji, who supported the pro-government and pro-market actors respectively.

In rural health insurance, the difference between a public and a market solution is closely linked to the administrative affiliation to either a government department or a commercial company. Ideal-typically, public insurance would be compulsory and aim at securing basic living standards, whereas commercial insurance would be voluntary and more differentiated regarding specific needs (cf. Gong 2003: 217f.). Public insurance in China today mainly appears in the form of parity-based social insurance or of tax-financed insurance systems such as the NRCMS or the URBMI, but during the 1980s and 1990s there also was a great variety of community-based CMS systems. Commercial insurance has always taken very diverse forms, including individual basic and complementary health insurance contracts, local governments purchasing standardized commercial insurance packages for the local population, and local governments contracting insurance companies for the administration of public insurance programs for a fixed fee.

The main bureaucratic stakeholder in public rural health insurance has been the MoH, under whose jurisdiction were the CMS and NRCMS schemes until its merger with the National Population and Family Planning Commission (NPFPC) in 2013, which created the Commission of Health and Family Planning (CHFP) (Guobanfa 2013: 22). Jurisdiction then passed to the Ministry of Human Resources and Social Security (MoHRSS), which is now in charge of all public insurance programs in China—that is, parity-based social insurance for (urban) employees, and tax-funded health and pension insurance for urban and rural residents. Despite its conflicts with the MoH with respect to jurisdiction over the NRCMS program, the MoHRSS is also a core pro-government actor. The MoCA is a third key actor: during the 1990s, it was in charge of public social security in the rural areas. During the 2000s, its competences shifted towards social assistance programs such as Dibao or Medical Assistance. In the wider field of health policy, the DRC and the NPFPC are interested in a strong role of the government due to their functional setup.

The MoH's core interests were determined by its institutional setup. On the one hand, it had regulatory authority over China's health providers, and large sections of the hospital system were directly subordinated to its line bureaucracy. Furthermore, large parts of its staff were recruited from the medical profession (Duckett 2011b). The MoH therefore has acted as a representative of the interests of the medical profession in national politics. On the other hand, the MoH had regulatory authority over most of China's cooperative medical systems until 2013 and beyond. It thus plays a double role as the representative of both the supply side and the demand side in China's healthcare markets.

Generally, the MoH had an interest in expanding its competences on both fronts. With regard to the question of health providers, the MoH spearheaded marketization reforms in the late 1970s and early 1980s, and largely maintained this course until the SARS crisis in 2003 (Duckett 2011b). Before the New Health Reform, when the status quo described above was openly called into question, it began to promote a National Health Service-like model in which hospitals would be largely state-financed again (Huang 2013). As this chapter will show, the pattern in risk-pooling was similar. The MoH by and large preferred a CMS system supported by state subsidies and aiming at universal coverage of the rural population, as will be shown in this chapter. However, it has also repeatedly abandoned the CMS program—in 1980 (Duckett 2011a) and again in 1998—when the political tides strongly empowered the pro-market actors and the CMS came under political attack.

The pro-market camp was more diversely structured and consisted of economic organizations and ministerial bodies with largely compatible preferences regarding rural social security. In the case of rural pension insurance, the coordination between the different actors in the national arena is well documented (Gong 2003). With regard to health insurance, previous research has mainly acknowledged the role of the MoA and its anti-burden campaign.

The main bureaucratic stakeholders in commercial health insurance are public and private insurance companies. The insurance companies had been establishing themselves as actors in the rural insurance markets since 1978, and in the early reform era the PICC basically enjoyed a monopoly. Since the 1980s, other companies appeared, among them Ping An and China Pacific (*Taipingyang Baoxian*). During the 1990s, the insurance industry underwent substantial restructuring: the CIRC was established and assumed regulatory authority, formerly held by the People's Bank of China (PBoC); the PICC was dissolved and China Life (*Zhongguo Renshou*) emerged as one of three succeeding companies. China Life retained strong personal ties with the PBoC and the CIRC after the reform, whereas less is known about the channels of political influence of other companies (New York Times Online, October 25, 2012; Pearson 2005). The rural areas offer vast and largely undeveloped markets for the Chinese insurance industry, and thus are crucial for domestic growth. However, local governments were often reluctant to cooperate with insurance companies, which created substantial barriers of access to the rural markets (Interview 101129; Hussain 1990; IBS Research Center 2009).

Wu Dingfu, the president of the CIRC, summarized the interests of the insurance industry in expanding into the rural insurance markets for health and other social risks as follows:

> By going to the countryside and marketing insurance to the farmers, we develop their consciousness for insurance, cultivate a massive potential of latent consumers, acquire valuable sources of data, accumulate management experiences and lay the foundations for a later spread of commercial insurance in the rural areas ... the urban insurance markets are already saturated, and there is desperate competition.
>
> (People's Daily, August 22, 2005)

Rural health insurance was part of a larger strategic portfolio of insurance products to be marketed in the rural areas, and part of a long-term development strategy.

Furthermore, financially conservative actors such as the MoF and the PBoC have traditionally favored non-public solutions over financial commitments of the state. The MoF was a super-ministry "unwilling to introduce policies that created open-ended commitments to fund health risk protection from general taxation—and generally supportive of user fees, commercialization and privatization" (Duckett 2011b: 17). This position has arguably been reinforced by the fiscal crisis the PRC went through during economic transition, and the dysfunctional public finance system that emerged from it (Wang and Hu 2001; Wong 2009). It opposed plans for expanding the funding of hospitals during the tenth and eleventh five-year plan periods "with concerns about the inability to control costs, waste of resources, and inefficient allocation" (Saich 2008: 100). As this chapter will show, it also played an important role in sabotaging the implementation of CMS policies during the 1990s. Its consent to funding could only be secured after the emergence of a stable consensus in the leadership core to expand public social security in 2001 (Duckett 2011b: 17f., 36f.; Liu and Yi 2004: 23).

The Ministry of Agriculture was another crucial yet ambivalent actor, as its preferences regarding rural healthcare depended on institutional self-interest, the general political climate and the preferences of its leadership. It supported the MoH's plans to expand public social security in the early 1990s. However, in the wake of the leadership change in 1992/93 and massive riots about illegal fees and charges in the rural areas, the MoA began to issue "anti-burden" policies that directly conflicted with the CMS, but to a lesser degree with the rural pension program. Those policies forbade the use of township and village fees for the CMS, and emphasized a strict interpretation of the rule of voluntary enrollment for the CMS and pension insurance. In terms of political communication, this opposition was framed as different visions of the appropriate approach to rural poverty reduction (Klotzbücher 2006: 201). Burden reduction and voluntariness was arguably a greater problem for the CMS, which operated with pooling accounts, and the effectiveness of which thus depended on high enrollment rates. Many villagers saw health and elderly care as family affairs, rather than affairs of public policy, and were generally reluctant to pool their resources with those of other families (Wu 2004). The pension program mainly operated with savings accounts, and could thus handle much lower rates of enrollment. Although the MoA's approach to the rural burden problem directly conflicted with the extension of health and pension insurance, its preferences were also highly dependent on the minister. It changed its allegiance twice after a change of the minister in charge: in 1993, it became an opponent of the CMS, and in 2001 it returned to supporting the CMS.

The Rural Welfare Regime: Status Quo and Policy Process

Between 1978 and 1985, rural China's commune-based welfare system collapsed. Until that time, the collective organization of the economy had provided a certain protection against the social risks connected to old age or ill health, but these risks were shifted to the households as it vanished. Since then, rural social security has been characterized by the conflicting interests of pro-government and pro-market actors. In the 1980s and 1990s, the main stakeholders in state-oriented policies were the MoCA and the MoH, while the pro-market camp included the PICC, the MoF and others. At the core of the conflict was the question whether rural insurance should be organized by government organs or by the PICC, and it characterized the fields of insurance against natural disasters, pension insurance and health insurance (Hussain 1990: 146; People's Daily, December 21, 1987). A central political motivation behind the development of a public rural social security system was to compensate the villagers for the one-child policy, which undermined the traditional and informal mode of social security via the family (*jiating baozhang*) (Huang 2009). The PICC, on the other hand, was interested in expanding into and developing the rural commercial insurance markets, which offered the potential of rapid and substantial growth (Griffin 1992).

The pro-government actors by and large promoted a rural CMS system supported by financial transfers from the central government. International experts realized during the 1980s that insurance schemes would be difficult to establish in the poorer areas of rural China without government subsidies

(Hussain 1990: 146). As early as 1980, a delegation of the World Bank was informed by the MoH that the Central Government planned to support the CMS in poor areas via financial transfers over the next ten years (World Bank 1983: 31). However, for a variety of reasons, including its inability to realize those preferences politically, the MoH subsequently abandoned its support for the CMS system (Duckett 2011a). Therefore, overall governmental budgetary support for the CMS in China decreased from around RMB 100 million in 1979 to about RMB 25 million in 1987 and remained low through most of the 1990s (Cao 2009: 24).

On the pro-market side, the insurance industry sought to create and maintain conditions for its growth in the rural markets. Insurance companies had a diverse portfolio, including individual contracts, administrative services in insurance programs such as the CMS for a fixed fee, and standardized commercial insurance packages for local governments to purchase with money they collected from the villagers. The fiscally conservative MoF tried to prevent large financial commitments of public budgets to social security. Furthermore, in the course of the 1990s the MoA and the MoF engaged in reducing the amount of fees and charges the rural population had to pay to sustain local government operations. The latter two points are closely connected to the fiscal crisis the Chinese party-state experienced in the course of the economic transition (Wang 2009; Wang and Hu 2001).

Both the pro-government and pro-market actors occupied influential positions in the bureaucracy and neither side was able to fully enforce its preferences on the other. Rather, the balance of power between them shifted in accordance with the balance of power in the bureaucratic leadership core. Through most of the 1980s and 1990s, it was the pro-market side that had the upper hand, and the outcome was a peculiar political consensus that can be summarized in three principles: the subsistence of local communities, the primary responsibility of the household and the voluntariness of public rural insurance programs.

1   Regarding the subsistence of local communities, rural insurance, as well as social security and public service provision in general, was to be primarily financed from local sources. Only poverty areas were entitled to intergovernmental transfers. This was reflected in the financing arrangements of health and pension insurance programs, and rural healthcare providers. Subsistence was an institutional heritage from the planned economy era, which remained valid in the context of the household responsibility system until the early 2000s. It institutionalized the responsibility of the communities—villages and townships—for their own population, and meant that the CMS systems were to be primarily financed from local resources. This principle was largely abandoned in the 2000s as a result of the introduction of governmental financial support via matching funds for the NRCMS and the new rural pension insurance.

2   The primary responsibility of the households for social security institutionalized the shift of social risks from the economic collectives to the
families. This and the concurrent shift of economic responsibility resulted
from the introduction of the household responsibility system in agriculture from the late 1970s on. With their rights to collective land, the
family and household were the primary units of economic production,
and thus assumed the primary responsibility for social security. Schemes
such as the CMS or pension insurance supported households as the main
carrier of responsibility, rather than becoming the main carriers themselves. This principle remains valid at the time of writing and is formally
stated in the policy documents of rural pension insurance, for example
(Guofa 2009: 32).

3   Rural insurance is to follow the principle of voluntary participation. On
the level of political communication, voluntariness constitutes a protection mechanism for the rural population against arbitrary fees and charges, and should pressure local cadres to implement the policy well and
establish relationships of trust with the rural population. It stands in the
context of the social conflicts connected to the "farmers' burden" (*nongmin fudan*) agenda in the 1990s (Bernstein and Lü 2003; Göbel 2010).
For local cadres, however, it was rarely practicable to organize a CMS on
a truly voluntary basis (Bloom et al. 1995). In the absence of effective
premium collection mechanisms based on the collective economy, factors
such as adverse selection, opposition to pooling and low trust in local
cadres constituted fundamental obstacles. Those obstacles could often
only be overcome by authority, pressure and coercion. This contradiction
was systematically exploited by the pro-market actors in the national
arena to sabotage and delegitimize the CMS by highlighting its involuntary aspects. The voluntariness and burden nexus in political communication coincides with the MoH dropping its support for the CMS in
1980 (cf. Bernstein and Lü 2003: 43; Duckett 2011a; People's Daily,
February 7, 1979) and 1998. Voluntariness remains a formal principle in
the NRCMS and rural pension insurance at the time of writing, but its
enforcement is limited by the requirement of full household participation,
participation targets in local cadre evaluations and an array of informal
practices (Müller 2016).

The interaction situation of the two coalitions is illustrated in Figure 3.1,
which uses a prisoner's dilemma for its reconstruction. The actors on both
sides were caught in a complex web of distributional conflicts, which
evolved around three key issues of the rural welfare regime: first, whether
health insurance should be public or commercial; second, whether public
insurance should be partly financed by taxes and communal resources; and,
third, whether insurance should be voluntary or mandatory. In the 1980s and
1990s, the status quo described above was the common framework of
reference.

Pro-market Actors

	Respect status quo	Disregard status quo
Respect status quo	3 (A) 3	4 (B) 1
Disregard status quo	1 (C) 4	2 (D) 2

Pro-government

Actors

Figure 3.1 The Two Coalitions in Agenda Setting

Due to the low political priority of rural social security, there was no institutionalized policy regime. Ministerial competences were not always clarified, and whether a violation of the status quo or an actor's role would be sanctioned depended on the political balance of power. Both sides could engage in either negative coordination—respecting the status quo described above and the opponents' core interests on this basis—or in unilateral action to pursue its own preferences in violation of the status quo. The viability of the non-cooperative strategies depended on the balance of power between the coalitions and within the leadership core.

Table 3.1 illustrates the course of interaction between 1985 and 2000, which will be analyzed more closely in this chapter. Between 1985 and 1989, the leadership core was dominated by market reformers. Under a rural health insurance agenda, the PICC and the health administration engaged in strategic policy experimentation with the CMS and commercial insurance (field A).

Table 3.1 Timeline of the Policy Process in the 1980s and 1990s

Five-year plan periods	*No. 7 (1986–1990)*	*No. 8 (1991–1995)*		*No. 9 (1996–2000)*	
Field in the matrix	Field A (1985–1989)	Field C (1989–1992)	Field D (1993)	Field A (1994–1996)	Field B (1997–2000)
Mode of interaction	Negative coordination	Unilateral action		Negative coordination	Unilateral action

When the market reformers in the leadership core were weakened between 1989 and 1992, the MoH built a coalition and launched a CMS reform that violated the status quo, as it installed intergovernmental transfers to support the CMS (field C). When the market reformers in the leadership core had regained strength in 1992, the pro-market coalition stopped the transfers and discredited the CMS as a burden, thus effectively dismantling the reform (field D). Between late 1993 and early 1997, the pro-government coalition launched a new CMS initiative, relying mainly on local sources of funding (field A). Between 1997 and 2001, the power balance in the leadership core shifted further towards the market reformers: the market coalition again discredited the CMS as a burden, and insurance companies expanded the coverage of commercial insurance in the rural areas (field B). By 2000, the pro-market actors appeared to emerge as the winning coalition.

Competing Policy Experimentation after 1985

In the course of the economic reforms of the early 1980s, the People's Communes in the rural areas largely disintegrated and the public social security system that was based on the collective economy largely collapsed. The households became the new units of economic production and also assumed comprehensive functions in social security. At the same time, the one-child policy began to undermine the traditional function of children for family-based social security. In 1985, the leadership core decided to build up a comprehensive formal social security system in China. The goal of creating the "embryonic" forms of a social security system with "Chinese particularities" was integrated into the seventh five-year plan from 1986 to 1990, including both social insurance and social welfare. The focus was to be on socialized administration, while the mutual aid of family, kin and neighbors would continue to remain a central pillar (Macrochina 2001).

Especially in the rural areas, public insurance was meant as an addition to the social security provided by family (*jiating baozhang*) and rights to collective land (*tudi baozhang*), and as compensation for the family planning policies and the introduction of the household responsibility system (Huang 2009: 62). In 1986, the Central Government formulated the target of achieving universal coverage of health insurance by 2000, which was operationalized in 50 percent of the rural population by 1995 and 70 percent by 2000, and continuously reiterated in the following years (Wang 2009: 387f; World Bank 1992: 98). China seemed determined to re-extend formal social security in the rural areas.

In 1987, the State Council formally put the MoCA in charge of rural social policy with the mandate to introduce social insurance schemes for natural disasters, healthcare and pensions in the developed areas (Gong 2003: 133). In healthcare, it shared jurisdiction over the CMS with the MoH, which came to play the dominant role in the following years. There was a broad range of bottom-up experimentation with insurance schemes in the rural areas, and the ministries selected some high-profile experimental sites to test new policies. The MoH cooperated with the World Bank and the RAND Corporation for a health insurance experiment, which was scheduled and executed between 1985 and 1990 in the counties of Jianyang and Meishan in Sichuan Province (Cretin et al. 2006). The MoCA selected Daxing County in Beijing and Dayun County in Shanxi Province as experimental sites for its pension policies in 1989 (Huang 2009). Policy options in both fields were developed in accordance with the central plan.

At the same time, local branches of the PICC started to penetrate the rural areas, which promised substantial opportunities for growth. Griffin (1992) noted that rural "and private sector insurance are now the fastest growing areas of insurance coverage in China, according to an internal World Bank report." In Jianli County in Hubei Province, the local branch of the PICC began to operate an insurance program for the rural population in cooperation with the local government: it started in 1986 and offered hospital insurance as a part of the local CMS program in six villages (Krieg and Schädler 1995: 196). In Shanghai's Jinshan County, the local insurance company and a local bank cooperated with government actors to provide "cooperative medical and health insurance" (*hezuo yiliao jiankang baoxian*) in one township from December 1986 (Zha 1987). The insurance company of Jiashan County in Zhejiang Province launched a health insurance program for the rural population (*nongmin yiliao baoxian*) in July 1988 (People's Daily, September 29, 1992). Besides that, the PICC also offered individual insurance contracts and other products. In Shunde County in Guangdong Province, for example, it began to offer hospital insurance as a part of life insurance benefits in 1988 (Krieg and Schädler 1995: 196).

As noted above, illness-induced poverty was to become the crucial conceptual description of the public policy problem that rural health insurance was to deal with. The phrase "illness-induced poverty" appeared on the public and academic agenda in the second half of the 1980s, and was almost immediately coupled to the concept of health insurance. It was mentioned in 1986 in a research article about the CMS system in Yuhang County in Hangzhou. The 1986 article was written by Zhang Chengmo from Yuhang's county bureau of health. It reported that 33 percent of the local poor had been impoverished by disease, and that the local "CMS system" (*hezuo yiliao zhidu*) was to combat this trend. In 1987, Zhang co-authored two very similar articles with Chen Yunfei from the office of health policy of Zhejiang's provincial health department, one of them in the *Journal of Rural Health Affairs Management*. The word "insurance" (*baoxian*) in connection to the CMS had a more market-oriented connotation, and pro-government actors tended to call the CMS a "system" (*zhidu*) (Wang 2009). The 1987 articles promoted Yuhang's CMS as a "rural health insurance system" (*nongcun yiliao baoxian zhidu*), whose funds were pooled at the township level and which mainly reimbursed catastrophic diseases in order to counter illness-induced poverty. Jintan County in Jiangsu also portrayed its CMS as insurance, and the

RAND experiment in Sichuan was portrayed in a similar way (Cheng and Zhang 1987a, 1987b; Wang 2009: 386; Zhang 1986).

People's Daily, too, began featuring articles discussing the problem of illness-induced poverty in 1987. One article in December featured the claim of MoCA for the jurisdiction over pension, disaster and health insurance in the rural areas, and portrayed it as an opponent of the PICC (People's Daily, December 21, 1987). Another article earlier that year discussed social problems associated with the institutional drift of the rural healthcare system with the example of Linli County in Hunan Province. The perspective of the article displays a strong preference for formalized, state-organized medicine as opposed to traditional forms of healing, and thus resembles the pro-government perspective of the MoH.

> The villages in Linli county used to have cooperative medical stations, but due to egalitarianism and other administrative malpractices, most of them have disintegrated . . . It is difficult for the peasants to see a doctor or have an illness treated. Some ailments are not treated in time, so they become catastrophic diseases. Illness-induced poverty is increasing gradually, 4,231 households were already affected in 1985. There are wandering doctors and salesmen of medicines, witches and sorcerers who take advantage of the situation. They engage in defraud with fake medicine and superstitious activities, and caused many peasants to lose their life and property.
>
> (People's Daily, April 8, 1987)

The PICC tried to develop both markets for its commercial insurance products and cooperative arrangements with local governments in which it administered health insurance funds, which were previously collected by rural cadres. Some of these cooperative projects operated under the label of the CMS, whereas others had different names (cf. Gu 2005: 372). Its vision for combatting illness-induced poverty with a national commercial insurance program was presented in 1987 in the *Journal of Rural Health Affairs Management*, just a few pages before Zhang Chengmo's article.

> The nature, tasks, goals and target population of rural health insurance are all identical with the former cooperative medical system, but the scope of participation will be broader . . . Its insurance funds will be more solid and have greater risk-pooling capacity than the old village and township funds of the CMS. It will be deposited in a bank to generate interest …
>
> (Zhu 1987: 19)

The system was to be managed by a small leadership group (*lingdao xiaozu*) headed by the county magistrate, which included, among others, the county bureaus of health and finance, the insurance company and the bank. This blueprint resembled policy experiments as conducted in Jinshan, and included a surprising number of elements that would later become part of the NRCMS policy.

The First Initiative to Reanimate the CMS (1989–1993)

The events around the student protests of 1989 sent shockwaves through the political system of the PRC and changed the balance of power in the leadership core and the field of health policy. Health policy in the period between 1988 and 1992 was dominated by pro-government actors, who worked towards the expansion of the role of the state in rural social security. The outline of the eighth five-year plan (1991–1995) called for a continuous development of social security with a focus on the pension system. In the rural areas, the focus was to be on establishing "diverse forms of old-age protection" (*butong xingshi de laonian baozhang*) and extending cooperative medical insurance (*hezuo yiliao baoxian*) (Macrochina 2001). In October 1988, Li Peng had clarified that, by 2000, healthcare protection was to be universal (Cao 2009: 21). The CMS was to cover 50 percent of the rural population by 1995 and 70 percent by 2000 (World Bank 1992: 98).

Towards the end of the 1980s, there were changes in the discussion of rural health policy. The word "insurance" was largely dropped when discussing illness-induced poverty, which points to the changing political tide.[1] But as the political language changed, the policy process for building up a new rural social security system continued according to plan. In preparation for the reform, the MoH conducted two evaluations of the different localities running CMS systems and of the Sichuan experiment, and published some results in 1990. It criticized the Cultural Revolution image of the CMS and portrayed it as clearly superior to the user-pay system (Cao and Zhang 1990). At the same time, *People's Daily* and other central media were reported to have received letters from peasants calling for the reintroduction of the CMS (Cao 2009: 16f.; Wang 2009: 387f.).

Within the MoH, there were differing political preferences and opinions, and pro-government actors were gaining the upper hand towards the end of the 1980s. This is reflected in a section of a 1990 evaluation report by two MoH officials:

> Within the MoH, there are many different views on how to answer to the challenges economic reforms brought for rural medical care, and how to strategically consider the problem of medical care in rural health. Some comrades with long experience in rural healthcare management advocate a comprehensive revival and improvement of the CMS. Other comrades have drawn lessons from the experiences of foreign healthcare management and advocate … installing a rural health insurance system. Yet other comrades think that the conditions in rural China do not allow for health insurance yet, and that a system of fundraising and risk-sharing

should be established first. Such a prototype can provide the basis for the transition to an insurance system. Those who insist on CMS argue that … there appears to be a trend that health costs rise year by year, and this has already become a factor preventing farmers from seeking care. The rise of rural incomes is much slower than the rise of health costs, so the farmers only consider seeing a doctor when illness has developed to a point that it affects their working ability.

(Cao and Zhang 1990: 6)

This section distinguishes three approaches: first, an insurance approach, arguably focusing on the PICC rather than the health administration; second, a prototype insurance model of CMS, which arguably points to a focus on catastrophic health spending as in Yuhang's CMS; and, third, the classic CMS, with a focus on primary and outpatient care. The promoters of the CMS had arguably gained the upper hand.

By 1990, the MoH had sufficient support in the leadership core and secured the cooperation of important ministries, including the State Planning Commission, the MoA, the Ministry of Human Resources and the Commission of Education. In March, five ministries specified the planning targets for reaching universal coverage by 2000: depending on their socio-economic status, rural localities were to achieve between 50 and 60 percent CMS coverage in ten years. A group of five ministries led by the MoH drafted a joint reform proposal for rural health reform, which was sent to the State Council in June 1990. Under the instruction of Politburo member Li Tieying, an additional investigation of the CMS was conducted in rural China in September 1990. The rural health reform was codified in document four of the State Council. In January 1991, document four was sent to the provincial authorities, and, at a subsequent conference in Beijing, the leaders of the provincial health departments reached a consensus on accepting the requirements of the document and implementing the reform. In the following months, various national leaders voiced their support for the reintroduction of the CMS publicly— including Premier Li Peng, Vice Prime Minister Zou Jiahua and the former minister of health Qian Xinzhong (Cao 2009; Wang 2009: 388).

Document four expressed a fundamental criticism of the market-oriented reforms in the rural healthcare system during the 1980s. Though accurate in its observations, its tone was not very diplomatic.

Not only did the rural health system not develop, but it has been weakened, and the urban–rural gap has widened. First, public and collective financing has further declined, which caused a loss in technical capacity and human capital. Second, the three-tier healthcare network has suffered a heavy blow. The cooperative healthcare system and grassroots facilities have dissolved in many areas. Both private and socialized providers are out of control and charge arbitrary and excessive fees. The masses are burdened with insurmountable health costs and there is a lack of medicines and doctors. Third, contagious diseases and parasites formerly extinct or controlled are breaking out and spreading again. These problems have to be thoroughly resolved, or they will not only impede rural development, but also leave the villagers displeased and thus impact negatively on the relations between the party and the masses.

(Guofa 1991: 4)

The document mentioned neither illness-induced poverty nor the term "insurance", and it specified only some of the administrative and financial details. Document four confirmed the principle of voluntary enrollment, and the appropriate level of premiums had been specified as 1.5 percent of farmers' annual incomes by the MoH (Cao and Zhang 1990).[2] It also explicitly mentioned village charges (*cun tiliu*) as sources of healthcare financing, and emphasized the role of local collective and state-owned enterprises in supporting the CMS and lowering the health expenditures of the rural citizens. Another State Council document in 1991 explicitly called for the village welfare funds to support the CMS (Guowuyuanling 1991). One crucial source of funding was, however, not specified in these documents—namely, a system of intergovernmental financial transfers to support the CMS. The central government provided RMB 20 million in transfers in 1991, and RMB 75 million in 1992, which were matched by 28 provinces with RMB 2.5 billion over both years. The 1991 reform constituted a considerable breach of the status quo, most notably for ignoring the principles of subsistence and of the primary responsibility of the households for social security by expanding the role of state actors in social security. As Wang notes, the reform managed to increase CMS coverage in 1991 and 1992 (Cao 2009; Wang 2009: 389).

However, the political support for this reform in the leadership core was not to last long, as the pro-market actors were strengthened again in the course of the leadership transition in 1992 and 1993. After Deng's Southern Tour, the central government began to send mixed signals regarding the CMS, and buzzwords from the second half of the 1980s reappeared. On September 23, the MoH issued a document that referred to the CMS as an "insurance system" (MoH 1992). On September 29, a *People's Daily* article discussed illness-induced poverty and the PICC-operated rural health insurance program in Jiashan County (Zhejiang Province). The Fourteenth Party Congress in October 1992 further strengthened the pro-market actors. Zhu Rongji became a member of the Standing Committee of the Politburo and—in 1993—the governor of the People's Bank of China, which had close connections with the PICC. With regard to rural healthcare, "the question whether to install a market-oriented insurance system or the CMS in the rural areas was again open for debate" (Cao 2009: 20).

The dismantling of the 1991 reform arguably began in December 1992, when Jiang Zemin and Li Peng emphasized the importance of reducing the burden of taxes, fees and charges on the rural population (Bernstein and Lü 2003: 130). On February 17, 1993, the minister of health, Chen Minzhang, met the minister of agriculture, Liu Zhongyi, at an informal meeting, where they discussed the CMS and other issues of rural health policy. Both sides agreed that farmers' health expenditures, premiums for CMS, and the standards (*dabiao*) for primary healthcare should not be interpreted as a burden for the farmers, and that public health should be interpreted as poverty alleviation. This consensus points to a considerable pressure against the CMS after the party congress, which was connected to the farmers' burden agenda. By the time of the meeting, the MoF and the Planning Commission had already announced the withdrawal of their financial support for the CMS. The looming fiscal crisis provided good arguments against expanding public financial commitments to social security, and in 1994 the government enacted a major tax reform to tackle this issue (Deng 1993; Wang and Hu 2001).

The pro-government actors around the MoH were substantially weakened in the course of 1993. In March, Liu Zhongyi was replaced by Liu Jiang as minister of agriculture, and the MoH lost the MoA as an ally. Furthermore, Li Peng—a crucial supporter of the CMS—had a heart attack on April 19 and remained absent from the political stage for several months (Johnston 2002: 157). The CMS had already lost intergovernmental transfers as a source of financing and relied primarily on villagers' premiums and village charges. The legitimacy of the remaining sources of financing would soon be called into question by interpreting them as a financial burden for the rural population and a source of instability.

In Renshou County of Sichuan Province, tensions between farmers and the local cadres over the collection of fees and charges had erupted in violent protests in early 1993. Although peace had apparently been restored in March and April, major riots erupted again in May. Renshou had become a case of national significance, which raised the profile of the burden issue. In May, the MoA under the new minister took the initiative to propose to the State Council a comprehensive burden reduction program. It abolished 43 "standard-upgrading activities" (*dabiao shengji huodong*) to ease the farmers' burden: among them were primary healthcare, the standard for "advanced health counties" (*weisheng xianjin xian dabiao*), birth control, and the CMS and health construction (*hezuo yiliao weisheng jianshe dabiao*) (People's Daily, May 27, 1993). A subsequent document in July further abolished fundraising (*jizi*) for health facility construction in townships and villages, village doctors' salaries, schistosomiasis prevention and other public health projects. In the following years, the MoF cooperated with the MoA to monitor the progress of burden reduction (People's Daily, October 27, 1996; Zhongbanfa 1993: 10).

Rural healthcare had been largely defunded and the 1991 reform crushed, and as a result CMS coverage decreased. The provinces interpreted the MoA's decree in different ways: some provinces, such as Sichuan, completely banned premium collection for the CMS, and such bans could last for several years (Liu et al. 2002: 36; World Bank 1997: 52). Coverage of the CMS shrank again after 1992, but a core of 5 to 10 percent of China's villages retained their CMS—mostly in the industrialized coastal areas. The effects of the 1991 reform had strong regional and local connotations, both in the extension and the decline of CMS coverage. According to the MoH's first national survey conducted in late 1993, CMS coverage was closely related to socio-economic development. It covered 9.8 percent of the surveyed population. Its coverage was highest in wealthy type-one counties with 28.8 percent, and lowest in the poorer type-three and type-four counties with 0.7 and 1 percent respectively. The coverage of commercial insurance only reached 0.3 percent nationally and was highest in type-one counties (0.6 percent) (MoH 1994: 7).

Towards the end of 1993, the balance of power between pro-market and pro-government actors gradually returned to normal. Like the CMS, birth control policies in rural China had been affected by burden reduction, and the NPFPC subsequently became an ally of the MoH in expanding the role of the state in rural health and social security. Its minister, Peng Peiyun—a member of the Central Committee—had supported the view that the CMS would not add to the farmers' burden in a *People's Daily* article in May 1993 and had fiercely criticized the standstill in rural healthcare and family planning in the wake of the burden reductions in July (People's Daily, May 8, 1993; People's Daily, July 3, 1993). Furthermore, Li Peng had recovered and returned to politics in December (Johnston 2002: 156f.).

On November 9, another article in *People's Daily* called for streamlining village organization by reducing the numbers of inactive committees and offices—explicitly mentioning the CMS and birth control—in order to reduce the burden of the farmers (People's Daily. November 9, 1993). On November 14, however, the decision by the Central Committee to establish the "socialist market economy" explicitly called for developing the CMS system and experimenting with voluntary pension insurance to develop the systems of social security in the rural areas—it did not mention the word "insurance" in connection with the CMS (Zhonggong Zhongyang 1993). In the following year, the national poverty plan assigned responsibility for social insurance in poverty areas to the MoCA, without mentioning the CMS (Guofa 1994: 30). Formally, the plan to build up a rural welfare system was back on track, but the goal of covering 50 percent of the rural population with health insurance by 1995 had by now become difficult to achieve.

The policy process for rural pension insurance was largely synched to that of rural healthcare. In 1990 and 1991, the MoCA built a coalition and secured consensus for its pension scheme at the central level, and directly contradicted the interests of the PICC with this. By 1992, its pension program covered 950 counties and 26 million farmers, indicating a higher coverage of jurisdictions and lower local enrollment rates than the CMS had (Bloom et al. 1995). While the CMS was based on social pooling and depended on high enrollment rates to be effective, the MoCA's pension scheme was based on individual savings accounts. In both the CMS and pension insurance, the principle of voluntariness was violated in local practice, and both were attacked as contributing to the "farmer's burden" in 1993 (Gong 2003: 143; Shi 2006: 797). The 1991 CMS program furthermore depended on subsidies from the central and provincial levels, which were discontinued in 1992. No such transfer payments have been reported for the pension program, which was arguably more sustainable on the basis of local subsistence. While the 1991 CMS program received a heavy blow, pension insurance continued to grow: it covered more than 1,100 counties in 1994 and 2,097 counties in 1997, with 82.9 million insured and 557,900 elderly citizens receiving pensions. Two factors related to the greater reliance of the CMS on social pooling may explain this development: first, pension insurance could handle low enrollment rates better than the CMS; second, genuine voluntariness for participation in pension insurance was probably higher, because the rural population tended to oppose household savings schemes less than social pooling schemes (Wu 2004). The CMS was in greater conflict with the political status quo than the pension program, and thus more vulnerable to political attacks denouncing it as adding to the farmers' financial burden, and to pressure on local cadres to uphold voluntary enrollment (Müller 2016).

The Second Initiative to Reanimate the CMS (1994–2000)

The preparations for the second initiative to extend the CMS in the rural areas began in early 1994, and this time the MoH was careful not to violate the principles of the status quo—that is, subsistence, the primary responsibility of the household and voluntary enrollment. By March, the MoH had initiated a pilot project for the CMS system in cooperation with the World Health Organization (WHO), Peking Medical University and Anhui Medical University. Peng Peiyun had conducted preceding investigations in Jiangsu and Henan, and filed a report which was reviewed and endorsed by three members of the State Council and the Central Committee: Jiang Chunyun, Wen Jiabao and Chen Junsheng. It concluded that government had a responsibility to give budgetary support for the CMS, and that the CMS was not per se dependent on a high level of local economic development. The project covered 14 counties in seven provinces, and the most important centers of policy development were Kaifeng County and Linzhou City in Henan, which were visited by more than 300 delegations from other counties for studying purposes (Cao 2009: 21f.; Carrin et al. 1999: 962f.; Wang 2009: 389f.; Wang and Ye 2004: 11).

A policy proposal by Chen Minzhang was published in *People's Daily* on July 2, 1994. Liu Zhongyi, the former minister of agriculture, had given Chen the advice to frame the CMS as poverty alleviation in early 1993 (Deng 1993). Chen took the advice and presented the CMS as combatting infectious diseases, the rise of informal and traditional medicine, and illness-induced poverty:

> [S]ince the disintegration of the CMS, farmers in many areas again find it difficult to see a doctor. Endemic and infectious diseases formerly extinguished … are breaking out again and even spreading. The burden of the farmers is growing heavier, and time and again illness causes poverty.

Presently, 85 percent of China's counties are affected by at least one endemic disease . . . and in poor and remote areas illness affects socio-economic development. Therefore, rebuilding and developing the CMS is of immediate significance.

(People's Daily, July 2, 1994)

The issue of illness-induced poverty was pivotal in the political communication of the CMS. Framing it as a policy combatting poverty connected to the public health situation, and as relief rather than a burden for the farmers, presented the CMS as being in line with the larger goals of economic and social development (Klotzbücher 2006: 197ff.). The proposal encouraged social pooling at the county level for the first time. It designated farmers' premiums as the main source of funding, complemented by township and village levies and contributions from township and village enterprises.[3] It differentiated between reimbursement models focusing exclusively on catastrophic expenditures (*buda bu buxiao*) or outpatient services (*buxiao bu buda*), as well as mixed models (*buda ye buxiao*). Furthermore, it mentioned detailed reimbursement catalogs, which could exclude specific items or types of items and called for reimbursement according to fixed rates rather than full reimbursement of the costs. Chen's proposal legitimized both premiums and township and village levies to be used for the CMS, but included no intergovernmental transfers (People's Daily, July 2, 1994).

The pilot project concluded in a conference in July 1996, where both Chen Minzhang and Peng Peiyun gave speeches, and opened out into an extension of the CMS in rural China. The project also delivered input for the policy formulation process of the 1997 comprehensive health reform: "as a result of the experience gained, the Ministry of Health has been able to draft plans for legislation and to submit them to the Legislation Department of the State Council" (Carrin et al. 1999: 965f.).

On October 23, 1996, a decision by the Central Committee and the State Council on poverty alleviation explicitly accepted the CMS as a poverty alleviation policy to be developed "in order to establish a basic system of health security, to decrease the farmers' medical burden, and to reduce illness-induced poverty" (Zhonggong Zhongyang 1996a). At a conference on national health policy in December 1996, Jiang Zemin and Li Peng emphasized the problem of illness-induced poverty and supported the CMS (People's Daily, December 10, 1996; People's Daily, December 11, 1996). The main reform was issued in January 1997 and was followed in May by a joint document of the MoH, the MoF, the MoCA, the MoA and the State Planning Commission about CMS administration and management (Guofa 1997: 18; Zhongfa 1997: 3; Cao 2009: 21ff.).

At the same time as the CMS was being legitimized, however, it came to be negatively associated with the farmers' burden again. On October 26, only three days after the CMS had been officially accepted as a poverty alleviation measure, vice-premier and Politburo member Jiang Chunyun addressed the

Standing Committee of the National People's Congress about the farmers' burden and clarified that the CMS and rural social insurance would qualify as illegitimate burdens unless enrollment was fully voluntary.[4] A decision by the Central Committee and the State Council on December 30 insisted on the voluntariness of the CMS and the rural insurance business (*baoxian yewu*), and forbade the use of mandatory payments and enrollment quotas (*baoxian zhibiao*) (Zhonggong Zhongyang 1996b). In localities and departments that raised the farmers' burden, the responsibility of the leading cadres was directly investigated, and those subjected to disciplinary measures were excluded from promotions and important posts. The 1997 initiative to reanimate the CMS was characterized by ambiguous policies from the start.

In the course of the leadership transition connected to the Fifteenth National Party Congress in 1997, the pro-market actors were strengthened again. Zhu Rongji remained in the Standing Committee of the Politburo and succeeded Li Peng as Premier in 1998. Two crucial promoters of the CMS resigned: Chen Minzhang and Li Peng. Chen was replaced by Zhang Wenkang, a personal friend of Jiang Zemin from Shanghai with apparently limited political experience (Liu and Rao 2006: 82f.). Zhang was an ambiguous figure: he was much less visible than his predecessor in publicly promoting the CMS, which was reflected in the low number of *People's Daily* articles mentioning his name in connection with the CMS, and the uncoupling of the CMS and illness-induced poverty in those articles. Zhang only touched on the subject briefly in two articles, one in 1998 and one in 1999, but he did not connect it to illness-induced poverty (People's Daily, April 7, 1998; People's Daily, January 7, 1999). On January 7, 1999, the name of Zhang Wenkang was connected to the CMS in *People's Daily* for the last time before October 2002 (People's Daily, January 7, 1999). On January 29, the deputy minister of agriculture, Liu Chengguo, suggested in *People's Daily* the promotion of rural sports to decrease illness-induced poverty, which indicates that the MoH had lost its monopoly of interpretation (People's Daily, January 29, 1999). Similar to 1980, the MoH, under new leadership, ceased to actively support the CMS in a politically difficult situation.

By the end of the 1990s, there was no clarity at the central level regarding who was responsible for the CMS program. Zhu Rongji's reforms of the central government apparatus, which also shifted jurisdiction over the rural pension program from the MoCA to the MoLSS, arguably contributed to this situation. The MoH officially denied being in charge of the program, arguing that it was under the jurisdiction of the MoCA (Klotzbücher 2006: 201f.). In 2001, Liu and Rao criticized the fact that there was no ministry in charge of the CMS at the central level and praised Guangdong for having formally put the provincial department of agriculture in charge of rural health protection (Liu et al. 2002: 56).

In terms of coverage, the second CMS initiative was at its peak in late 1996 and early 1997, reaching more than 350 counties, 17 percent of the administrative villages and 9.6 percent of rural citizens (Cao 2009). Decline in coverage began gradually in 1997 and accelerated in 1998 (Wang 2009). In the course of 1997, the MoA drafted a blacklist of illegal rural fees which included CMS premiums, and in 1998 the State Council issued new burden reduction policies similar to those of 1993. In 1998 and 1999, the new leadership core around Jiang and Zhu resolved its preference for a rural tax-for-fee reform—a shift from township and village levies to an agricultural tax—the agenda status of which was elevated accordingly (Göbel 2010). The MoA and the MoF continued to issue documents emphasizing the voluntariness of the CMS and discrediting premium collection on an annual basis until 2001 (Guobanfa 2000: 33; Guowuyuan 1999).

With those negative signals from the central level, the CMS brought few benefits and high political risk for local governments, undermining their readiness to implement and maintain it (Cao 2009; Wang 2009: 378). Most localities abandoned their CMS projects, including the two model counties in Henan (Liu et al. 2002: 36). The decline in coverage accelerated after 1997, but its dynamics differed between provinces and localities. The 1997 documents on the CMS had recommended the introduction of a financial transfer system to support the CMS in poor areas: they were to be financed by all subnational levels of government, and the MoF would not contribute to them (Guofa 1997: 18). Only one provincial unit did follow this recommendation: the Autonomous Region of Tibet. It launched a CMS program supported by matching funds, which previously had been designated "free healthcare fund" (*mianfei yiliao zhuangxiang jingfei*). Pilots were launched in two counties after local leaders had been sent to Henan for investigations and training. The program achieved a swift increase in coverage that was first acknowledged by a *People's Daily* article in 1999. By that time, it already covered most counties and townships as well as about 55 percent of Tibet's rural population (Liu et al. 2002: 38). In the Tibetan CMS, transfers of RMB 15 per capita amounted to 54 percent of the overall funding (People's Daily, October 22, 1999).

The decline after 1997 was probably steeper than the decline after 1992 in most of rural China. When coverage arguably reached the lowest level of 5 to 7 percent of China's villages in 2001, a substantial share of them were jurisdictions in Tibet. The 2003 MoH survey indicated that CMS coverage since 1998 had declined in wealthy counties, but increased dramatically in poverty counties, as illustrated in Figure 3.2 and Figure 3.3.[5] The CMS also survived in the industrialized coastal areas, most notably around Shanghai. The norm of voluntary enrollment applied to farmers, but not necessarily to workers in local enterprises, which reduced the problems of operating the CMS in such areas (Klotzbücher 2006: 216f.). The existence of local industry and governmental transfers stabilized the CMS and had a strong influence on its spatial distribution in the period between 1997 and 2002.

The Asian crisis increased the sensitivity of Chinese leaders to the risks in their own financial sector, including the insurance industry (Shi 2006: 798; Walter and Howie 2011). Among Zhu Rongji's core projects were rural tax reforms and financial sector reforms, including a restructuring and differentiation of China's insurance industry, which quickly began to expand its presence in the rural insurance markets. The PICC had already been

restructured as the PICC Group with three separate companies and subordinated to the PBoC in 1996, after the passing of the Insurance Law in
1995. In 1998, after the governor of the PBoC, Zhu Rongji, had become
Premier, the CIRC was established and assumed regulatory authority from
the PBoC. In 1999, the PICC Group was dissolved and China Life emerged
as one of three succeeding companies. The insurance companies subsequently
expanded into the rural areas, selling individual insurance contracts and
managing health insurance systems such as the CMS for local governments
(Gu 2005: 372; People's Daily, October 11, 2003). China Life retained strong
personal ties with the PBoC and the CIRC after the reform, while less is
known about the channels of political influence of other companies (Bird and
Wong 2005; Göbel 2010; IBS Research Center 2009; Pearson 2005; Wang and
Ning 2010; Zhang and Wang 2007: 46f.).

Figure 3.3 illustrates the substantial rise in coverage of commercial health
insurance in rural China. By 2003, overall coverage of the CMS was 9.5 percent. Commercial insurance covered 9.4 percent of rural citizens, of which 1.1
percent were complementary insurances to the CMS or other types of health
insurance (MoH 2004: 16f.). The CMS was particularly strong in the coastal
and industrialized regions and in poverty counties. Commercial insurance was
generally strong in all but the poverty counties and clearly surpassed the CMS
in the middle-income areas, which represented the majority of Chinese counties.
Gu and colleagues found substantial local variation in the composition and
designation of public and commercial health insurance systems in 2002. The
CMS was strongest in Shanxi and Zhejiang, whereas commercial insurance
was particularly strong in Sichuan, Zhejiang and Guangdong. Various studies
contradict the idea that commercial insurance was restricted to the wealthy
regions of China (Gu 2005: 353–72; MoH 2004: 16ff., 93; MoH 2009: 18).[6]

Much like the CMS, the MoCA's pension program encountered a serious
setback around 1998, when jurisdiction over public rural pensions was transferred to the MoLSS. As a reaction to the Asian Crisis, a "Rectification
Group on Insurance Industry" was organized to assess the risks inherent in
public and commercial insurance programs. It was headed by Zhang Zuoji,
who was promoted to minister of the MoLSS in 1998. Its final report criticized several points about the MoCA's pension program, including local
power abuse, coercive enrollment and misleading information given to the
villagers about the program. Financial interest rates in China had been
declining since the middle of the 1990s, and the programs were unlikely to
deliver the promised pension levels. Furthermore, local management practices
gave rise to concerns. Zhu Rongji had used his influence to worsen this evaluation against the more moderate standing of Wen Jiabao, and directly
recommended replacing the MoCA scheme with a commercial scheme. Like
the CMS, the MoCA's pension program reached its peak in 1997—with 82.8
million insured—and saw its coverage decreasing to 61.7 million in 2000 and
to 54.3 million in 2003 (Gong 2003: 215–21; Huang 2009; Shi 2006).

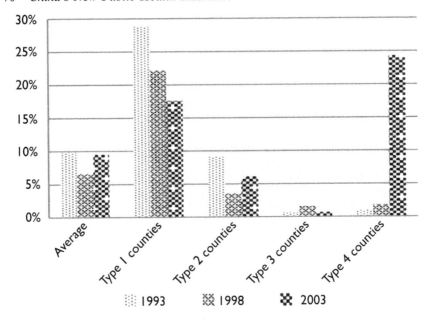

Figure 3.2 CMS Coverage
Sources: MoH 1994: 7; 1999: 23f.; 2004: 16f.

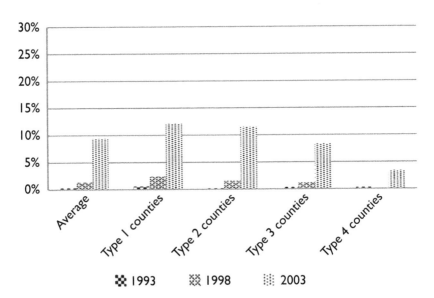

Figure 3.3 Coverage of Commercial Insurance
Sources: MoH 1994: 7; 1999: 23f.; 2004: 16f.

Summary

The policy processes for the CMS and public pension insurance largely developed in a synchronized way. Strategic experimentation in both areas kicked off in 1985 after the decision to install a rural system of public social security. The main policy initiatives in both fields were launched in the aftermath of 1989, when pro-government actors had temporarily gained the upper hand in the leadership core. Those initiatives were subsequently attacked and abandoned in 1998, when the pro-market actors gained power in the leadership core and promoted the creation of rural insurance markets.

The CMS had been a reform project of the pro-government actors, and of the MoH in particular. Despite the MoH abandoning support for the program in politically difficult situations, the CMS remained its main social security system for the rural areas. The MoH launched two national initiatives to reanimate the CMS, one in 1991 and one in 1996. The CMS was more vulnerable to burden accusations than the rural pension program, which may be rooted, among other things, in its greater reliance on social pooling. Many villagers opposed it, as they saw health as a family affair and did not want to share resources with other families. Effective social pooling requires high enrollment rates, which were difficult to achieve with genuinely voluntary participation. The MoH envisioned a CMS system supported by financial transfers from different levels of government, similar to the NRCMS. However, it was only able to realize this briefly in the aftermath of 1989, when the pro-government actors were strengthened. In the late 1990s, when the pro-market actors became strong enough to unilaterally sabotage the CMS, the MoH backed down from its support and left the field.

Political and academic discourse in China has strongly emphasized the role of practical constraints. The fiscal crisis provided valid arguments against an expansion of government-funded social security through most of the 1990s. Villages and townships lacked the administrative capacity for effective risk-pooling programs. Many rural cadres solicited illegitimate fees from the population, which often did not trust their abilities and was reluctant to enroll. Many local cadres violated the voluntary enrollment rule. Although these factors remain valid and important, an exclusive emphasis on them draws attention away from the politics of rural social policy. In fact, trust, voluntariness and administrative capacity remained important problems in the NRCMS, but the NRCMS enjoyed stable financial and political support from the central government.

The biggest gap in research so far has been the role of the Chinese insurance industry as the implicit antagonist of the MoH and the MoCA. The insurance industry had excellent political connections and was the main beneficiary of the 1998 leadership change and the subsequent demise of the CMS. Although the common political narratives suggest that commercial insurance was only suitable for wealthy people, there are various indicators that even in middle- and low-income areas the companies managed to turn social security into a lucrative business. Around 2000, the pro-market actors seemed to have won the battle over China's rural welfare regime, and the insurance industry expanded into the rural areas with fewer obstacles than ever.

List of Interviews

Interview 101129: Interview with a city-level NRCMS administrator in Shandong Province, November 29, 2010

Notes

1 In 1989 there were only two articles about illness-induced poverty listed in the China Academic Journals index—one published by Zhang Chengmo from Yuhang—that did not mention insurance but discussed "CMS systems" (*hezuo yiliao zhidu*) (Zhang 1989). Beginning in 1990, the presence of illness-induced poverty in the China Academic Journals index increased, and *People's Daily* returned to the subject in 1991 with two more articles, both of which related the problem to the CMS without the word "insurance" (People's Daily, October 29, 1991; People's Daily, October 31, 1991).

2 In practice, farmers' annual incomes were difficult to determine, which left the local cadres a considerable amount of discretion (Cao and Zhang 1990; Tang et al. 1994: 45f.).

3 Villages contributed in ten counties of the 14 pilots, township governments in eight counties, and the county government in two counties (Carrin et al. 1999: 965f.).

4 Jiang Chunyun's role regarding CMS remains ambiguous, as he had previously promoted it along with Wen Jiabao and Chen Junsheng (People's Daily, October 27, 1996).

5 The CMS-related figures of the 2003 National Health Service Survey should be interpreted carefully. On the one hand, the NRCMS initiative had been prepared in some provinces by supporting CMS since late 2001; on the other hand, the formal implementation had already begun when the survey was conducted. Governmental support for poverty counties had been part of the 1997 initiative, but the World Bank noted that it had not been broadly implemented by 2001. There were, however, international projects targeting poverty counties and sometimes also supporting CMS, as Wang and Klotzbücher noted. They probably raised CMS coverage in poor areas along with the Tibetan program (Klotzbücher 2006; MoH 1999: 23f.; MoH 2004: 16; Wang 2009; World Bank 2002).

6 In Henan, there was a CMS-like system with very low funding and little effect. In Gansu, a system named *dabing tongchou* (catastrophic disease plan)—largely managed by the local insurance industry—covered much of the rural population. Commercial insurance differed strongly with regard to the level of premiums and the insurance plans in the different socio-economic contexts. Coverage was higher among men than women, and particularly high among those younger than 14 years. By September and October 2003, when the data for the National Health Service Survey was being collected, coverage of commercial insurance was already declining in some regions due to the ongoing implementation of the NRCMS. A *People's Daily* article in 2003, for example, describes the situation in Yunfu City of Guangdong province, where the former cooperation of the local government and China Life to provide rural health insurance was dissolved: pure commercial insurance was not eligible for financial transfers, and the company was not ready to settle for the reduced amount of premiums it was offered under a new scheme (People's

Daily, November 10, 2003). As noted above, the high coverage of the CMS in poverty counties in the MoH survey may be an indicator that some financial support for the CMS in poverty counties was actually organized, for there were no sample counties in Tibet (MoH 2004: 185–203). However, the figures need to be interpreted carefully. For comparison, data from a survey conducted by Beijing University with a smaller and wealthier sample found the coverage of the CMS at 2.4 percent and commercial insurance at 2.5 percent in 2002. Coverage of the CMS was highest in the low-income group, whereas coverage of commercial insurance surpassed that of the CMS in the middle- and high-income groups.

Bibliography

Bernstein, Thomas P. and Xiaobo Lü 2003, *Taxation without Representation in Contemporary Rural China*, Cambridge: Cambridge University Press.

Bird, Richard M. and Christine Wong 2005, China's Fiscal System: A Work in Progress, online: http://papers.ssrn.com/sol3/papers.cfm?abstract_id=875416 (accessed October 20, 2012).

Bloom, Gerald, Shenglan Tang and Xingyuan Gu 1995, Financing Rural Health Services in China in the Context of Economic Reform, in: *Journal of International Development*, 7, 3, 423–441.

Cao, Guirong and Bin Zhang 1990, Woguo nongcun yiliao baojian zhidu de yanbian ji fazhan yanjiu (Progression and Development of China's Rural Cooperative Medical Care System), in: *Zhongguo Chuji Weisheng Baojian (Chinese Primary Health Care)*, 4, 7, 5–10.

Cao, Pu 2009, 20 shiji 90 niandai liang ci "Chongjian" nongcun hezuo yiliao de changshi he xiaoguo ("Rebuilding" CMS Twice in the 1990s—Attempts and Results), in: *Dangshi Yanjiu yu Jiaoxue (Party History Research and Education)*, 4, 18–26.

Carrin, Guy *et al.* 1999, The Reform of the Rural Cooperative Medical System in the People's Republic of China: Interim Experience in 14 Pilot Counties, in: *Social Science and Medicine*, 48, 7, 961–972.

Cheng, Yunfei and Chengmo Zhang 1987a, Qianlun "fengxianxing" nongcun yiliao baoxian zhidu (About a Rural "Risk-Type" of Health Insurance), in: *Zhongguo Weisheng Shiye Guanli (China Health Affairs Management)*, 5, 38–41.

Cheng, Yunfei and Chengmo Zhang 1987b, Qianlun "fengxianxing" nongcun yiliao baoxian zhidu (About a Rural "Risk-Type" of Health Insurance), in: *Zhongguo Nongcun Weisheng Shiye Guanli (Chinese Rural Health Affairs Management)*, 10, 32–35.

Cretin, Shan, Albert P. Williams and Jeffrey Sine 2006, China Rural Health Insurance Experiment Final Report, WR-411, online: www.rand.org/pubs/working_papers/2007/RAND_WR411.pdf (accessed July 2, 2012).

Deng, Yuzhen 1993, Weishengbu, Nongyebu jiu jiaqiang weisheng gongzuo qude gongshi (The Ministries of Health and Agriculture Reach a Consensus on Strengthening Rural Healthcare), in: *Zhongguo Nongcun Weisheng Shiye Guanli (Chinese Rural Health Affairs Management)*, 4.

Duckett, Jane 2011a, Challenging the Economic Reform Paradigm, Policy and Politics in the Early 1980s' Collapse of the Rural Co-operative Medical System, in: *The China Quarterly*, 205, 80–95.

Duckett, Jane 2011b, *The Chinese State's Retreat from Health: Policy and the Politics of Retrenchment*, London: Routledge.

Göbel, Christian 2010, *The Politics of Rural Reform in China, State Policy and Village Predicament in the Early 2000s*, London: Routledge.

Gong, Sen 2003, *The State and Pension Instability People's Republic of China*, Doctoral thesis, Sheffield: University of Sheffield.

Griffin, Charles C. 1992, *Health Care in Asia, A Comparative Study of Cost and Financing*, Washington, DC: World Bank.

Gu, Xin, Gao, Mengtao and Yang Yao. 2005, *Zhenduan yu chufang: Zhimian Zhongguo yiliao tizhi gaige (China's Health Care Reforms: A Pathological Analysis)*, Beijing: Shehui Kexue Wenxian Chubanshe (Social Sciences Academic Press).

Guobanfa 2000, 33, Guowuyuan Bangongting zhuanfa Nongyebu deng bumen guanyu gonggu da jiancha chengguo jinyibu zuohao jianqing nongmin fudan gongzuo baogao de tongzhi (Notification from the General Office of the State Council about the Work Report of the Ministry of Agriculture and Other Ministries about Consolidating the Achievements of the Major Inspection and Further Reduce the Farmers' Burden).

Guobanfa 2013, 22, Guowuyuan Bangongting guanyu shishi "Guowuyuan jigou gaige he zhineng zhuanbian fang'an" renwu fengong de tongzhi (Notification from the General Office of the State Council about the Task Assignments to Implement the "Program of the Reform and Functional Transformation of the State Council Organs").

Guofa 1991, 4, Pizhuan Weishengbu deng bumen guanyu gaige he jiaqiang nongcun yiliao weisheng gongzuo qingshi de tongzhi (Notification from the MoH and other Departments about Inviting Instructions for Reforming and Strengthening Rural Healthcare).

Guofa 1994, 30, Guojia ba qi fupin gongjian jihua: 1994–2000 nian (The National Eight-Seven Plan to Combat Poverty: 1994 to 2000).

Guofa 1997, 18, Guowuyuan pizhuan Weishengbu deng bumen guanyu fazhan he wanshan nongcun hezuo yiliao ruogan yijian de tongzhi (Notification from the State Council about the Opinion of the MoH and Other Ministries on Developing and Perfecting the CMS).

Guofa 2009, 32, Guowuyuan guanyu kaizhan xinxing nongcun shehui yanglao baoxian shidian de zhidao yijian (Leading Opinion of the State Council on Initiating Experimentation with the New Rural Social Pension Insurance).

Guowuyuan 1999, Guowuyuan Bangongting zhuanfa Nongyebu deng bumen guanyu zuohao dangqian jianqing nongmin fudan gongzuo yijian de tongzhi (Notification from the General Office of the State Council about the Opinion of the Ministry of Agriculture and Other Ministries on Easing the Present Peasant's Burden).

Guowuyuanling 1991, Nongmin chengdan feiyong he laowu guanli tiaoli (Regulation on the Administration of Costs and Labor Services to be Assumed by Villagers).

Hsiao, William C. and Xianglin Du 1985, Zhongguo baojian shiye de zhuanbian (The Transformation of Chinese Health Protection), in: *Zhongguo Shehui Yixue Zazhi (Chinese Journal of Social Medicine)*, 2, 3, 185f.

Huang, Jiahao 2009, Jianguo 60 nian lai nongcun yanglao baoxian zhidu de lishi tansuo zhi lu (Historical Experimentation with Rural Pension Insurance Since the 1960s), in: *Juece Zixun Tongxun (Policy Advice Newsletter)*, 6, 61–66.

Huang, Yanzhong 2013, *Governing Health in Contemporary China*, New York: Routledge.

Hussain, Athar 1990, Rural Social Welfare in China. In *Remaking Peasant China. Problems of Rural Development and Institutions at the Start of the 1990s*, eds Jørgen

Delman, Clemens S. Østergaard and Flemming Christiansen, 139–156, Aarhus, Denmark: Aarhus University Press.

IBS Research Center 2009, *Eyeing the Rural Insurance Market: Will China Life hit the Bull's Eye?, ECCH—The Case for Learning*, online: www.ibscdc.org/Case_Studies/ Marketing/Marketing%20Strategies/MKS0138IRC.htm (accessed January 10, 2014).

Johnston, M. F. 2002, Elites and Agencies: Forgeing Labor Policies at China's Central Level, in: *Modern China*, 28, 2, 147–176.

Klotzbücher, Sascha 2006, *Das ländliche Gesundheitswesen der VR China: Strukturen, Akteure, Dynamik (The Rural Health Sector of the People's Republic of China: Actors, Structures, Dynamic)*, Frankfurt: Peter Lang.

Krieg, Renate and Monika Schädler 1995, *Soziale Sicherheit im China der neunziger Jahre (Social Security in China in the 1990s)*, Hamburg: Institut für Asienkunde.

Liu, Xingzhu and Yunni Yi 2004, The Health Sector in China—Policy and Institutional Review, Background Paper of the World Bank Rural Health Study.

Liu, Yuanli and Keqin Rao 2006, Providing Health Insurance in Rural China: From Research to Policy, in: *Journal of Health Politics, Policy and Law*, 31, 1, 71–92.

Liu, Yuanli, Keqin Rao and Shanlian Hu 2002, *People's Republic of China: Towards Establishing a Rural Health Protection System*, Manila: Asian Development Bank.

Macrochina 2001, Guomin jingji he shehui "ba wu" (1991–1995) fazhan jihua gangyao (Summary of the 8th Five-Year Plan (1991–1995) for the Development of the Economy and Society), online: www.macrochina.com.cn/fzzl/ckwx/20010514005369.shtml (accessed July 9, 2015).

MoH 1992, *Weishengbu guanyu shenhua weisheng gaige de jidian yijian (Some Opinions of the MoH on Deepening Health Reform)*.

MoH 1994, *Guojia weisheng fuwu yanjiu—1993 nian guojia weisheng fuwu zong diaocha fenxi baogao (Research on National Health Services—An Analysis Report of the National Health Service Survey)*, online: www.moh.gov.cn/publicfiles/business/ htmlfiles/mohwsbwstjxxzx/s8560/201009/49159.htm (accessed June 7, 2012).

MoH 1999, *Guojia weisheng fuwu yanjiu—1998 nian di er ci guojia weisheng fuwu diaocha fenxi baogao (Research on National Health Services—An Analysis Report of the Second National Health Service Survey in 1998)*, online: www.nhfpc.gov.cn/ cmsresources/mohwsbwstjxxzx/cmsrsdocument/doc9907.pdf (accessed June 7, 2012).

MoH 2004, *Di san ci weisheng fuwu diaocha fenxi baogao (The Third National Health Service Survey Analysis Report)*, online: www.nhfpc.gov.cn/cmsresources/m ohwsbwstjxxzx/cmsrsdocument/doc9908.pdf (accessed July 18, 2016).

MoH 2009, *2008 Zhongguo weisheng fuwu diaocha—di si ci jiating jiankang xunwen diaocha fenxi baogao (The 2008 National Health Service Survey—The Fourth Household Health Survey Analysis Report)*, online: www.nhfpc.gov.cn/cmsre sources/mohwsbwstjxxzx/cmsrsdocument/doc9911.pdf (accessed July 18, 2016).

Müller, Armin 2016, Premium Collection and the Problem of Voluntary Enrollment in China's New Rural Cooperative Medical System (NRCMS), in: *Journal of Current Chinese Affairs*, 45, 1, 11–41.

New York Times Online 2012, Billions in Hidden Riches for Family of Chinese Leader. October 25, 2012, online: www.nytimes.com/2012/10/26/business/global/fam ily-of-wen-jiabao-holds-a-hidden-fortune-in-china.html?pagewanted=all&_r=0 (accessed November 29, 2012).

Pearson, Margaret M. 2005, The Business of Governing Business in China, Institutions and Norms of the Emerging Regulatory State, in: *World Politics*, 57, 296–322.

People's Daily 1979, Guanyu nongcun hezuo yiliao, chijiao yisheng de jige wenti (On Problems Regarding CMS and the Barefoot Doctors), February 7, 1979.

People's Daily 1987, Linli Xian shiying xin xingshi chongjian cunji yiliao zuzhi, caiqu gezhong xingshi banyi, fangbian nongmin fangbing, zhibing (Linli County Adapts to the New Terrain, Rebuilds the Village Health Organization, Utilizes Multiple Forms of Medical Practice and Makes Preventive and Curative Care More Comfortable for the Farmers), April 8, 1987.

People's Daily 1987, Shiying guangda nongmin sheng lao bing can si deng fangmian xuqiu—Nongcun shehui baozhang shiye xunsu fazhan (Adapt to the Needs of the Peasants Regarding Birth, Age, Death, Illness and Disability—Swiftly Develop Rural Social Security), December 21, 1987.

People's Daily 1991, Jiejue nongmin kanbing nan de youxiao tujing—Cong Wuxue Shi de jingyan kan huifu he fazhan hezuo yiliao de biyaoxing (An Effective Way to Solve the Problem of Access to Healthcare—The Necessity to Renew and Develop the CMS in Wuxue City's Experience), October 29, 1991.

People's Daily 1991, Nongmin huhuan hezuo yiliao (The Peasants Call for CMS), October 31, 1991.

People's Daily 1992, Nachu jibao xiangyan qian, shengle dabing bu fachou—Jiashan Xian shixing nongmin yiliao baoxian (For the Price of a Few Packs of Cigarettes, the Worries about Catastrophic Illness Are Gone—Jiashan County Tests Rural Health Insurance), September 29, 1992.

People's Daily 1993, Peng Peiyun zai Jiangsu Anhui kaocha shi zhichu tuijin yiliao zhidu gaige gaohao nongcun jisheng gongzuo (Peng Peiyun Promotes Health System Reform to Accomplish Birth Planning Work During an Investigation in Jiangsu and Anhui), May 8, 1993.

People's Daily 1993, Nongyebu shouquan xuanbu: quxiao sishisan xiang nongcun dabiao shengji huodong (Ministry of Agriculture Authorized to Announce the Cancellation of Fourty-Three Rural Standard-Upgrading Activities), May 27, 1993.

People's Daily 1993, Qude chenggong jingyan chansheng guoji yingxiang—12 shengshi nongcun weisheng gongzuo chengji tuchu (Acquiring Successful Experience with International Impact—The Outstanding Merits of Rural Healthcare in Twelve Provinces and Cities), July 3, 1993.

People's Daily 1993, Cunbu paizi buneng duo (There Should Not Be Too Many Plaques in the Villages), November 9, 1993.

People's Daily 1994, Jiakuai nongcun hezuo yiliao baojian zhidu de gaige he jianshe (Accelerating the Reform and Construction of the Rural Cooperative Health Insurance System), July 2, 1994.

People's Daily 1996, Jiang Chunyun xiang Quanguo Renda Changweihui zuo baogao shi zhichu jianqing nongmin fudan bixu biaoben jianzhi (During his Work-Report to the Standing Committee of the National People's Congress, Jiang Chunyun Points Out the Necessity of Treating Both, Roots and Symptoms of the Farmers' Burden), October 27, 1996.

People's Daily 1996, Jiang Zemin zai quanguo weisheng gongzuo huiyi shang jiang hua (The Speech of Jiang Zemin on the National Healthcare Conference), December 10, 1996.

People's Daily 1996, Li Peng zai quanguo weisheng gongzuo huiyi shang jiang hua (Speech of Li Peng on the National Healthcare Conference), December 11, 1996.

People's Daily 1998, Xinren Weishengbu buzhang Zhang Wenkang tan weisheng shiye de gaige he fazhan—Rang renren xiangshou chuji weisheng baojian (The Newly

Appointed Minister of Health Zhang Wenkang Discusses the Reform and Development of the Health System—Let Everybody Enjoy Primary Healthcare), April 7, 1998.

People's Daily 1999, Jinnian weisheng gongzuo zhongdian renwu queding—Zhuaji chengzhen yiliao jigou peitao gaige, tuijin weisheng jiandu tizhi gaige, jiaqiang nongcun chuji weisheng baojian (Deciding this Year's Focus in Health Work—Grasp the Reform of Urban Health Providers, Promote the Reform of the Health Supervision System, and Strengthen Primary Healthcare in Rural China), January 7, 1999.

People's Daily 1999, Kaizhan nongcun tiyu tigao nongcun tizhi Zhongguo nongmin tixie renzhong daoyuan (The Chinese Farmers' Athletic Association will Shoulder Heavy Responsibilities in Developing Rural Sports to Improve the Physical Constitution of the Farmers), January 29, 1999.

People's Daily 1999, Xizang tuijin nongmuqu yiliao baozhang zhidu gaige—yiyou yiban yishang nongmumin canjia hezuo yiliao (Tibet Promotes Rural Healthcare System Reform—More Than Half of the Farmers and Herdsmen Already Participate in the CMS), October 22, 1999.

People's Daily 2003, Jiankang baoxian zai Yunfu (Health Insurance in Yunfu), November 10, 2003.

People's Daily 2005, Baojianhui zhuxi Wu Dingfu changtan baoxianye redian wenti—Guli geng duo baoxian gongsi "xiaxiang, rushi, chuhai" (Wu Dingfu, Director of the CIRC, Talks Freely about Core Problems of the Insurance Industry—Encouraging More Insurance Companies to "Go to the Rural Areas, the Stock Markets and Overseas"), August 22, 2005.

Saich, Tony 2008, *Providing Public Goods in Transitional China*, New York: Palgrave Macmillan.

Shi, Shih-jiunn 2006, Left to Market and Family—Again? Ideas and the Development of the Rural Pension Policy in China, in: *Social Policy and Administration*, 40, 7, 791–806.

Tang, Shenglan *et al.* 1994, *Financing Health Services in China, Adapting to Economic Reform*, Brighton: Institute of Development Studies.

Walter, Carl E. and Fraser J. Howie 2011, *Red Capitalism, The Fragile Financial Foundations of China's Extraordinary Rise*, Singapore: John Wiley & Sons (Asia).

Wang, Boya and Lutao Ning 2010, Corporate Governance Reform through Internationalization, Case Study of a State Owned Insurance Company, China Life, online: www.ceauk.org.uk/2010-conference-papers/full-papers/Boya-Wang-+-Lutao-Ning-final.pdf (accessed July 9, 2012).

Wang, Shaoguang 2009, Adapting by Learning, The Evolution of China's Rural Health Care Financing, in: *Modern China*, 35, 4, 370–404.

Wang, Shaoguang and Angang Hu 2001, *The Chinese Economy in Crisis: State Capacity and Tax Reform*, New York: M.E. Sharpe.

Wang, Shidong and Yide Ye 2004, Nongcun hezuo yiliao zhidu huigu yu fazhan yanjiu (Looking Back at the Development of the CMS), in: *Zhongguo Chuji Weisheng Baojian (Chinese Primary Health Care)*, 18, 4, 10–12.

Wong, Christine 2009, Rebuilding Government for the 21st Century: Can China Incrementally Reform the Public Sector?, in: *The China Quarterly*, 200, 929–952.

World Bank 1983, *Socialist Economic Development (vol. 3 of 9): Annex B—Population, Health and Nutrition*, online: http://documents.worldbank.org/curated/en/1982/03/2002852/china-socialist-economic-development-vol-3-9-annex-b-population-health-nutrition (accessed April 5, 2012).

World Bank 1992, *China—Strategies for Reducing Poverty in the 1990s*, Washington, DC: World Bank.

World Bank 1997, *Financing Health Care, Issues and Options for China*, Washington, DC: World Bank.

World Bank 2002, *China—National Development and Sub-National Finance*, online: www.worldbank.org/research/2002/04/1768217/china-national-development-sub-na tional-finance-review-provincial-expenditures (accessed February 8, 2012).

Wu, Ming 2004, *Nongcun hezuo yiliao zhidu de zhengce fenxi (A Policy Analysis of the Rural CMS)*, Beijing: Zhongguo Xiehe Yike Daxue Chubanshe (China Harmony and Medicine University Press).

Yip, Winnie and William Hsiao 2015, What Drove the Cycles of Chinese Health System Reforms?, in: *Health Systems and Reform*, 1, 1, 52–61.

Zha, Zheng 1987, Jinshan Xian Tingxin Xiang hezuo yiliao jiankang baoxian (The Cooperative Medical and Health Insurance in Tingxin Township, Jinshan County), in: *Zhongguo Nongcun Weisheng Shiye Guanli (Chinese Rural Health Affairs Management)*, 7, 18–21.

Zhang, Chengmo 1986, Shilun xin xingshi xia de hezuo yiliao zhidu (Testing CMS in a New Situation), in: *Zhongguo Nongcun Weisheng Shiye Guanli (Chinese Rural Health Affairs Management)*, 4–5, 56–59.

Zhang, Chengmo 1989, Yuhang Xian nongcun hezuo yiliao zhidu de zhuangkuang, wenti he duice (The Situation, Problems and Solutions of the CMS System in Yuhang County), in: *Zhongguo Nongcun Weisheng Shiye Guanli (Chinese Rural Health Affairs Management)*, 8, 1–4.

Zhang, Shuo and Meiling Wang 2007, The World Trade Organization and China's Health Insurance Sector. In *WTO, Globalization and China's Health Care System*, eds Meiling Wang, Shuo Zhang and Xiaowan Wang, 40–54. Basingstoke: Palgrave Macmillan.

Zhongbanfa 1993, 10, Guanyu sheji nongmin fudan xiangmu shenhe chuli yijian de tongzhi (Notification about the Opinion on Examining and Disposing of Projects Involving a Burden for the Farmers).

Zhongfa 1997, 3, Zhonggong Zhongyang, Guowuyuan guanyu weisheng gaige yu fazhan de jueding (Decision of the Central Committee and the State Council on Healthcare Reform and Development).

Zhonggong Zhongyang 1993, Zhonggong Zhongyang guanyu jianli shehui zhuyi shi-chang jingji tizhi ruogan wenti de jueding (Decision of the Central Committee on Several Problems on Establishing a Socialist Market Economy).

Zhonggong Zhongyang 1996a, Zhonggong Zhongyang, Guowuyuan guanyu jinkuai jiejue nongcun pinkun renkou wenbao de jueding (Decision of the Central Committee and the State Council on Solving the Problems of the Rural Poor).

Zhonggong Zhongyang 1996b, Zhonggong Zhongyang, Guowuyuan guanyu qieshi zuohao jianqing nongmin fudan gongzuo de jueding (Decision of the Central Committee and the State Council on Practically Decreasing the Farmers' Burden).

Zhu, Xianxiang 1987, Jianli Zhongguo nongcun yiliao baoxian zhidu zhi wo yijian (My Opinion about Establishing a Rural Health Insurance System in China), in: *Zhongguo Nongcun Weisheng Shiye Guanli (Chinese Rural Health Affairs Manage-ment)*, 10, 18–20.

4 The Enactment and Implementation of the NRCMS

By 1999, the pro-market actors clearly emerged as the winners from the conflict concerning rural China's health insurance system, with the MoH abandoning the CMS program after two failed policy initiatives. Only three years later, the Central Committee and the State Council enacted a new policy that ultimately realized the long-held demand of the pro-government forces—that is, extending a state-subsidized CMS program in the rural areas. The document came out only weeks before the Sixteenth Party Congress and the transition to the Hu and Wen administration, which emphasized social policy and a concern for the rural areas in its political self-description. Jiang Zemin had presided over two failed CMS initiatives, and Zhu Rongji had arguably played a crucial role in those failures. By the end of their term, however, a political compromise for the pro-government solution of the MoH had been formed, and preparations for the implementation of the new CMS program—the NRCMS—were already proceeding in several provinces. The first part of this chapter will analyze the conditions under which this change of orientation occurred, and the details of the resulting policy compromise.

After the 2002 decision, the evaluation of the NRCMS program began with a pilot stage that lasted from 2003 to 2005. In the national arena, the pilot stage was characterized by the lingering tensions between the pro-government and pro-market forces. While the MoF and the MoA had been integrated into the new policy regime, the insurance industry had been left out at first. Furthermore, after the SARS crisis the MoH leadership was divided between a pro-market minister and a pro-government party secretary. During the pilot stage, the issue of voluntary enrollment became a problem again and delayed the implementation. By 2005, however, both sides reached a new compromise: the insurance industry was integrated into the NRCMS policy regime, the pro-market minister of health resigned, and the extension of the program was scheduled.

Between 2006 and 2008, the NRCMS program was evaluated and extended. It covered all jurisdictions in rural China by early 2008, two years ahead of the original schedule. The evaluation focused on the early cohorts of pilot counties with above-average implementation conditions. Among other things, it recommended the toleration of minor violations of the rule of voluntary enrollment. It criticized the use of MSAs for outpatient reimbursement as ineffective and pointed to rising health costs as a problematic development threatening to neutralize the effects of the new insurance system.

Policy Formulation and Decision-Making

The Political Climate around the Year 2000

As Chapter 3 has shown, by the end of the 1990s two initiatives to reanimate the CMS in the rural areas had largely resulted in failure. Commercial insurance was on the rise and overtook the CMS in terms of coverage in many middle-income areas. It appeared as if the market coalition had won the political struggle over the welfare regime in rural China. By the end of 2002, however, the Central Committee and the State Council issued a decision on rural health reforms that promoted the extension of a new CMS initiative. The NRCMS realized many long-standing demands of the pro-government coalition, most notably a formalized system of tax-funded transfers to support the local insurance funds (Zhongfa 2002: 13).

The timing of the 2002 decision was surprising in various ways. First, it preceded the leadership transition in the course of the Sixteenth Party Congress and therefore was not an initiative of the new Hu and Wen administration, which put a greater emphasis on public social security than the preceding ones. Second, the policy preceded the outbreak of SARS in mainland China by several months. It was thus also not a reaction to the acute public health crisis, even though the SARS crisis arguably further strengthened the government's commitment to the policy, as the lack of insurance coverage was one factor that intensified the crisis (Gu 2004). Third, the NRCMS was followed by a rural pension insurance program with similar funding arrangements in 2009. This indicates both a general upgrading of rural social security in the early 2000s and a separation of the issues of health insurance and pension insurance. Furthermore, pro-government actors and their ideas gained ground vis-à-vis pro-market actors.

These shifts arguably had multiple causes, which were rooted in a larger political-situational logic around the millennium. First, Zhu Rongji lost some of his political influence at the end of the 1990s. Besides the financial reforms mentioned above, he was also a crucial promoter of reforms in the state-owned enterprise sector and of China's accession to the World Trade Organization (WTO). This economically liberal political agenda increasingly encountered opposition in the wake of the Asian crisis, when state-owned enterprises began to lay off workers, township and village enterprises began to lose their dynamics as job creators, and falling grain prices exerted pressure on rural incomes. Urban workers, the unemployed, women and the rural population became increasingly visible in the public consciousness as losers of the reforms. As Zweig notes, Zhu Rongji's "political problems peaked after President Clinton walked away from the promised WTO deal" (Zweig 2001: 236) during the former's visit to Washington in April 1999, and the subsequent bombing of the Chinese embassy in Serbia. Once there was an agreement, left-wing critics of liberalization and WTO accession became increasingly influential. In their view, WTO accession would intensify regional inequalities, income inequality, downward pressure on rural incomes and unemployment. The rise of Wang Tiejun's idea of the "three rural problems" and the political priority of public social security under the Hu and Wen administration have to be interpreted in this context (Fewsmith 2001; Zweig 2001).

Second, the NRCMS was enacted seven years before the rural pension insurance program. This indicates that the pro-market actors had lost their dominance in the field of healthcare earlier on. The incidents around Falun Gong may have contributed to this loss of influence. The problems of access and affordability of Western scientific medicine had given rise to traditional forms of healing since the collapse of the CMS and the large-scale privatization of grassroots health service provision (Heberer 2001). Organizations based on Qi Gong and the Pentecostal Churches had been thriving by offering their followers traditional interpretations of health and sickness, as well as cheap ways of supposedly attaining good health (Kupfer 2008; Oblau 2011). The pro-government actors around the MoH had always been strong critics of informal medicine and treatment, as Chapter 3 has shown. Zhu Rongji and other pro-market politicians, on the other hand, had welcomed Qi Gong groups, for they saw them as decreasing government expenditure in healthcare by promoting good health. The deputy minister of agriculture displayed a similar mind-set when he recommended rural sports as a means to conquer illness-induced poverty in January 1999 (People's Daily, January 29, 1999). Incidents related to Falun Gong in April 1999 arguably caused contradictions between top leaders: Jiang Zemin favored a harsh crackdown on the movement, whereas Zhu Rongji favored a more moderate approach (Keith and Lin 2003: 231f.). To the hardliners, the incident arguably illustrated the potential of political mobilization inherent to health issues. The interpretations by Western scholars and Chinese media of the NRCMS as an attempt to re-extend state-organized scientific medicine against informal healthcare and social security largely fit this view (Bunkenborg 2012).

Third, in 2000 the WHO officially criticized China for the organization of its healthcare system in an evaluation of its member countries. The failure to achieve universal access to primary care by 2000 was also related to the problems with the CMS. In the category "fairness in financial contribution," China was ranked 188 out of 191 (WHO 2000). This was connected to the heavily biased patterns of health spending of the Chinese state, which strongly focused on the cities, large urban hospitals and financing healthcare for state cadres (Huang 2013: 67). The WHO rating arguably came as a shock to many in the central government and contributed to the rising awareness of the problem (Liu and Rao 2006: 86f.). The Chinese government had missed its goal of covering 70 percent of the rural population with health insurance by a long way. At the same time, the successful extension of the CMS in the

Autonomous Region of Tibet from 1997 demonstrated that the program could be sustained even in the most adverse environments with a certain amount of public financial support (Wang 2009).

Furthermore, two important arguments of the pro-market actors began to lose their potency around 2000. First, the fiscal crisis that had dominated the 1990s was, at least at the central level, slowly coming to an end. This made it more difficult for the MoF and other pro-market ministries to argue that there was no fiscal capacity to back up the MoH's calls for fiscal support of the CMS. Second, the rural tax-for-fee reform abolished a vast array of fees and charges for the rural population, and replaced them with an integrated agricultural tax, which was subsequently abolished. It was piloted in Anhui in 2000, and its national extension began in 2002. With the enactment of this policy, the political priority of the burden agenda began to decrease (Göbel 2010; Wang 2009).

Inside Initiation and Policy Formulation (2000–2002)

The previous sections have analyzed remote causes of the NRCMS policy decision in 2002, which created a political climate conducive to its enactment. The most important proximate cause for the decision was the inside initiation strategy that convinced Jiang Zemin to become a supporter of the pro-government approach to the CMS in 2001. As noted above, the problem of illness-induced poverty was crucial in the agenda-setting process for legitimizing the CMS as a measure of poverty alleviation in the 1990s. Among the most important scholars conducting research on the problem were William Hsiao and Liu Yuanli (Hsiao and Du 1985; Liu et al. 1995; Liu et al. 1996). Together with Hu Shanlian, a professor at Fudan University, and Rao Keqin, a research director of the MoH, Liu contributed to convincing Jiang Zemin of the importance of illness-induced poverty (Liu and Rao 2006).

Between 2000 and 2002, the CMS Best Practice Task Force conducted an evaluation of the 1997 CMS initiative, which in itself could be interpreted as a manifestation of the changing political tides compared with the lethargy of 1998 and 1999. The task force was a joint project involving the WHO, the MoH, the UNDP, as well as Chinese and international experts in rural healthcare and the CMS. Between June 2000 and June 2001, it launched two conferences in Beijing and Nanjing, followed by fieldwork in the rural areas. The task force drafted reports of the different models of the CMS and gave detailed policy recommendations, which were subsequently published (Carrin et al. 2002a, 2002b, 2002c, 2004; CMS Best Practice Task Force 2003). Furthermore, Zhang Wenkang and the Planning Commission also arranged for an engagement of the Asian Development Bank (ADB). In January 2001, the ADB then entrusted Liu to conduct a study on rural healthcare, sponsored by the Planning Commission. Liu, Rao and Hu presented their findings at an international conference in Beijing in July. The conference was organized by the Planning Commission and attended by experts of the State Council, the

MoA, the MoF, the MoH, Harvard University and the WHO, as well as by representatives of various line ministries and provincial governments (Liu and Rao 2006: 79f.).

At that time, a new CMS initiative was already on the way. In 2000, the MoA and the MoF had declared that CMS premium collection ought to be illegal. By May 2001, they had drafted a joint document on rural health with the MoH and the Planning Commission, which called for strengthening multiple forms of health protection to counter illness-induced poverty, including the CMS (Guobanfa 2000: 33; Guobanfa 2001: 39).

The ADB study strongly emphasized the role of government support for the CMS and the public nature of the problem of rural risk protection. The executive summary clarified this point:

> Some policymakers, especially those in support of a voluntary community-based rural health protection system, hoped that with economic growth people's demand for health protection will increase, which will automatically lead to community initiatives to address the health protection issues. This has not happened yet. Despite steady economic growth since the 1980s and the announced policy directions on rural health protection in 1996, the majority of the rural population remains uninsured today. All existing CMS schemes succeeded because of a strong government support. We have yet to find one single example in the PRC, where government support is not needed and the scheme is totally initiated and operated on a sustainable basis by a nongovernment organization.
>
> (Liu et al. 2002: 1)

It saw further reasons for government support in the inter-regional inequalities of economic and social development and the need for authority, skills and trust to organize premium collection and risk pooling. Neither problem could be solved by the market alone. The study further highlighted the role of illness-induced poverty, and used data from the 1998 National Health Service Survey to assess its impact via the headcount method (Liu et al. 2002: 17–21). It asserted that commercial insurance was suitable for the wealthy coastal areas, but not for China's interior. Furthermore, it highlighted the connection between the MoA's burden reduction initiatives and the problems of the CMS.

After the conference, Liu and colleagues drafted a policy briefing paper in cooperation with the Planning Commission's Health and Social Security Division. It was sent to the office of Premier Zhu Rongji, who did not respond. Zhang Wenkang then took the initiative and wrote a summary of the ADB report, together with Liu's co-author Rao, as a personal letter to Jiang Zemin. The letter highlighted the role of illness-induced poverty and family bankruptcies as the cause of one-third of rural poverty, which reportedly came as a shock to Jiang. Soon after this, Rao and others involved with the report were visited and interviewed by members of the Policy Research Office of the Central Committee.

In August 2001, there was a sudden leadership change in the MoA, which had been pivotal in the anti-burden agenda. Minister Chen Yaobang—in office since 1998—was replaced by Du Qinglin before the end of his term (People's Daily, September 1, 2001). The MoA was later assigned responsibility to support the propaganda for the NRCMS (Guohan 2003: 95). In August and September 2001, the National People's Congress authorized an investigation of the implementation of the Agricultural Law, which recommended the strengthening of rural social security to prepare China for WTO accession (Renda 2001). In November, the State Council Office for Economic System Reform was officially assigned responsibility to coordinate policy formulation for a new CMS initiative. In the same month, two articles in *People's Daily* mentioned Tibet's CMS system, the extension of coverage and the importance of intergovernmental transfers (People's Daily, November 9, 2001; People's Daily, November 27, 2001). By the end of 2001, various provinces were already supporting local CMS projects financially in preparation for a new policy initiative (World Bank 2002: 118).

It was also in November 2001 that two insurance companies started strategic experiments to get a foot in the door of the new CMS initiative. In Jiangsu Province, the government of Jiangyin City contracted China Life to manage the CMS. Jiangyin had gained experience with commercial hospital insurance for farmers during the 1990s. Its approach was a delegation model: the government delegated the administration of the CMS to China Pacific for a fixed annual fee. In Fujian Province, Tong'an District of Xiamen City launched a project with Ping An Insurance. The company was contracted to manage the CMS funds and reimbursement in four townships. The so-called "Pingbao model" (*Pingbao Moshi*) allowed the company to retain profits from the CMS operations, and thus resembled earlier models of commercial rural health insurance. The Fujian pilot was portrayed in a *People's Daily* article in July 2002, during the policy formulation process. Commercial health insurance coverage in rural China was at an all-time high at the time, but the new policy constituted a risk for the commercial insurance companies. They adapted quickly to the new situation to get a foot in the door and to retain an influence on the new policy (Lin 2010: 153ff.; People's Daily, July 21, 2002; People's Daily, August 18, 2004).

The cooperation of the MoF was facilitated in the formal process of policy formulation and decision-making. It began in November 2001, when the State Council Office for Economic System Reform was given the mandate to coordinate the formulation of a new policy, and ended in October 2002, when the reform was officially announced at a national policy conference on rural health. Liu and Rao described it as follows:

> The national policy-making process generally includes the following steps: First, relevant line ministries are urged by the Central Party Committee or the State Council to draft policy documents, with one national agency serving as coordinator. Second, draft policy documents are

discussed during several rounds of politburo meetings. Third, when the policy documents are finalized, a national conference is scheduled to publicly announce the new policies.

(Liu and Rao 2006: 85)

They furthermore noted that "the central government was keen to hold the rural health policy conference right before the Party's Sixteenth Congress to demonstrate the Chinese Communist Party's commitment to the people and their needs" (Liu and Rao 2006: 85).

While the leadership core was actively involved in policy formulation, the processes of compromise-building and securing cooperation occurred in inter-ministerial negotiations, rather than being facilitated directly by the leader-ship core via hierarchical direction:

Since the beginning of that year, the Ministry of Health, negotiating and fighting with other ministries (especially the Ministry of Finance), had begun working diligently to create and maintain the momentum for developing China's new rural health policies. ... Minister Zhang was advised that holding the conference before the big party meeting should be conditional on the real resource commitment behind the new policies from the Ministry of Finance. The political negotiation was helped by the fact that the State Council person in charge of scheduling major national conferences, Gao Qiang, happened to be a former deputy finance minis-ter who was very supportive of the idea that government should do more to help the rural populations improve their access to health care. Gao Qiang was able to assist in influencing and garnering the Ministry of Finance's attention and potential financial support, so the conference was scheduled with some real resource commitment.

(Liu and Rao 2006: 85f.)

Document 13 was officially passed on October 19, 2002. It proposed a com-prehensive reform of the rural healthcare system, of which the NRCMS was a central element. Article two specified the main targets of the reform: until 2010, China was to establish a basically complete rural health service net-work, a highly skilled rural health service workforce, a capable and highly efficient rural health administration system, new CMS and Medical Assis-tance systems focused on pooling the risks of serious illness, to create access to primary healthcare for all Chinese farmers and to achieve the health indi-cators suitable for an advanced developing country. The main purpose of the NRCMS was to solve the problem of illness-induced poverty (*yinbing zhipin, fanpin wenti*) by pooling the risks of infectious, endemic and other cata-strophic diseases. Its sources of funding were farmers' individual premiums, collective support and governmental contributions. The central government would support the NRCMS from 2003 on with transfers of RMB 10 per capita to the NRCMS funds in the rural regions of Central and Western

China, which were to be matched by the subnational levels of government. The NRCMS was furthermore complemented by a social assistance program called Medical Assistance. Its purpose was to assist poor households with health costs or NRCMS premiums. Both policies should basically cover all of the rural population by 2010 (Zhongfa 2002: 13).

On December 28, the revised version of the Agricultural Law passed by the National People's Congress confirmed that the state encouraged the development of cooperative medical care and other forms of health security (*yiliao baozhang*) (Renda 2002). On January 16, the State Council issued a joint document of the MoH, the MoF and the MoA with complementary provisions about the NRCMS and the implementation process (Guobanfa 2003: 3). Complementary provisions for the Medical Assistance program were issued later that year, in November, in a joint document of the MoCA, the MoH and the MoF (Minfa 2003: 158).

The NRCMS Policy as a Compromise

The NRCMS policy was a negotiated compromise between core actors of the pro-government and pro-market coalitions. The regulatory cornerstones for the NRCMS and the complementary Medical Assistance system were document 13 of the Central Committee and the State Council in October 2002, and a series of complementary documents drafted by the State Council and various ministries in 2003 and 2004 (Caishe 2003: 112; Guobanfa 2003: 3; Guobanfa 2004: 3; Guohan 2003: 95; Minfa 2003: 158; Zhongfa 2002: 13). The regulatory framework largely followed the recommendations specified in the evaluations of the CMS policy by the Best Practice Task Force (Carrin et al. 2002a, 2002b, 2002c, 2004; CMS Best Practice Task Force 2003) and the ADB (Liu et al. 2002). The NRCMS policy has been adapted on an annual basis since 2003 and is in a constant process of change.

Document 13 defined two goals for the NRCMS: first, to extend the coverage of health insurance to the vast majority of the rural population; second, to protect the rural population from illness-induced poverty due to catastrophic illness and public health issues. State Council document three in 2003 formulated the goals slightly differently: to decrease the burden of medical expenditure of the rural population, and to improve its health status. For Medical Assistance, document 13 specified that it should provide relief for Five-Guarantees households[1] and poverty households by contributing either to their catastrophic health expenditures or to their NRCMS premiums. Document 13 specified that both policies should basically cover all of the rural population by 2010, and document 158 by the MoCA, the MoH and the MoF called for a full roll-out of Medical Assistance by 2005 (Guobanfa 2003: 3; Guobanfa 2004: 3; Minfa 2003: 158; Zhongfa 2002: 13).

The NRCMS policy provided a new framework for rural health insurance, with matching funds from various levels of government, county-level pooling and administration, and a focus on catastrophic illness and inpatient services as the key policy innovations. Apart from this, the policy largely confirmed the traditional practices and policy experimentation of the CMS, and to a large extent followed the recommendations of the policy evaluations. Overall, it built on the experimentation of the 1990s and realized long-standing demands of the pro-government actors. Medical Assistance was to target poverty households and Five-Guarantees households and would either subsidize their out-of-pocket payments for healthcare or their NRCMS premiums. The funding was to primarily come from local budgets. As complementary policy documents specified, the NRCMS was to rely on positive lists of drugs and services eligible for reimbursement to reduce health costs and ensure efficient treatment. Furthermore, the shift to bidding and bulk purchases for drugs, which was pursued parallel to the NRCMS implementation and briefly described in Chapter 2, was to decrease drug prices and make treatment more affordable. Chapter 6 will analyze in greater detail the interplay between these reforms.

A crucial feature of the NRCMS was the institutionalization of inter-ministerial negotiations and cooperative decision-making. During the 1990s, the CMS administration at the central level had been problematic, as there was no stable and institutionalized cooperation mechanism between the different ministries. Towards the end of the 1990s, it was even unclear which ministry was actually in charge of the CMS. A cooperation mechanism was established with the NRCMS inter-ministerial conference (*xinxing nongcun hezuo yiliao buji lianxi huiyi*), which was founded in September 2003 to oversee the implementation (Guohan 2003, 95). At the provincial and prefectural level, the line administrations of health, finance, agriculture, civil affairs, audit and poverty alleviation would form coordination groups (*xietiao xiaozu*), and the health administrations would create internal organs for NRCMS administration.

The NRCMS policy also standardized the administrative framework in the local state. The CMS of the 1990s was characterized by a diverse array of different models regarding pooling and administration of the funds. The most common forms involved healthcare facilities or government organs at the township or village level managing township- or village-level insurance funds (Yang 2009: 67f.). The NRCMS was to be managed by administrative committees (*guanli weiyuanhui*) and carrier organs (*jingban jigou*) at the county level. The county bureaus of civil affairs were put in charge of the Medical Assistance program.

Institutionalizing financial support from all levels of government was among the most crucial changes of the NRCMS policy. The provincial, prefectural and county levels were to support Medical Assistance and the NRCMS funds on a per capita basis, and the central government would support the NRCMS in the central and western regions with transfers of RMB 10 per capita. The provincial governments were required to enact regulations for governmental contributions to the funds, and the subnational levels of government were to match the central transfers of 10 RMB in accordance with provincial regulations. Premiums remained a crucial part of NRCMS funding: they accounted for about 33 percent of the overall financial input, and financial transfers were conditional on previous premium payment. Only entire households were to enroll, the minimal individual premium was to be RMB 10, and allowing township and village enterprise workers to enroll was to be optional for county governments.

The NRCMS policy was a compromise between key ministerial actors of the pro-government and pro-market coalitions. It represented a milestone in pushing through key pro-government demands and creating a cooperative and consensual framework for the implementation of the NRCMS. However, two fundamental points of conflict were only partially addressed: the problem of voluntary enrollment and premium collection, and the role of the insurance industry.

With regard to premium collection, document 13 clarified that NRCMS premiums could not be considered a burden, thus shielding one of the policy's most vulnerable points. Nevertheless, enrollment was still supposed to be voluntary. The CMS evaluations had recognized the problematic nature of voluntary enrollment as well as the political obstacles to a compulsory rural health insurance. The ADB study recommended the incentivization of villagers to enroll via governmental subsidies for the funds (Liu et al. 2002: 52f.). The Task Force recommended only allowing entire households enroll, and making the enrollment rate a key performance indicator for local governments (Carrin et al. 2002c). As the pro-government actors' political influence was not sufficient to push through a compulsory system in 2002, the central and provincial governments acted in accordance with these recommendations during the implementation, thus delegating the contradiction between voluntariness and universal coverage to the local governments to resolve (Müller 2016).

The role of the insurance industry was the second point of conflict which remained largely unresolved in the NRCMS policy. By 2002 commercial insurance was at an all-time peak, especially in the middle-income regions, where it covered higher shares of the population than the CMS. But both the ADB proposal and document 13 ignored this, and saw commercial insurance as a system for wealthy areas only. In local practice, commercial insurance companies had pursued different approaches to health insurance in rural China: selling individual contracts and managing hospital insurance systems on behalf of the local government for either a fixed annual fee or on a for-profit basis. The administrative documents furthermore did not explicitly acknowledge the cooperation with local governments, despite the recent pilot projects in Jiangsu and Fujian.

Interestingly, insurance companies only played a minor role in the NRCMS policy. Although commercial insurance programs were usually much more expensive than the CMS, they nevertheless displayed a substantial local variation in terms of costs. This arguably facilitated their expansion in the rural middle-income areas discussed in the Chapter 3. More importantly, insurance companies had comparative advantages that were highly valuable for the NRCMS: commercial insurance usually focused on inpatient treatment, and company staff were experienced in pooling funds and forecasting expenditures. The bureaus of health, which came to manage the NRCMS, often lacked the human and financial resources for effective management (cf. Gu 2005: 373ff.).

The Pilot Stage: Institutionalizing Cooperation and Resolving Conflicts (2003–2005)

2003

In early 2003, the leadership transition and the preparations for the implementation of the NRCMS were proceeding when the SARS crisis struck China. It reshuffled the balance of power in the subsystem of health policy, which became immediately visible in the political leadership change in the MoH. The minister of health and party secretary of the MoH, Zhang Wenkang, was removed from office in April 2003. Whereas Chen Minzhang and Zhang Wenkang had both been doctors by training, neither of Zhang's successors was. Gao Qiang—the former deputy minister of finance, who was involved with the policy negotiations on the NRCMS—became his successor as party secretary and the deputy minister of health. Zhang had been a friend and protégé of Jiang, but Gao's loyalty arguably shifted between Jiang and Hu Jintao (Jia 2006: 56f.). Wu Yi, who had become vice premier in the cabinet of Wen Jiabao in March, now also became the successor of Zhang Wenkang as minister of health. Wu was a member of the Central Committee and the Politburo, and a protégé of Zhu Rongji and Li Lanqing (Dittmer 2003: 17; Thacik 2004: 117). Between 2003 and 2005, the leadership of the MoH was divided, with the pro-government forces represented by Gao and the pro-market forces represented by Wu. Within the MoH, both appeared to be equally strong (Nanfang Zhoumo, August 4, 2005).

In January, the State Council ordered that a first cohort of pilot counties should prepare the implementation, which was in line with the suggestions of the ADB proposal. It called on all provinces to select at least two or three counties or cities to "precede the others as pilots and acquire experiences before the roll-out" (*xianxing shidian, qude jingyan hou zhubu tuikai*). The pilot counties were to explore the administrative, financial and operational mechanisms of the NRCMS. They were to be characterized by a high readiness of the rural citizens to enroll and solid fiscal and administrative capacity, to provide a good basis for the NRCMS. All provinces were required to present lists of their pilot counties with the numbers of rural residents and the pilot program plans to the center by the end of May 2003. The pilot work officially began in July. The first cohort in 2003 consisted of 256 counties—97 in Eastern China, 87 in Central China, 72 in Western China. These figures did not include Liaoning Province, where the implementation only began in 2004, and the Autonomous Region of Tibet, where the government-supported CMS had already covered a large share of the jurisdictions. Altogether, the number of NRCMS counties was 304 in September 2003 (Guobanfa 2003, 3; PEG 2006: 21, 172, 191f.).

Even in Eastern and Central China, the distribution of NRCMS pilots across different provinces was very uneven. This arguably reflects differences in previous CMS coverage, in their preparations for the NRCMS implementation and in the level of political support the policy enjoyed. Among the 256 pilots, 130 pilots were located in eight provinces: 23 in Beijing and Shanghai, 27 in Zhejiang, 26 in Shandong,[2] 25 in Henan, 20 in Yunnan, and 15 in Shanxi. The provincial governments were to choose the pilot counties according to their fiscal and administrative capacity, and the readiness of the local population to enroll with the NRCMS (Guobanfa 2003, 3). It thus made sense to select counties with previous experience of operating the CMS or, ideally, operational CMS systems in one or more of their townships (PEG 2006: 191f.),

The insurance industry operated a number of (NR-)CMS pilot counties by 2003, not all of which, however, were immediately recognized as official pilot counties. Ping An Insurance and China Pacific Insurance had engaged in local experiments as managers of the CMS in Jiangyin City in Jiangsu and in Tong'an District of Xiamen City in Fujian. Jiangyin was not registered as a pilot of the first cohort. In Fujian, either the launch or formal acceptance of the first cohort was delayed until July 2004; by then, Tong'an was a part of it.[3] The successor of the PICC in the field of health insurance, China Life, now also engaged in managing the NRCMS on behalf of local governments. By June 2003, the government of the county-level city of Taizhou in Zhejiang had reached an agreement with China Life: it would delegate the financial management of the NRCMS to the company. In July, China Life had reached agreement with Beilun District in Ningbo City, Zhejiang, to initiate a commercial insurance model of the NRCMS: the company would provide insurances for a fixed annual premium, bear the risk and retain the profits. In the counties of Xinxiang City of Henan Province, China Life engaged in a mixed model of NRCMS administration that displayed patterns of both the delegation and the commercial model. Overall, eight local sub-branches of China Life concluded agreements with 31 county-level jurisdictions in seven provinces in 2003: 28 of them followed a delegation approach, in which the company offered administrative services for a fixed fee. The rest followed a commercial model, in which the company would fully or partially assume the financial risks and profits of the endeavor (CIRC 2006; Lin 2010: 87; Zhang 2006: 87–93).

In September, the State Council announced the official institutionalization of the NRCMS inter-ministerial conference, which was in charge of the organization, coordination and macro-level guidance of the NRCMS operations, the research and formulation of the NRCMS policies, and the supervision of the collection of the funds. It comprised representatives of 11 ministerial bodies involved with the NRCMS: the MoH, the MoF, the MoA, the MoCA, the DRC, the FDA, the Office of the National Conference on Poverty and Development (*Fupinban*), the Ministry of Education, the Traditional Chinese Medicine (TCM) Administration, the Ministry of Personnel and the NPFPC. It was headed by Wu Yi as vice premier; her deputies came from the MoH, the MoF, the MoA and the MoCA; the representatives of the other organs were ordinary members. The members were assigned different responsibilities: the MoH was responsible for policy formulation, leadership and coordination, and operative work; the MoF was responsible for inter-governmental transfers in Central and Western China, and the MoA was responsible for supporting the propaganda for the NRCMS. Zhejiang, Jilin, Hubei and Yunnan were given the status of pilot provinces, in which policy development would be monitored closely by the center. The CIRC was not integrated into the inter-ministerial conference, which points to the lack of acknowledgement of the insurance industry and its emerging role in the NRCMS (Guohan 2003, 95).

In the following months, conflicts about the voluntariness of the NRCMS again emerged. The events somewhat resembled the dynamics of the implementation processes of the two CMS initiatives in the 1990s. On November 10, while the implementation was officially proceeding, *People's Daily* featured an article about a commercial health insurance project between China Life and the government of Yunfu City in Guangdong Province, which had been aborted earlier that year. Under the new regulatory institutions of the NRCMS, both parties had been unable to negotiate a consensus, and the project was abandoned. At one point, the article asked: "Why does a good thing have to encounter so much trouble?" (People's Daily, November 10, 2003).

On November 14, the MoH distributed a document it had received from the provincial government in Hunan about irregularities in the premium collection process connected to voluntary enrollment of one pilot. According to the document, the townships had received an enrollment target of 40 percent. Where the quota could not be reached, cadres and THCs had prepaid the missing amount to reach the target. On November 25, the MoH disseminated another similar document, which criticized the premium collection practices in Guangnan County of Yunnan Province. Teachers in one township had arguably been pressured to participate in the premium collection process, and their salaries were withheld until they reached the quotas. Many if not most provincial governments had issued target quotas for NRCMS enrollment, as had been recommended by the Best Practice Task Force. County governments had to achieve those targets and handed them down to the township cadres. In the document, the MoH—now under the leadership of a pro-market minister—criticized the use of enrollment targets, granting loans, apportion, prepayment and coercive enrollment in the premium collection process (Müller 2016; Weibanjifufa 2003, 147; Weijifufa 2003, 317).

2004

On January 13, 2004, the State Council announced a stop to the extension of piloting in its document three (Guobanfa 2004, 3). It criticized the practice of fixed enrollment quotas, and suggested not further extending the NRCMS in 2004. It emphasized the importance of voluntariness and condemned the use of pressure, force, the target-responsibility system and the coercive drafting of health staff to aid in the collection process. Rural cadres were to convince the villagers to enroll by propaganda, reasoning and the dissemination of information about the NRCMS. The criticisms targeted a series of informal practices, by which rural cadres tried to cope with the contradictory goals of voluntary enrollment and universal coverage (Müller 2016). These problems were long known at the central level, and the criticisms and pilot stop were a manifestation of the continuing conflicts between pro-government and pro-market actors about the nature of the NRCMS and the role of commercial insurance companies.

In April 2004, the technical guidance group (*jishu lingdao zu*) was set up under the leadership of the State Council, the inter-ministerial conference and the MoH's department of rural health. It was to guide and assist the implementation process in all of China, with a special focus on the pilot provinces.[4] Each was to select two contact counties (*lianxi xian*) for direct supervision through the technical guidance group. It would conduct inspections for at least two weeks every three months and submit a report to the MoH within one week after the inspection. Furthermore, it was to assist the contact counties to develop models (*peiyu dianxing*) and to summarize successful experiences (Weibannongweifa 2004, 46).

On May 23, a television report exposed prepayment and other irregularities regarding voluntary enrollment and premium collection in Taikang County in Henan. On the following day, the MoH issued an urgent notification announcing an evaluation of the financial situation and a verification of NRCMS enrollment in all the pilot counties. The evaluation consisted mainly of a questionnaire to be filled out by the local NRCMS administrators. Furthermore, random investigations to verify the figures were announced. The further extension of NRCMS piloting in 2005 was made conditional on the respective province successfully passing the evaluation. By June, the number of NRCMS pilots had only marginally increased to 310 counties. The central government used its financial transfers to steer the implementation of the NRCMS in Central and Western China. Its influence in these areas was greater than in the coastal provinces, where the provincial governments were responsible for most of the transfers (PEG 2006; Weifadian 2004, 37; Weinongweifa 2004, 256).

The CIRC also conducted investigations of NRCMS pilots, even though it was not part of the inter-ministerial conference. In August 2004, its director Wu Dingfu conducted an investigation of the Xinxiang Pilot in Henan, and the CIRC subsequently submitted a work report to the State Council and received supportive comments from Wu Yi (vice premier and minister of health) and Huang Ju (vice premier and member of the Politburo's Standing Committee). In Xiamen, Tong'an District was now acknowledged as a part of the first cohort of NRCMS pilot counties, and the model was extended (Anonymous 2011; Lin 2010: 87).

By December 2004, there were officially 333 NRCMS pilot counties. On average, there was one per prefecture-level jurisdiction, but their distribution had a regional bias. Beyond the official NRCMS pilots, a substantial number of counties implemented locally financed CMS systems in preparation for the

NRCMS extension. Entering the NRCMS framework would merely add central transfers to the funding. According to internal studies of the MoH, in 2004 there were 15 counties where the NRCMS was managed by the social insurance centers, and 21 counties where it was managed by insurance companies. Especially with regard to the insurance companies, these figures may either understate their involvement or indicate that many projects had been given up during the first year (MoH 2009a: 59f.; PEG 2006: 21).

2005

The year 2005 was a turning point for the NRCMS and for Chinese health policy. Wu Yi resigned as minister of health, and Gao Qiang became minister and party secretary of the MoH, which subsequently began to clearly communicate pro-government preferences in health policy (Nanfang Zhoumo, July 21, 2005). The Development Research Center of the State Council released a research report that argued that the reforms of marketization and commercialization in the Chinese healthcare system had failed (Guowuyuan 2006). This report sparked an extensive and critical policy debate about the development of China's health system after 1978, and the role the state was to play in it (Huang 2013). While China's health policy as a whole was now called into question, the tensions regarding the NRCMS were receding.

The second cohort of pilot counties was launched largely during the first half of 2005. By June, there were 641 NRCMS pilots altogether. According to Gao and Han (2007), the NRCMS was now managed by insurance companies in 68 counties in eight provinces. The MoH (2009a) counted only 24 counties. In August, the MoH and the MoF announced that the main evaluation of the pilot work would be organized by the inter-ministerial conference in the second half of 2005. The provinces were to first conduct evaluations of their own pilot counties, summarize the experiences and problems, and report the information to the MoH and the MoF by September 10. The extension of the NRCMS in 2006 for each province was conditional on passing the evaluation. Furthermore, each province was to select two or three models of the NRCMS for extension (Weinongweifa 2005, 319).

During August 2005, Xu Shaoshi (secretary general of the State Council) and Wu Dingfu of the CIRC both conducted inspections in Xinxiang City of Henan province. On August 22, when the annual NRCMS conference of the State Council was held, *People's Daily* published an interview with Wu Dingfu. He explained the participation of the CIRC in the inter-ministerial conference as part of a strategy to encourage China's insurance companies to engage in NRCMS administration and to expand from the saturated urban markets to the still undeveloped rural markets. He pointed to the insufficiencies of local governments' financial administration, information processing and supervision capacities, and praised the insurance companies as a superior alternative (Anonymous 2011; People's Daily, August 22, 2005).

On September 8, 2005, the State Council released a document that formally integrated the CIRC in the inter-ministerial conference and thus formally legitimized the insurance industry's involvement with the NRCMS (Guobanhan 2005, 81). Wu Yi repeatedly mentioned the topic in speeches during September. On October 10, the CIRC held a conference on the role of insurance companies in the NRCMS, and on October 26 it released a document with a basic regulatory outline for the insurance companies' engagement. The focus was to be on the delegation model, in which the government assumed all financial risks and profits, and the insurance company only offered administrative services for a fixed fee. The local government in Beilun District of Ningbo City experimented with a for-profit contracting model of NRCMS administration, in which the government bought insurance with the NRCMS funds and the company assumed the risks. The contradiction between the government's regulatory authority and the company's responsibility for financial losses caused by governmental regulations, however, ultimately led to the termination of the experiment. A mixed model in Xinxiang City of Henan Province gave rise to similar conflicts of interest, such as the distribution of profits and losses between the company and the government, the level of administrative fees for the company and the administrative competences of the government. The delegation model prevailed with regard to the administration of the NRCMS. As Chapter 7 will show, the contracting model was resurrected in 2012 for the Catastrophic Disease Insurance program (*dabing yiliao baoxian*) within the NRCMS and the URBMI (Baojianfa 2005, 95; Interview 111129; Wang 2008: 144ff.).

By the end of 2005, the political conflict about the role of the insurance industry in the NRCMS had been resolved. The CIRC had been integrated in the inter-ministerial conference, and the role of insurance companies as management organs for the NRCMS had been legitimized by the central government. The main pro-government and pro-market actors were now integrated in the cooperative framework of the inter-ministerial conference, and the implementation could proceed without further problems. By December 2005, the goal of extending the NRCMS nationwide until 2008 had been integrated in the eleventh five-year plan and the Construction of a New Socialist Countryside initiative (Zhonggong Zhongyang 2005).

At the same time, a greater conflict had emerged concerning the general nature of China's healthcare system. Its roots lay in the SARS crisis and disputes about the privatization of public healthcare facilities, the focus of which was Suqian City of Jiangsu Province. In this larger conflict, ministerial actors more openly than before entered symbiotic relationships with academic actors—mainly professors and universities—who would support their policy preferences with scientific arguments. The MoH and the DRC supported a tax-funded health service oriented towards the British model. The MoLSS, on the other hand, promoted the approach of a coordinated market economy focused on health insurance as a financing mechanism (Huang 2013: 68f.; Nanfang Zhoumo, July 21, 2005; Nanfang Zhoumo, August 4, 2005).

Evaluation and Extension (2006–2008)

Evaluation of the First Cohort (2006)

On January 10, 2006, the MoH and six other ministerial bodies announced the acceleration of the implementation process and presented specific targets: the NRCMS was to cover 40 percent of China's counties by the end of 2006, 60 percent by 2007 and 100 percent by 2008. While the level of premiums was to remain at 10 RMB per capita, the matching funds would be doubled to 40 RMB per capita. Urban districts with a high population share having an agricultural household registration were entitled to join the NRCMS framework, and the Eastern provinces were entitled to receive an unspecified amount of central transfers for the NRCMS. Among other things, the document also criticized various informal practices in the administration of the NRCMS (Weinongweifa 2006, 13).

On January 25, the MoH and the MoF released a document summarizing the outcomes of the 2005 auditing inspection, which had targeted 20 counties in 15 provinces. It listed a number of problems regarding the processes of financing, premium collection and reimbursement, and it criticized informal practices and rising health costs. It reiterated the call for guiding the villagers to voluntary enrollment and demanded that the regulations were observed in local administration and the transfers of matching funds. The various supervision mechanisms of the NRCMS were to be strengthened and all problems that came up during the investigation were to be solved by March. On March 15, a MoH document criticized irregularities regarding premium collection, check-ups and the supervision of hospitals in Nayong County of Guizhou Province. The document did not feature the issue of voluntariness, which indicates that the issue was dying down by now (Weibannongweifa 2006, 42; Weinongweifa 2006, 40).

In March, the MoH announced the comprehensive evaluation of the first cohort of pilot counties in 29 provinces—excluding Tibet and Liaoning. It was supported by international actors such as the World Bank, and by different administrative and academic organizations on different levels of China's administrative system. The evaluation was organized in four evaluation groups. First, a general evaluation was to be provided by the Chinese Academy of Social Sciences. Second, a report on service provision in the NRCMS was to be delivered by Peking University. Third, a report on health service consumption was to be delivered by the Center of Statistical Information of the MoH. Fourth, an analysis of poverty reduction, the Medical Assistance system and the NRCMS was to be delivered by the Rural Economy Research Center of the MoA. The first official evaluation report was published in 2006, followed by a second report in 2007, which was mainly prepared by the research groups of Peking University and the MoH's Center for Statistical Information (MoH 2007; PEG 2006).

In June 2006, the NRCMS research center was officially set up as a permanent organ under the MoH and the Health Economics Research Institute. It was located on the campus of Peking University and entrusted with the tasks of collecting, arranging and analyzing statistical information on the NRCMS, as well as assisting in the construction of the NRCMS information network and tasks related to staff training and human resources. These studies were strongly based on data of the NRCMS information system, which had been gradually built up during the implementation. The pilot counties had to conduct baseline surveys about the local rural healthcare system and the impact of the NRCMS, and the MoH had begun to systematically collect this information. In late 2009, the research center submitted an internal compilation of 20 research reports ordered by different MoH departments about specific problems such as NRCMS administration, operations and cost control (MoH 2009a; Weinongweifa 2006, 453).

The two evaluation reports delivered a detailed analysis of the first wave of pilot counties. The evaluation highlighted the achievements of the NRCMS: the system attracted high numbers of villagers and enjoyed broad support in the population. The scope of its benefits had broadened in recent years, and it was decreasing the health costs of the villagers and strengthening their capacity to resist financial shocks. It constituted an opportunity for the development of rural healthcare providers by increasing the effective use of rural health resources and the demand for health services: many counties granted higher reimbursement rates for health providers on lower levels, thus incentivizing patients to consume cheaper services. Finally, an institutional framework and administrative system had been established and was continuously improved (PEG 2006: 44ff.).

The evaluation also pointed to problems. Among other things, the financing mechanisms were still unstable and incomplete, and premium collection remained a problem. Enrollment quotas were used widely on the sub-national levels, and were generally higher on the lower levels of government. If the counties were to operate fully voluntary systems, they could not achieve the enrollment targets. The premium collection process remained cumbersome and costly. Prepayment and other informal practices remained common phenomena, and the reports recommended the toleration of informal practices (MoH 2007: 145; PEG 2006: 46ff.).

Furthermore, while the focus on catastrophic illness helped to focus the system on combatting illness-induced poverty, the narrow distribution of the funds negatively affected the attitude of the villagers towards the NRCMS. The inpatient pooling funds often retained high surpluses due to conservative and risk-averse fund management, most notably in the early years of the implementation. Many local governments had selected MSAs for outpatient reimbursement, which had little effective function in terms of risk protection due to their small pooling capacity, low utilization and informal practices. There were substantial problems with controlling the hospitals, which were further intensified by their problematic relationships with governmental and administrative organs. The villagers had few opportunities to participate in the administration. High copayment rates disadvantaged the poor among the insured, and the Medical Assistance system usually only paid for their premiums, which did not necessarily improve their access to health services. Finally, the rural healthcare markets remained characterized by monopolistic supply structures, informal practices and rising costs (PEG 2006: 49–55).

The evaluation found numerous governance problems and informal practices, but it did not analyze all aspects of the NRCMS. It evaluated the first cohort of pilots, which implemented under above-average conditions, as they were selected according to administrative and fiscal capacity and the positive attitude of the population to the NRCMS. The problems it found can thus be expected to have intensified in the following cohorts. Furthermore, it did not provide a systematic comparison of different administrative models—that is, administration by the bureau of health, an insurance company or the social insurance offices. Remarkably, the reports did not only openly discuss the problems of voluntary enrollment, but they advised against excessively tight controls in this area. This indicates that the issue was now less politically sensitive than it had been in previous years, when the status of the insurance companies was still less secure and clarified.

The evaluations provided a number of policy recommendations for the further implementation and adaptation of the NRCMS. The NRCMS was to continue to provide a standardized framework that would allow for local diversity, most notably for raising financial input and integrating urban and rural insurance systems in the more wealthy areas. In the long run, the share of premiums in the overall financing was to be raised, and the level of premiums was to be connected to the level of household income. The Medical Assistance program was to be strengthened to allow the poor not merely to formally participate in the NRCMS, but also to gain better access to medical services. Furthermore, the NRCMS was to enhance the protection of the so-called "hidden poor"—households only slightly above the poverty line that were particularly threatened by health-induced financial shocks, but not covered by the Medical Assistance system. Healthcare facilities on the township and village levels were to be strengthened, to adapt their service profiles to the ongoing disease transition, and to focus more strongly on public health and prevention (MoH 2007: 148; PEG 2006: 55–9).

The rising costs of healthcare were an issue of particular concern, most notably due to the provision of unnecessary care. They threatened to neutralize the benefits of the new insurance system, as the measures of cost containment taken in recent years had by and large been ineffective. Coping with the rising costs would require substantial adaptations in the systems of healthcare provision, health insurance and drug provision and circulation, as the NRCMS could only control costs to a very limited extent. Also, enhanced mechanisms of supervision and transparency, and greater participation of the villagers were required (PEG 2006: 59f.).

The reports furthermore recommended higher utilization rates of the pooling funds and the abolition of the MSAs. Administrative expenditures were to be reduced in order to free local fiscal resources for the insurance funds. At the same time, more financial, personal and material resources were needed for the administration. Furthermore, the financial transfer processes for the matching funds were to be simplified. Administrative capacity was highlighted as a core problem in the extension phase: because the pilot counties were selected on the basis of experience in health policy, good administrative and fiscal capacity, and populations with a positive attitude towards the NRCMS, the later cohorts would encounter larger problems than the earlier cohorts. As speeding up the implementation would raise the risks, a gradual approach based on regulatory standards was recommended (MoH 2007: 145f.; PEG 2006: 61f.).

Extension (2006–2008)

In the course of 2006, the number of counties implementing the NRCMS had more than doubled—from 678 to 1,451. In the course of 2007, another 1,000 counties began implementation. In 2008, their number rose from 2,451 to 2,729, before it started to gradually decline again in the following years. Until 2006, the largest share of implementing counties was located in Eastern China, where the pace of the implementation was substantially faster. The vast majority of central and western counties only implemented in or after 2006. Some of them had already implemented a locally financed system in advance, and the formal extension only meant that they would finally receive central and provincial subsidies, as in the case of C District. Furthermore, there was also a considerable number of urban districts among the later cohorts, which only became eligible for transfers when the required share of agricultural population was decreased. Nevertheless, in general the implementation conditions deteriorated in the later cohorts, and the problems highlighted in the evaluation reports arguably intensified (CHFP 2014; MoH 2009b).

The implementation process of the Medical Assistance program proceeded more slowly than that of the NRCMS. Originally, the program was to be rolled out completely by 2005 (Minfa 2003, 158). The implementation started with 130 counties in 2003, and after substantial expansion in the following years covered 65 percent of the county-level jurisdictions by 2006 (Wagstaff et al. 2009: 38). The implementation process was arguably further delayed after 2006, as at least in one province—Heilongjiang—full coverage of Medical Assistance was rescheduled for 2015 in 2009 (Guo 2009).

The central government heeded much of the policy advice given in the evaluation in the following years, most notably in two areas. First, it substantially decreased the local use of MSAs, which will be discussed in more detail in Chapter 5. Second, it showed greater flexibility regarding the problem of voluntariness, most notably by changing the dominant vocabulary by which it criticized informal premium collection practices. Furthermore, the expansion of provider payment reforms in the NRCMS adapted the financial incentives it presented to healthcare providers. With the enactment of the New Health Reform, the center finally initiated a comprehensive reform of the healthcare system as a whole, which substantially altered the context in which the NRCMS operated. These changes will be discussed in greater detail in Chapters 5 and 6.

Summary

After the pro-market forces had emerged as politically dominant by the end of the 1990s, the early 2000s saw a substantial shift in preferences in the leadership core of the party-state regarding rural health insurance. On the one hand, rural social security was re-evaluated in general due to the WTO entry and the changes it brought: an increasing influence of critical ideas regarding economic globalization and the potential social costs of the world trade regime. However, the NRCMS program was enacted before the Sixteenth Party Congress in 2002, which is regarded as a milestone for many other rural social security programs. The NRCMS was an initiative of the Jiang Zemin administration, not the Hu Jintao administration.

This indicates that around 2000 the status of rural health insurance was elevated above other rural social security programs. The general political situation at the time displayed two particularities that favored such a development: first, the bad rating of China's healthcare system by the WHO in 2000, which was followed by an evaluation program for the failed 1997 CMS initiative (Wang 2009); second, the fast development of religious and spiritual organizations with a focus on health and illness in their teachings, such as Pentecostal Churches or Qigong groups. The latter had been supported by pro-market actors during the 1990s as a cheap alternative to government spending on healthcare, which potentially contributed to a loss of authority of the pro-market forces in the field of healthcare. In 2001, the MoH and a group of affiliated academics used an inside initiation strategy to convince Jiang Zemin to support the CMS program with public financial transfers, and succeeded. The issue of illness-induced poverty—that is, the poverty-generating aspects of illness—was reported to be pivotal in this approach.

Between 2001 and 2005, the pro-government and pro-market coalitions gradually dissolved. As a first step, the MoF and the MoA entered negotiations with the MoH about the new policy in late 2001. The policy was enacted in 2002, and the inter-ministerial conference was formed as a decision-making forum for the NRCMS in 2003. At this time, the CIRC was excluded from the inter-ministerial conference, even though several insurance companies had strategically positioned themselves as partners for local governments in the NRCMS administration by 2001. It was not until 2005 that the CIRC was integrated into the inter-ministerial conference.

The phase of conflict concerning the voluntary nature of the NRCMS coincided with the phase of ambiguity regarding the status of the insurance industry in the NRCMS. The leadership of the MoH was divided between a pro-market minister and a pro-government party secretary. On the one hand, the provinces followed the recommendation of the CMS evaluation reports and largely made enrollment rates a performance target for local governments to compensate for the non-compulsory nature of the NRCMS. The MoH criticized the use of such targets and pressure and coercion in the premium collection processes. This stalled the implementation in 2004, when the extension of piloting was preliminarily stopped. In the course of 2005, the status of the insurance industry in the NRCMS was confirmed, the pro-market minister resigned and left the MoH to the pro-government forces, and the conflict about voluntary enrollment died down. In the following years, informal practices related to premium collection were still criticized by the MoH, but with different and less loaded vocabulary and less severe consequences.

Overall, by 2005 the main conflict between pro-government and pro-market forces over rural health insurance was resolved. All major actors had their interests formally represented after the integration of the CIRC into the inter-ministerial conference and the formalization of the insurance companies' status in the NRCMS framework. In recent years, the role of the insurance industry appears to be increasing again, for it is mentioned in various administrative documents. Administrative documents in 2012 that preceded the Eighteenth Party Congress specified the regulatory guidelines for insur-ance companies' participation in the NRCMS, and mandated certain shares of the NRCMS funds to be spent on purchasing Catastrophic Disease Insur-ance from commercial companies. The example of Ningbo's contracting model illustrates the pitfalls of such endeavors. Nevertheless, it is possible that state management will be but a transitory stage in the development of rural health insurance.

List of Interviews

Interview 101129: Interview with a city-level NRCMS administrator in Shandong Province, November 29, 2010
Interview 111129: Interview with a civil servant in Beilun District of Ningbo City, November 29, 2011

Notes

1　"Five-Guarantees households" are households targeted by a basic social assistance system called the Five-Guarantees program. This program mainly targets people unable to work and without a family to rely on, and provides material benefits in five areas: food, clothing, shelter, healthcare and funerals.
2　The 2006 NRCMS evaluation report counts 26 counties for Shandong Province. According to Guo, CMS in Shandong already covered 37 percent of the townships and towns in 2000, which arguably served as the basis for the large first cohort. A part of those counties arguably only implemented NRCMS in one or several townships in 2003—a so-called city-level pilot, as financial support came only from the city, not from the higher levels (Guo 2008: 63–71; Interview 101129; PEG 2006: 191f.).
3　The literature provides contradicting claims regarding the launching and/or official acknowledgement of 13 pilots in three provinces: three in Fujian, seven in Inner Mongolia and three in Liaoning (cf. Liaoning Ribao, January 23, 2006; Lin 2010; Neimeng Weishengting 2006; PEG 2006: 21, 191f.; Qu and Liu 2006).
4　Zhejiang, Jilin, Hubei and Yunnan were selected as pilot provinces for direct supervision in 2004; Sichuan was added in 2005.

Bibliography

Anonymous 2011, Guanyu wanshan baoxianye yu xinxing nongcun hezuo yiliao shi-dian gongzuo de ruogan zhidao yijian (Some Leading Opinions on Completing the

Pilots of the Insurance Industry and NRCMS), online: www.doc88.com/p
-17385351119.html (accessed January 13, 2013).

Baojianfa 2005, 95, Zhongguo Baoxian Jiandu Guanli Weiyuanhui guanyu wanshan
baoxianye canyu xinxing nongcun hezuo yiliao shidian gongzuo de ruogan zhidao
yijian (Some Leading Opinions from the Chinese Insurance Regulatory Commission on Completing the Participation of the Chinese Insurance Industry in NRCMS
Experimentation).

Bunkenborg, Mikkel 2012, Organizing Rural Health Care. In *Organizing Rural China,
Rural China Organizing*, eds Ane Bislev und Stig Thøgersen, 141–156. Lanham:
Lexington Books.

Caishe 2003, 112, Caizhengbu, Weishengbu guanyu zhongyang caizheng zizhu zhongxibu diqu nongmin canjia xinxing nongcun hezuo yiliao zhidu buzhu zijin bofu
youguan wenti de tongzhi (Notification from the MoF and the MoH about Problems Concerning the Allocation of the Central Financial Contributions to Aid
Rural Residents in Central and Western China).

Carrin, Guy, Philip Davies and Qin Jiang 2002a, Zhongguo nongcun hezuo yiliao
zuijia shijian fenxi kuangjia—Fuwu tigong, ziyuan chansheng yu guanli—Er (Best
Practices of China's Rural CMS—Service Provision and the Generation and
Administration of Resources—Part Two), in: *Zhongguo Weisheng Jingji (China
Health Economics)*, 21, 3, 22–3.

Carrin, Guy, Philip Davies and Qin Jiang 2002b, Zhongguo nongcun hezuo yiliao
zuijia shijian fenxi kuangjia—Jixiao pingjia—San (Best Practices of China's Rural
CMS—Performance Evaluation—Part Three), in: *Zhongguo Weisheng Jingji
(China Health Economics)*, 21, 4, 12–14.

Carrin, Guy, Philip Davies and Qin Jiang 2002c, Zhongguo nongcun hezuo yiliao
zuijia shijian fenxi kuangjia—Weisheng xitong de gongneng yu chouzi zuzhi—Yi
(Best Practices of China's Rural CMS—Functions and Financial Organization of
the Healthcare System—Part One), in: *Zhongguo Weisheng Jingji (China Health
Economics)*, 21, 2, 7–10.

Carrin, Guy, Philip Davies and Qin Jiang 2004, Zhongguo nongcun hezuo yiliao zuijia
shijian fenxi (Best Practices of China's Rural CMS), in: *Guoji Yiyao Weisheng
Daobao (International Medicine and Health Guide)*, 1, 9–12.

CHFP 2014, *Zhongguo weisheng he jihua shengyu tongji nianjian (China Statistical
Yearbook of Health and Family Planning)*, Beijing: Zhongguo Xiehe Yike Daxue
Chubanshe (China Harmony and Medicine University Press).

CIRC 2006, *Zhongguo Renshou canyu xinxing nongcun hezuo yiliao shidian gongzuo
qingkuang diaoyan baogao (Report on China Life's Engagement in the NRCMS
Pilot Work)*, online: www.circ.gov.cn/web/site0/tab5267/info34785.htm (accessed
July 18, 2016).

CMS BestPractice Task Force 2003, Zhongguo nongcun hezuo yiliao zuijia shijian
moshi de yanjiu (Best Practices and Models of China's Rural CMS), in: *Zhongguo
Chuji Weisheng Baojian (Chinese Primary Health Care)*, 17, 6, 15–16.

Dittmer, Lowell 2003, Chinese Leadership Succession to the Fourth Generation. In
China after Jiang, eds Gang Lin und Xiaobo Hu, 11–38. Chicago, IL: Stanford
University Press.

Fewsmith, Joseph 2001, The Political and Social Implications of China's Accession to
the WTO, in: *The China Quarterly*, 167, 573–591.

Gao, Guangying and Youli Han 2007, Woguo xinxing nongcun hezuo yiliao zhidu
fazhan (The Development of China's NRCMS). In *Yiliao weisheng lüpishu—*

Zhongguo yiliao weisheng fazhan baogao No. 3 (Green Book of Health Care—Annual Report on China's Health Care No. 3), ed. Lexun Du, 85–112. Beijing: Shehui Kexue Wenxian Chubanshe (Social Sciences Academic Press).

Göbel, Christian 2010, *The Politics of Rural Reform in China, State Policy and Village Predicament in the Early 2000s*, London: Routledge.

Gu, Xin 2004, Healthcare Regime Change and the SARS Outbreak in China. In *The SARS Epidemic. Challenges to China's Crisis Management*, eds John Wong und Yongnian Zheng, 123–156. Singapore: World Scientific.

Gu, Xin, Gao, Mengtao and Yang, Yao 2005, *Zhenduan yu chufang: Zhimian Zhongguo yiliao tizhi gaige (China's Health Care Reforms: A Pathological Analysis)*, Beijing: Shehui Kexue Wenxian Chubanshe (Social Sciences Academic Press).

Guo, Minghua 2009, Minzheng bumen li mubiao: 2015 nian nongcun yiliao jiuzhu shixian quan fugai (Heilongjiang's Department of Civil Affairs Sets a Target: Full Coverage of Rural Medical Assistance by 2015), online: www.hljnews.cn/fouxw_yw/2009-03/13/content_89308.htm (accessed July 18, 2016).

Guo, Zhenzong 2008, *Wanshan xinxing nongcun hezuo yiliao zhidu wenti—Yi Shandong Sheng wei li (Improving NRCMS—The Example of Shandong Province)*, Beijing: Zhongguo Nongye Chubanshe (China Agricultural Press).

Guobanfa 2000, 33, Guowuyuan Bangongting zhuanfa Nongyebu deng bumen guanyu gonggu da jiancha chengguo jinyibu zuohao jianqing nongmin fudan gongzuo baogao de tongzhi (Notification from the General Office of the State Council about the Work Report of the Ministry of Agriculture and Other Ministries about Consolidating the Achievements of the Major Inspection and Further Reducing the Farmers' Burden).

Guobanfa 2001, 39, Guowuyuan Bangongting zhuanfa Guowuyuan Tigaiban deng bumen "Guanyu nongcun weisheng gaige yu fazhan zhidao yijian de tongzhi" (Notification from the General Office of the State Council about the Leading Opinion of the State Commission for Restructuring on Rural Health Reform and Development).

Guobanfa 2003, 3, Guowuyuan Bangongting zhuanfa Weishengbu deng bumen guanyu jianli xinxing nongcun hezuo yiliao zhidu yijian de tongzhi (Notification from the General Office of the State Council about the Opinion of the MoH and Other Departments on Establishing the NRCMS).

Guobanfa 2004, 3, Guowuyuan Bangongting zhuanfa Weishengbu deng bumen guanyu jinyibu zuohao xinxing nongcun hezuo yiliao shidian gongzuo zhidao yijian de tongzhi (Notification from the General Office of the State Council about the Leading Opinion of the MoH and Other Departments on Further Improving the NRCMS Pilot Work).

Guobanhan 2005, 81, Guowuyuan Bangongting guanyu zengbu he tiaozheng Guowuyuan xinxing nongcun hezuo yiliao buji lianxi huiyi chengyuan de fuhan (Reply from the General Office of the State Council about Augmenting and Adjusting the Members of the NRCMS Interministerial Conference of the State Council).

Guohan 2003, 95, Guowuyuan guanyu tongyi jianli xinxing nongcun hezuo yiliao buji lianxi huiyi zhidu de pifu (Answer of the State Council Regarding the Common Establishment of a Joint Inter-Ministerial Conference System).

Guowuyuan (ed.) 2006, Dui Zhongguo yiliao weisheng tizhi gaige de pingjia yu jianyi (Evaluation and Recommendations for Health System Reform in China), Beijing.

Heberer, Thomas 2001, China: Der Markt sprengt das alte Sozialsystem (The Market Blows Up the Old Social System), in: *Der Überblick*, 1, 54–59.

Hsiao, William C. and Xianglin Du 1985, Zhongguo baojian shiye de zhuanbian (The Transformation of Chinese Health Protection), in: *Zhongguo Shehui Yixue Zazhi (Chinese Journal of Social Medicine)*, 2, 3, 185f.

Huang, Yanzhong 2013, *Governing Health in Contemporary China*, New York: Routledge.

Jia, Wenshan 2006, The Wei (Positioning)-Ming (Naming)-Lianmian (Face)-Guanxi (Relationship)-Renqing (Humanized Feelings) Complex in Contemporary Chinese Culture. In *Confucian Cultures of Authority*, eds Peter D. Hershock and Roger T. Ames, 49–64. Albany, NY: State University of New York Press.

Keith, Ronald C. and Zhiqiu Lin 2003, The "Falun Gong Problem": Politics and the Struggle for the Rule of Law in China, in: *The China Quarterly*, 175, 623–642.

Kupfer, Kristin 2008, Soziale Sicherung in der Volksrepublik China und die Rolle spirituell-religiöser Gruppen (Social Security in the PRC and the Role of Spiritual and Religious Groups). In *Ost- und Südostasien zwischen Wohlfahrtsstaat und Eigeninitiative: Aktuelle Entwicklungstendenzen von Armut, Alterung und sozialer Unsicherheit (East and Southeast Asia between the Welfare State and Individual Initiative: Current Development Trends of Poverty, Ageing, and Social Insecurity)*, eds Karl Husa, Rolf Jordan and Helmut Wohlschlägl, 201–215. Vienna: Universität Wien Institut für Geographie und Regionalforschung.

Liaoning Ribao 2006, Liaoning quanmian qidong xinxing nongcun hezuo yiliao, jiang fugai quansheng nongmin (Liaoning Rolls Out NRCMS and will Cover the Rural Citizens in the Entire Province), January 23, 2006.

Lin, Shuzhou 2010, *Xinxing nongcun hezuo yiliao baozhang zhidu yanjiu—Yi yanhai diqu wei shijiao (The NRCMS from the Perspective of the Coastal Regions)*, Beijing: Zhishi Chanquan Chubanshe (Intellectual Property Rights Press).

Liu, Yuanli *et al.*1995, Transformation of China's Rural Health Care Financing, in: *Social Science and Medicine*, 41, 8, 1085–1093.

Liu, Yuanli *et al.* 1996, Is Community Financing Necessary and Feasible for Rural China?, in: *Health Policy*, 38, 3, 155–171.

Liu, Yuanli and Keqin Rao 2006, Providing Health Insurance in Rural China: From Research to Policy, in: *Journal of Health Politics, Policy and Law*, 31, 1, 71–92.

Liu, Yuanli, Keqin Rao and Shanlian Hu 2002, *People's Republic of China: Towards Establishing a Rural Health Protection System*, Manila: Asian Development Bank.

Minfa 2003, 158, Minzhengbu, Weishengbu, Caizhengbu guanyu shishi nongcun yiliao jiuzhu de yijian (Opinion of the Ministries of Civil Affairs, Health and Finance on the Implementation of Rural Medical Assistance).

MoH 2007, *Zhongguo xinxing nongcun hezuo yiliao jinzhan ji xiaoguo yanjiu (Research on the Progress and Outcomes of the NRCMS), 2005 nian xinxing nongcun hezuo yiliao shidian diaocha baogao (2005 NRCMS Pilot Evaluation Report)*, Beijing: Zhongguo Xiehe Yike Daxue Chubanshe (China Harmony and Medicine University Press).

MoH (ed.) 2009a, *Weishengbu xinxing nongcun hezuo yiliao yanjiu zhongxin keti yanjiu baogao huibian, 2006–2008 (Compilation of Research Reports of the NRCMS Research Center of the MoH, 2006–2008)*, Beijing.

MoH 2009b, *Zhongguo weisheng tongji nianjian (China Statistical Yearbook of Health)*, Beijing: Zhongguo Xiehe Yike Daxue Chubanshe (China Harmony and Medicine University Press).

Müller, Armin 2016, Premium Collection and the Problem of Voluntary Enrollment in China's New Rural Cooperative Medical System (NRCMS), in: *Journal of Current Chinese Affairs*, 45, 1, 11–41.

Nanfang Zhoumo 2005, Suqian yigai—Wu nian jibian (Health Reform in Suqian—Five Years of Change), July 21, 2005, online: www.southcn.com/weekend/economic/200507210027.htm (accessed January 1, 2013).

Nanfang Zhoumo 2005, Zhongguo yigai 20 nian (20 Years of Chinese Health Reform), August 4, 2005, online: http://news.sina.com.cn/h/2005-08-04/10427410736.shtml (accessed June 8, 2011).

Neimeng Weishengting 2006, Xinxing nongcun muqu hezuo yiliao shidian gongzuo (Pilot Work for the New CMS in Agricultural and Herding Districts), previously online: www.nmwst.gov.cn/html/tslm/wsnj/2007/ncmqws/200811/02-7753.html (accessed January 20, 2013).

Oblau, Gotthard 2011, Divine Healing and the Growth of Practical Christianity in China. In *Global Pentecostal and Charismatic Healing*, ed. Candy G. Brown, 307–327. New York: Oxford University Press.

PEG (ed.) 2006, *Fazhan zhong de Zhongguo xinxing nongcun hezuo yiliao—Xinxing nongcun hezuo yiliao shidian gongzuo pinggu baogao (China's NRCMS in Development—The NRCMS Pilot Evaluation Report)*, Beijing: Renmin Weisheng Chubanshe (People's Health Press).

People's Daily 1999, Kaizhan nongcun tiyu tigao nongcun tizhi Zhongguo nongmin tixie renzhong daoyuan (The Chinese Farmers' Athletic Association will Shoulder Heavy Responsibilities in Developing Rural Sports to Improve the Physical Constitution of the Farmers). January 29, 1999.

People's Daily 2001, New Minister of Agriculture Appointed, September 1, 2001, online: http://english.peopledaily.com.cn/200109/01/eng20010901_79063.html (accessed January 13, 2013).

People's Daily 2001, Xizang de xiandaihua fazhan (The Modernization and Development of Tibet), November 9, 2001.

People's Daily 2001, Xizang bufen diqu jinru laoling shehui (The Ageing Society in a Part of Tibet's Districts), November 27, 2001.

People's Daily 2002, Baoxian gongsi nengfou jieru nongcun yibao (Is it Possible for Insurance Companies to Get Involved with Rural Health Insurance?), July 31, 2002.

People's Daily 2003, Jiankang baoxian zai Yunfu (Health Insurance in Yunfu), November 10, 2003.

People's Daily 2004, Jiangsu Sheng Jiangyin Shi cong 2001 nian kaishi tansuo xinxing nongcun hezuo yiliao moshi (Jiangyin City in Jiangsu Province Started Exploring an NRCMS Model in 2001), August 18, 2004.

People's Daily 2005, Baojianhui zhuxi Wu Dingfu changtan baoxianye redian wenti—Guli geng duo baoxian gongsi 'xiaxiang, rushi, chuhai' (Wu Dingfu, Director of the CIRC, Talks Freely about Core Problems of the Insurance Industry—Encouraging More Insurance Companies to 'Go to the Rural Areas, the Stock Markets and Overseas'), August 22, 2005.

Qu, Shaoxu and Xudong Liu 2006, Liaoning sheng nongcun xinxing hezuo yiliao zhidu jianshe shidian qingkuang kaocha—Yi Huanren wei li (Inspecting the Situation of NRCMS Pilot Counties in Liaoning Province—The Example of Huanren County), in: *Guangxi Shehui Kexue (Guangxi Social Sciences)*, 3, 176–180.

Renda 2001, Quanguo Renda Changweihui Zhifa Jianchazu guanyu jiancha "Zhonghua Renmin Gongheguo Nongyefa" shishi qingkuang de baogao (Report from the

Enforcement and Inspection Group of the Standing Committee of the National People's Congress about the Implementation Situation of the "Agricultural Law of the PRC"), Beijing.

Renda 2002, Zhonghua Renmin Gongheguo Nongyefa (Agricultural Law of the People's Republic of China).

Thacik, John 2004, Premier Wen and Vice President Zeng: The "Two Centers" of China's "Fourth Generation". In *Civil-Military Change in China Elites, Institutes, and Ideas after the 16th Party Congress*, eds Andrew Scobell and Larry Wortzel, 95–178, Darby, PA: DIANE Publishing.

Wagstaff, Adam *et al.* 2009, *Reforming China's Rural Health System*, Washington, DC: World Bank.

Wang, Shaoguang 2009, Adapting by Learning, The Evolution of China's Rural Health Care Financing, in: *Modern China*, 35, 4, 370–404.

Wang, Shuguang 2008, *Shehui canyu, nongcun hezuo yiliao yu fan pinkun (Social Participation, NRCMS and Poverty Reduction)*, Beijing: Renmin Chubanshe (People's Press).

Weibanjifufa 2003, 147, Weishengbu Bangongting zhuanfa Yunnan Sheng Weishengting guanyu Wenshan Zhou Guangnan Xian A'ke Xiang xinxing nongcun hezuo yiliao shidian gongzuo zhong budang zuofa de qingkuang tongbao de tongzhi (Notification from the General Office of the MoH Regarding the Circular from the Health Department of Yunnan Province about Inappropriate Measures in the NRCMS-Experimentation in Ake Township in Guangnan County, Wenshan Prefecture).

Weibannongweifa 2004, 46, Weishengbu Bangongting guanyu chengli Weishengbu xinxing nongcun hezuo yiliao jishu zhidaozu de tongzhi (Notification from the General Office of the MoH about Establishing the NRCMS Technical Guidance Group of the MoH).

Weibannongweifa 2006, 42, Weishengbu Bangongting zhuanfa "Guizhou Sheng Xinxing Nongcun Hezuo Yiliao Gongzuo Lingdao Xiaozu Bangongshi guanyu dui Nayong Xian xinxing nongcun hezuo yiliao shidian gongzuo guanli bushan, jianguan buli youguan wenti de tongbao" de tongzhi (Notification from the General Office of the MoH about the "Notice Brief from the NRCMS Small Leadership Group of Guizhou Province about Problems Regarding Bad Administration and Perfunctory Supervision of the NRCMS Pilot Work in Nayong County).

Weifadian 2004, 37, Weishengbu, Caizhengbu guanyu kaizhan xinxing nongcun hezuo yiliao shidian youguan gongzuo jiancha de jinji tongzhi (Urgent Notification from the MoH and the MoF about the Initiation of Inspections of NRCMS-Related Experimental Work).

Weijifufa 2003, 317, Weishengbu zhuanfa Hunan Sheng Renmin Zhengfu Bangongting guanyu Guiyang Xian xinxing nongcun hezuo yiliao shidian gongzuo youguan wenti tongbao de tongzhi (Notification from the MoH about the Circular by the General Office of the People's Government of Hunan about Problems in the NRCMS Experimentation in Guiyang County).

Weinongweifa 2004, 256, Weishengbu zhuanfa Henan Sheng Renmin Zhengfu guanyu Taikang Xian zai xinxing nongcun hezuo yiliao shidian gongzuo zhong weigui chouzi wenti tongbao de tongzhi (Notification from the MoH about the Circular from the People's Government of Henan Province about the Problems with Irregular Premium Collection for NRCMS in Taikang County).

Weinongweifa 2005, 319, Weishengbu, Caizhengbu guanyu zouhao xinxing nongcun hezuo yiliao shidian youguan gongzuo de tongzhi (Notification from the MoH and the MoF about Accomplishing the Experimental Work for NRCMS).

Weinongweifa 2006, 13, Weishengbu deng qi buwei lianhe xiafa "Guanyu jiakuai tuijin xinxing nongcun hezuo yiliao shidian gongzuo de tongzhi" (The MoH and Seven Other Ministries and Commissions Jointly Transmit the "Notification about Accelerating the NRCMS Pilot Work").

Weinongweifa 2006, 453, Weishengbu guanyu xinxing nongcun hezuo yiliao xinxi xitong jianshe de zhidao yijian (Leading Opinion of the MoH on Building Up an NRCMS Information System).

Weinongweifa 2006, 40, Weishengbu, Caizhengbu guanyu jiaqiang xinxing nongcun hezuo yiliao guanli gongzuo de tongzhi (Notification from the MoH and the MoF about Strengthening NRCMS Administration).

WHO 2000, *The World Health Report 2000, Health Systems Improving Performance*, Geneva: World Health Organization.

World Bank 2002, *China—National Development and Sub-National Finance*, online: www.worldbank.org/research/2002/04/1768217/china-national-development-sub-na tional-finance-review-provincial-expenditures (accessed February 8, 2012).

Yang, Hongyan 2009, *Zhongguo nongcun hezuo yiliao zhidu kechixu fazhan yanjiu (The Sustainable Development of the NRCMS)*, Beijing: Zhongguo Shehui Kexue Chubanshe (China Social Science Press).

Zhang, Jianping 2006, *Zhongguo nongcun hezuo yiliao zhidu yanjiu (Research on China's NRCMS)*, Beijing: Zhongguo Nongye Chubanshe (China Agricultural Press).

Zhongfa 2002, 13, Zhonggong Zhongyang, Guowuyuan guanyu jinyibu jiaqiang nongcun weisheng gongzuo de jueding (Decision of the Central Committee and the State Council on Further Strengthening Rural Health Work).

Zhonggong Zhongyang 2005, Zhonggong Zhongyang, Guowuyuan guanyu tuijin shehui zhuyi xinnongcun jianshe de ruogan yijian (Opinions of the Central Committee and the State Council on Extending the New Socialist Countryside).

Zweig, David 2001, China's Stalled "Fifth Wave", Zhu Rongji's Reform Package of 1998–2000, in: *Asian Survey*, 41, 2, 231–247.

5 Designing the NRCMS in a Local Context

Chapter 5 will begin the analysis of the local implementation of the NRCMS. It reconstructs the dynamics of policy design decisions, which are of greatest magnitude during the early years of a local implementation, and are most relevant for the time between 2003 and 2008. Over the years, the system of regulatory guidelines has become increasingly dense, and therefore the formal decision space of local governments has gradually decreased. Furthermore, the later cohorts of implementing counties systematically imitated the NRCMS models devised by the earlier cohorts. The earlier cohorts had the greatest leeway in designing the system and provided models for the following cohorts. Nevertheless, as the NRCMS system is being modified and adapted on an annual basis, the basic dynamics of the decision-making process reconstructed in this chapter form a social mechanism that continues to repeat itself.

The first part of this chapter will introduce the main actors and structures of the local policy arenas with a focus on the county as jurisdiction. It thus provides a foundation for the analysis in this chapter and in Chapter 6. County- and township-level governments are treated as integrated actors, whose preferences are strongly determined by the dysfunctional public finance system and the leading cadre evaluations. In health policy, their political priorities are on family planning and public health, whereas health insurance and the provision of curative care services are of subordinate priority. Adequately funding their healthcare providers is neither a priority nor an attractive choice for most local governments in both poor and wealthy areas.

The healthcare providers, on the other hand, are strongly affected by the institutional misfits between health sector regulation and the public finance system. They are required to adhere to the pricing system, but governmental funding is insufficient to support such adherence. County hospitals are in a comparatively comfortable position, as they can rely on a diverse clientele including wealthy urbanites, and because their portfolio comprises profitable diagnostic services. Village clinics rely almost entirely on drug sales, but benefit from their proximity to the patients and their low costs of operation. THCs are in a difficult position in between, competing with village clinics for outpatient service provision, and with the county hospitals for inpatient service provision. Overall, the competitive relations inhibit the mutual aid and cooperation that once facilitated the strength of the rural health services.

In the course of the implementation, the county governments made strikingly homogeneous decisions across very diverse socio-economic settings. The vast majority chose to integrate outpatient services into the NRCMS reimbursement catalog, despite the additional administrative workload and the funds being diverted from the main policy goal—the reimbursement of catastrophic health costs caused by inpatient services. Furthermore, most localities chose MSAs as the method of outpatient reimbursement, which is rather ineffective: MSAs only pool risks at the household level, and thus provide little protection. The most common policy design in Eastern, Central and Western China thus diverted scarce administrative and financial resources away from productive use, which appears counterintuitive at first.

Analyzing the policy design as the outcome of negotiations between the local governments and the healthcare providers can explain this pattern of decision-making. Local governments were responsible for the administrative expenditures of the NRCMS. Delegating administrative services to the providers, and the THCs in particular, brought the NRCMS closer to the rural population and lightened the financial and administrative burden of the county health administration. In exchange for this, county governments could compensate the THCs by integrating outpatient services into the reimbursement plans. As village clinics were mostly excluded from NRCMS reimbursement, the NRCMS outpatient funds were often exclusively allocated to the THCs. The administration of the MSAs could be entirely delegated to the THCs, and thus provided no administrative burden for the county health administration.

The motivation of county governments to delegate administrative services to THCs and use MSAs for outpatient reimbursement was also enhanced by the problems of premium collection. Due to the contradiction between voluntary enrollment and universal coverage, and the reluctance of a large part of the rural population to enroll with the NRCMS, grassroots cadres were caught in a trap. If they observed voluntariness, they risked not achieving their enrollment targets. If they coerced people to enroll, they risked political criticism from the higher levels. Therefore, local governments and grassroots cadres devised an array of innovations and informal practices to mitigate this problem. Using MSA funds to pay for the premiums was a simple, effective and thus highly attractive measure. Having the funds administered at the township level further withdrew them from the scrutiny of higher levels.

Bureaucratic Actors and Institutional Structures in the Local Arenas

County and Township Governments

The term "local government" in this study mainly refers to the organs of government and administration at the county and township level. The formal institutions of county government largely reproduce the structural model of the higher levels. Political power is concentrated in the party committee and disciplinary commission, but the functional differentiation between party and government in rural counties is less pronounced than in urban areas or at higher levels. The county is the most important level of local government and politically and administratively dominant vis-à-vis the township and village levels. Despite their relatively low position in the administrative hierarchy, county leaders have considerable discretionary power and strategic agency in the political system. Township governments have a less differentiated bureaucratic structure and have lost much of their former autonomy since the 1980s. Political power on both levels is concentrated in the position of the party secretary (Heberer and Schubert 2012; Lam 2010; Zhong 2003: 51–71).

This study treats county and township governments as integrated actors due to their high capacity to act strategically as a unit and the lower impact of factionalism and bureaucratic rivalries. The pressure created by the leading cadre evaluation system and misfit institutional structures of the state and the public sector reinforces the shared interests of the leading cadres, and thus the integration of bureaucratic interests between different line administrations and between the county and township levels. Exceptions confirm the rule: in localities where factionalism and bureaucratic conflict are stronger than the integrative pressures, the capacity for strategic action and effective coordination of the administrative organs decreases (Heberer and Schubert 2012).

The orientations of local governments and their administrative organs are crucially determined by the evaluation system. Although all state cadres have to face evaluations, there is a distinction between normal cadres, for whom the personnel departments (*renshibu*) are responsible, and leading cadres, for whom the organization departments (*zuzhibu*) are responsible. The evaluations of the latter include policy and program evaluations (*mubiao kaohe*) and leading cadre evaluations (*lingdao ganbu kaoping*). Policy and program evaluations comprise performance contracts (*mubiao zeren shu*), which are signed by the government and party leaders of a jurisdiction with the next higher level (Edin 2003a, 2003b; Heberer and Trappel 2013; Whiting 2004).

The performance contracts are a means of communicating the hierarchy of political goals through the hierarchy of government. There are different kinds of contracts for different fields of policy, and they contain different types of performance targets. The performance contracts create highly powered incentives, as they are directly connected to the cadres' remuneration, prestige and career perspectives. Soft targets (*yiban zhibiao*) are usually applied to policies of subordinate priority, or to targets which are difficult to quantify. Hard targets (*ying zhibiao*) are usually quantified targets from the plans of economic and social development, which strongly focus on economic development. Priority targets under the "one item veto-rule" (*yipiao foujue*) are reserved for special political priorities, typically birth planning and social stability. Failure to achieve the targets in these areas will revoke the achievements in the other fields. The weighting of targets—and of hard targets in particular—reflects the political priorities of the central and local government, as well as the specific local development situation. The evaluations display strong local idiosyncrasies, both with regard to the composition of goals and the definition of complex targets such as social stability. They reflect both local development problems and the specific policy preferences of the different subnational levels of government. By and large, however, the core issues during the period of observation were usually economic development, social stability and birth planning.

The structure of targets in health policy crucially determines the allocation of human and financial resources in the rural healthcare system. Birth planning traditionally has the highest priority, falling under the "one item veto-rule" (*yipiao foujue*). Public health targets, such as infant mortality rates or immunization rates, are often hard targets, which are either defined quantitatively at the national level and operationalized in local development plans, or defined according to local conditions, as for endemic disease prevention. A more implicit requirement is maintaining a comprehensive three-tier network of healthcare facilities—with one public THC per township that integrates village doctors into the provision of public health (Zhongfa 2002, 13). The foreclosure of a county hospital—due to corruption issues, for example—can be prevented by concerns about social stability, namely the stability of health service provision in the county (Tam 2011: 275). Public health outcomes and the existence of a comprehensive three-tier system of healthcare facilities are connected to core targets in the evaluation system, and local governments will allocate their resources in accordance with those targets (Saich 2008: 67ff; Zhongfa 2002, 13).

The strategic interests of county governments are furthermore crucially influenced by their position in the intergovernmental financial system and the local level of economic development. Both budgetary and extra-budgetary sources of funding are most abundant in the industrialized regions of Eastern China, whereas they are scarce in the agricultural regions of Central and Western China. Expenditures for PSUs constitute a heavy budgetary burden for local governments—estimates suggest that 45.6 percent of actually conducted county and township expenditures in 2002 were dedicated to PSUs (World Bank 2007b: 38). PSUs and healthcare facilities in particular have suffered from budget cuts and commercialization during the reform era. This is closely related to the general structure of incentives for local government spending:

> [C]entral directives for rural public service provision compete directly with local preferences for spending on infrastructure. In all localities there is a strong incentive to increase revenues, especially own revenues that local governments can allocate freely. Given the tax structure emphasizing industry and commerce, and especially since agricultural taxes have been abolished, seeking local revenue growth means that governments engage in growth-enhancing investments in infrastructure to attract businesses to the area. This incentive is reinforced by the convergence of

interests in growth-promoting infrastructural investments for mobilizing both on-budget and off-budget revenues, as these investments raise the value of land locally—the main source of extra-budgetary revenues for local governments.

(World Bank 2007a: 31)

The general structure of incentives thus encourages local governments to invest their available financial resources in projects yielding financial and political profits, such as land development, rather than public services and social policy.

These incentives can be reinforced by fiscal imbalances and the level of fiscal stress in a given locality. Where budgetary and extra-budgetary revenues are plentiful, there is potentially more fiscal capacity available for the health sector, and vice versa. Fiscal stress is reinforced by fiscal imbalances and by the local level of debt. There is little precise information on the local levels of debt available; according to World Bank estimates, even before 2008 they exceeded international standards several times over (World Bank 2007a: 90). Some estimates suggest that 25 percent of China's counties are in a good fiscal condition, another 25 percent in average condition, and about 50 percent either in deficit or officially designated poverty counties (Lam 2010: 151f.). Deficits and debt tend to undermine the ability and commitment of local governments to finance the health sector, as Zou notes:

> Because a part of the county-level governments is over-indebted or has been "running deficits" for a long time, they cut down the budgetary spending for the health facilities. In most counties in H Province, budgetary allocations to county hospitals are insufficient even for the basic salaries, and county hospitals entirely depend on own revenues for construction, new equipment … and qualified personnel. THCs are PSUs only in name and hardly receive any funding. Among the village stations, 90 percent appear and vanish without being taken any care of (*zisheng zimie*).
>
> (Zou 2008: 232)

Fiscal imbalances can thus substantially undermine local government spending on health.[1]

Long-term fiscal imbalances also have an important effect on intergovernmental relations: they undermine the accountability of local governments to the higher levels. This concerns primarily the institutional role of local governments and the expectations directed at them by higher levels, but it also touches on changes in professional values and organizational culture sparked by continued exposure to fiscal imbalances.

> The difficulties of central policies not being fully implemented at the grassroots level have existed for a long time. When for several years the centralization of revenues left expenditure responsibilities for local

government that far exceeded their revenue capacities, there emerged an acceptance that local governments could not be expected to fulfill all of their assigned tasks. This notion persists and is in itself a hindrance to any effort to enforce local accountability.

(World Bank 2007b: 30)

Underfinancing of local public service facilities—most notably hospitals—is often perceived as a legitimate course of action by county and city governments.

Fiscal capacity and the absence of large fiscal imbalances are a precondition for strong accountability between the county government and its superiors, at least with regard to general policy implementation and budgetary spending. The evaluation system furthermore specifies a number of targets on policy fields of core priority, which need to be accomplished. But it does not exclusively function as a sanctioning mechanism: actually sanctioning cadres who fail to achieve their targets was a measure applied in exceptionally severe cases of misconduct, rather than on a regular basis (Heberer and Trappel 2013). The behavior of local governments with low fiscal capacity is more predictable, as the scope of possible actions and the effective factors causing variation are more limited. Strong accountability is unlikely in poor areas, unless they receive special support. It is more likely in wealthier areas, but also dependent on more complex causal settings.

The Three-Tier Healthcare System

The three-tier healthcare network—illustrated in Figure 5.1—is the organizational framework of the medical profession in rural China.[2] The corporate actors on the county level are hospitals (*yiyuan*) and public health facilities (*zhuanye gonggong weisheng jigou*) for disease prevention and maternal and child healthcare. The THCs and village clinics are classified as "grassroots health facilities" (*jiceng yiliao weisheng jigou*), and their administrative status is more ambiguous than that of the county facilities. The vast majority of these facilities are classified as non-profit providers and thus expected to adhere to the pricing system, as described in Chapter 2.

As Figure 5.1 illustrates, the local service units are embedded in a complex system of administrative responsibility called the *tiaotiao kuaikuai* system. The term *kuaikuai* represents a horizontal jurisdiction of the local government on the same level, while the term *tiaotiao* represents a vertical jurisdiction of the line administration on the next higher level. A dual jurisdiction (*shuangchong lingdao*) refers to a sharing of administrative responsibility between the township government and the county line administration. Since 2000, the county level has been strengthened vis-à-vis the township level: the rural tax-and-fee reform weakened the townships' autonomy, and the rural health reform of 2002 assigned more comprehensive responsibilities to county governments (Klotzbücher 2006: 205–72; Zhong 2003: 71–85; Zhongfa 2002, 13).

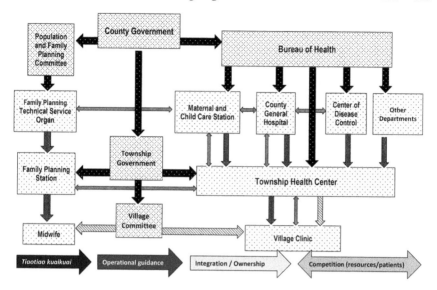

Figure 5.1 Local Government, the Three-Tier Healthcare System and the Family Planning Organs
Aource: adapted from: Teng 2010; Zheng et al. 2010.

At the county level, the bureau of health forms the administrative head of the network, and represents the interests of the medical profession organized in the public sector in the local government, with its own staff partly recruited from the medical profession.[3] Just like its central counterpart, the bureau of health is usually a relatively weak actor in the county government, which is associated with its difficulties in lobbying for funding for hospitals. At the township level, the THCs represent the county bureau of health in its administrative functions, most notably vis-à-vis the village clinics. In many areas, the birth-planning organs used to form a separate structure of administrative organs and PSUs. The merger of the MoH and the CPFP in 2013 potentially enhances integration in the local arenas as well.

Administrative monitoring is much more fragmented. Different line administrations are responsible for the supervision of their own separate fields. They include the planning commission, the price administration, the FDA, the administration of industry and commerce, the bureau of finance and the bureau of audit. Most of them conduct annual evaluations, which may include inspection tours to the respective PSUs that are often perceived as a burdensome process by hospital directors. The different line administrations in turn do not usually cooperate or share information. Local governments therefore often lack a comprehensive overview of the operations of their healthcare PSUs, despite extensive monitoring activities (Fang 2008; World Bank 2007b: 38).

The health providers are empowered vis-à-vis their patients and the local government mainly due to the information asymmetry between medical specialists and laymen. A substantial part of doctors' salaries stems from bonus payments which are linked to the revenues and profits of the hospital, and which in turn are generated by drug sales and high-tech diagnostic services (Hsiao 2008). For example, in a hospital in D District of B City, each department received an annual revenue target, and the department staff was entitled to 10 percent of the revenues that exceeded the target (Yuanfa 2011, 20). Doctors have powerful incentives to exploit the knowledge asymmetry vis-à-vis their patients to induce demand—that is, to over-prescribe drugs and diagnostic tests. Administrative tasks and services in public health in turn bring little or no profit and tend to be neglected (cf. Zou 2008: 230f.). There is a strong contradiction between the economic incentives and the normative role orientations: the Chinese medical curriculum includes medical ethics, Chinese doctors take an oath similar to the Hippocratic Oath, and communist ideology and the propaganda efforts of the MoH emphasize devotion and altruism (Hsiao 2008).

Figure 5.1 illustrates the different administrative and operational actors in the three-tier network and their relationships. The institutional misfits have undermined important processes of cooperation in the three-tier network and thus decreased the overall level of welfare production in the rural areas. Maternal and child healthcare stations and centers for disease control and prevention have often gone beyond the provision of public services and expanded into profitable niches of general medical care, which facilitates competitive relations with the county hospitals. The vertical relations of THCs with the county hospitals above and the village clinics below are equally characterized by competition. Furthermore, there are potential resource conflicts between the family-planning facilities and the healthcare facilities. This potentially undermines service provision in public health, weakens the referral mechanisms between the levels, and enhances the creation of over-capacities and the misallocation of resources.

The institutional setup of Chinese healthcare providers can be differentiated along three dimensions. First, the formal ownership status (*dengji zhuce leibie*) can be state-owned (*guoyou*), collective (*jiti*), mixed (*lianying*) or private (*siying*). Second, the operating unit (*zhuban danwei*) can be governmental (*zhengfuban*), societal (*shehuiban*) or private (*gerenban, sirenban*). Finally, the business model can be formally for-profit (*yinglixing*) or non-profit (*fei yinglixing*). Depending on current regulatory trends, these differentiations can determine core issues. Most notably, the distinction between for-profit and non-profit status largely determines whether a facility has to conform to the pricing system. Recently, ownership status increasingly takes over this function.

County Hospitals

County hospitals are mainly providers of curative care. According to the 2006 development plan for the rural healthcare system:

[C]ounty hospitals are the center of curative care and operational guidance of the county; they are responsible for basic medical care and
emergency cases; they receive referrals from the healthcare facilities on
the township and village levels, assume tasks in the training and operational guidance of township and village health staff, and engage in education and research.

(Weiguicaifa 2006, 340)

The plan functionally distinguishes county hospitals from the specialized public
health facilities, and from the TCM hospitals, which provide services in both areas.

Both comprehensive county hospitals and TCM hospitals are financed primarily through operational revenues. County hospitals of all types generated
more than 90 percent of their revenues themselves, and drug revenue usually
accounted for 47 to 55 percent of this operational income. The rate of debt to
assets for county hospitals usually oscillated between 25 and 30 percent. The
county hospitals are economically self-reliant and have substantial business
autonomy with regard to capital investment and their own position in the
market. Although they compete with public health facilities for the profitable
niches of curative care, their own market position is comfortable compared
with lower-level facilities, as their customer base is more diversified and their
attractiveness is higher than that of the THCs. County hospitals have limited
interest in training THC staff or directing resources to operational guidance
and supervision (MoH 2004: 146–51, 2006).

The vast majority of county hospitals are formally state-owned and their
personnel administration is covered by the *bianzhi* system. Typically, they are
partially funded PSUs formally entitled to some governmental budgetary
support for salaries and personal costs. The specific *bianzhi* regulations are
under the jurisdiction of provincial and sub-provincial levels, and the compliance of local governments with formal regulations may be constrained by
problems of fiscal capacity or political commitment. Despite the rigidity of
the *bianzhi* system, county hospitals have substantial autonomy in human resource
management. First, they can hire contracted staff on a self-financing basis, whose
employment conditions depend on local regulation and the respective contract. Second, the hospital director has substantial jurisdiction over salary
allocation. A part of doctors' salaries is paid in bonuses and depends on the
overall revenue generated by the doctor or his department, which allows
hospital directors to set operational priorities. The local arrangements in
county hospitals can vary substantially, depending on the socio-economic
conditions and the policies of the province and the local government.

The county hospitals play a role in the policy process and are often
involved in negotiations with the local government and in policy formulation.
In health policy, the local government often depends on their professional
expertise. Individual factors also play an important role: hospital directors
upholding good relations with leading county cadres can be very influential
actors (PEG 2006: 77ff.).

THCs

The institutional status of the THCs is much more ambiguous than that of the county hospitals, an issue that is to some extent rooted in their historical development. The term "township health center" (*xiangzhen weishengyuan*) refers to generalist healthcare facilities, whose focus is officially on public health, although they also provide curative care. Furthermore, they administratively represent the bureau of health on the township level, as the MoH's line administration only reaches to the county level. THCs are active in public health—preventive and mother and child healthcare—as well as birth planning, basic curative care, TCM and the training and operational guidance of village doctors. There is an important distinction between central and general THCs, with central THCs assuming some functions similar to those of county hospitals as centers of operational guidance and curative care, while also fulfilling the functions of a regular THC. They are typically larger facilities with more qualified staff and more sophisticated equipment, and, unlike regular THCs, tend to be covered by the *bianzhi* system. Central THCs are more consolidated service units with better capacities to generate revenues (Klotzbücher 2006: 161–5; Weiguicaifa 2006, 340; Zhongfa 2002, 13).

THCs generated around 80 percent of their overall revenue themselves between 2000 and 2009. The overall amount of budgetary support from local governments gradually rose from about 10 to about 20 percent of THC revenues, and from about 40 to about 60 percent of their personnel expenditures (see, for example, MoH 2006). Budgetary allocations have been reported to be ad hoc and arbitrary, and dependent on the relationship between the THC director and local leading cadres (Audibert et al. 2008). The THCs' official focus is on public health and administrative tasks. As non-profit facilities, they are expected to adhere to the pricing system, and their portfolio of profitable service items is limited (Guobanfa 2001, 39).

The political influence of THC directors is much lower than that of their county hospital counterparts, and representation by the county bureau of health is arguably of crucial importance for them. However, they may also take part directly in policy negotiations at the county level (PEG 2006: 79). THC directors' duration of service at the same township is important for their political influence at the township government (Audibert et al. 2008: 95f.). The decision space of the township government depends on its division of labor with the county level, and these arrangements are generally in the course of centralization.

Village Doctors and Other Practitioners

The village clinics are the most basic unit of the three-tier healthcare network and were thoroughly privatized in the early 1980s. The term "village clinic" covers a broad range of facilities, from well-equipped outposts of THCs manned with salaried medical college graduates to former barefoot doctors practicing independently in their own homes, often still retaining a parcel of land and engaging in agriculture. According to the 2006 development plan, the responsibilities of village clinics include reports on infectious and epidemic diseases, planned immunizations, maternal and child services, health education, basic curative services and referrals (Weiguicaifa 2006, 340).

Village clinics' ownership status and operating unit have relatively little impact on their mode of operations. In C District, for example, most village clinics were formally operated by the villages, even though 60 or 70 percent of the village doctors practiced in their own homes and received no support from the village whatsoever; a minority of doctors may practice in village facilities or receive support in cash or kind from the village committee (Interview 111010). The lack of public funding has very detrimental effects on the provision of services in public health (Qu et al. 2006: 34f.).

Figure 5.1 points to the complexity of the relations between village clinics and THCs. Both are competing for patients in outpatient care. Their administrative relationships unfold in a continuum between operational guidance (i.e. regulatory oversight) and vertical integration. In the former case, "the central THC regularly holds meetings with the village doctors and teaches us about the working guidelines . . . Mostly it is about healthcare issues: how to avoid medical malpractice, how to purchase and sell medicine, and how to arrange the station—the rooms for pharmacy, diagnosis and infusions need to be strictly separated" (Interview 110906).

Vertical integration covers an array of administrative models in which the THC has stronger regulatory and administrative authority. The focus is usually on controlling the village clinics' drug portfolio, procurement channels and pricing. Vertical integration is most common in some coastal provinces such as Shandong and Jiangsu (Liu and Zhang 2010). Unless a village clinic is fully integrated into the THC organization, however, such approaches are often instable due to the competitive nature of the relation between the two actors and the structural changes it requires in the villages. In the absence of financial compensations for the policy-related financial losses, the village stations often maintain informal channels of drug supply. THC staff in a township in E District, for example, explained that one of their two vertical integration projects had to be abandoned due to administrative problems. A villager in A County reported that the government had built a new group station for the two village doctors, but both had soon returned to practicing separately in their homes and so the facility was not being used even though drugs were still delivered by the THC (Interviews 101126, 111127; Xu 2001).

The Implementation Process and Local Policy Designs

Phased Implementation and Policy Development

The first cohort of counties played a crucial role in policy development by rearranging the instruments of the former CMS in the new policy framework of the NRCMS. These counties often had previous experience with CMS systems at the village or township levels. The large variety of practices developed under the CMS umbrella thus became a direct input for the NRCMS. The NRCMS policy substantially narrowed the decision space of local governments regarding the level of financing and pooling, and the general administrative approach. However, it left considerable leeway in the design of the benefit packages and reimbursement procedures.

As specified by document three of the State Council in 2003, the pilot counties were to be selected by the provincial governments according to their administrative and fiscal capacity and the willingness of the local villagers to enroll (Guobanfa 2003, 3). In 2004, the criteria became more specific: the local government was to take the initiative in the application process and have a focus on health policy; the farmers were to have the necessary financial capacity—the average household income in the first cohort of pilots was RMB 4,161 by 2005, compared with a national average of RMB 3,255 (MoH 2006; PEG 2006: 154). The implementation began in localities with favorable conditions and proceeded to more difficult ones. Many of them had previously operated CMS schemes, and could thus refer to their previous experiences and administrative practices (Guobanfa 2004, 3).

Previous experience with the CMS was not only a crucial asset for the selection of pilot counties, but was also systematically generated throughout the implementation process. As Table 5.1 illustrates, many of the field counties had previous experience with CMS systems when they entered the NRCMS program and became eligible for financial transfers. A County had operated CMS systems in several of its towns and townships since the 1990s. It launched the NRCMS as a provincial pilot in 2003, whereas the neighboring counties were ordered to launch CMS pilots on the township level first. The cadres in B County mentioned no such preparations. C District had an agricultural population of about 60 percent and only became eligible for

Table 5.1 The NRCMS and Pilot Preparations in Five Field Counties

	A County	B County	C District	F County	G County
Cohort	First out of three	Second out of three	Third out of four	Fourth out of five	Fifth out of five
Preceding CMS	1990s (town)				
City pilot			2005 (county)	2005 (town)	2006 (town)
NRCMS county	2003	2006	2007	2006	2007
Pilot selection	Voluntary	Voluntary	Drafted		

Source: Mao 2005: 14

NRCMS transfers in 2007, after having run a locally funded CMS on the county level for two years. F County and G County were both late implementers under the same prefectural city and followed the same model: before becoming a formal NRCMS county, or provincial pilot (*shengji shidian xian*), each county needed to select one township for testing a CMS for one year in advance—a so-called city-level pilot (*shiji shidian xian*), as only the prefectural city would financially support the funds during that year, but not the higher levels (Interviews 101129, 101202).

The selection procedures differed locally and between the cohorts. In the early cohorts, the selection process was usually steered via negotiated agreements: the counties were offered the pilot program or volunteered for it, and they could decline the offer. Hierarchical steering was applied during the extension. Launching preparatory pilots in single townships could be mandatory, and in some cases counties were just drafted as pilots. Negotiated agreements lowered the risk of selecting counties with internal administrative problems in the first cohort (cf. Wu 2004). C District was actually drafted by the province, rather than volunteering for the implementation (Interview 111010). A County had a history of piloting rural health policy initiatives and gaining model status (*shifan xian*), and accepted the offer of the provincial department of health to join the first cohort in 2003 (Interview 101105). The cadres in B County merely pointed out that they applied for the second cohort in 2005 and were accepted in 2006. It was the only poverty county in their prefectural city. G County was in the last cohort in its prefectural city.

There is a direct connection between the time of implementation of the NRCMS in a locality on the one hand, and the conditions of implementation on the other. The earlier counties had comparatively solid administrative and fiscal capacity, and often previous experience with the CMS. The exceptions from this rule are, primarily, urban districts that only became eligible for NRCMS transfers in the later cohorts. The center's guidelines required a certain share of agricultural population, which gradually decreased in the years before 2008 (Caishe 2005, 2; Weinongweifa 2006, 13; Weinongweifa 2007, 82). Overall, however, the later cohorts can be expected to have encountered more severe problems in the implementation process. The field sites visited for this study are thus not fully representative, but rather above average.

Policy Development, Innovation, Dissemination and Diffusion

The first cohort of pilot counties had developed a basic set of pooling and reimbursement models, which were rooted in the practices of the old CMS systems. They came to dominate the NRCMS in the first years, before the MoH and the State Council began to draft more systematic and detailed regulations about the NRCMS. In January 2004, the State Council encouraged the integration of smaller health expenditures in the NRCMS reimbursement catalogs and the use of MSAs (Guobanfa 2004, 3).

The old CMS program had operated different types of funds for reimbursement. Pooling funds redistributed the financial resources of the contributors and allocated them according to financial need as specified by the regulations. They typically were to be depleted by the end of the year. Risk funds retained a strategic reserve of financial resources over the years to stabilize the pooling funds in times of increased pressure. MSAs for households pooled resources only on the household level. The substantial variation in the combination and functional purposes of the different fund types that characterized the CMS was substantially limited by the NRCMS policy framework. The main part of the resources was to go into a pooling of funds for catastrophic health costs and inpatient services. Arrangements for outpatient services were optional and left local governments with a considerable distributive leeway (Klotzbücher 2006: 218–21; Liu et al. 2002: 34f.).

Within the decision space the NRCMS policy granted, four general types of reimbursement models emerged: some exclusively focused on catastrophic diseases and covered inpatient services, and sometimes also catastrophic outpatient expenditures typically related to chronic diseases. Other models covered small health expenditures via outpatient pooling or MSAs. A small number of counties also operated MSAs along with large-sum outpatient expenditures. Table 5.2 illustrates strikingly homogenous selection patterns in the first and second cohorts: in central and western regions, between 80 and 90 percent of the pilot counties selected a MSA model. The official evaluations, however, presented samples with lower shares. The share of MSAs increased in the second cohort, and probably reached its peak in 2007. By then, MSAs covered 73.2 percent of all NRCMS counties and 83.1 percent of national poverty counties (MoH 2009: 475; cf. PEG 2006: 70).

The preference for the MSA models was striking against the background of the large local and regional differences of Central and Western China. Two issues are especially puzzling in this regard: first, models covering catastrophic expenditures exclusively require much less administrative work in a local context, and thus should be a rational choice for local governments; second,

Table 5.2 Models of Pooling and Reimbursement in 354 Pilot Counties in 2005

Pooling and reimbursement model		China	East	Center	West
Catastrophic expenditures	Inpatient pooling (hospital insurance)	15%	27.3%	3.4%	0%
	Inpatient plus large-sum outpatient pooling	12.4%	16.4%	6.8%	9.6%
Broad coverage	Inpatient plus outpatient pooling	7.3%	11.5%	4.6%	1.2%
	Inpatient pooling plus MSA	65.3%	44.8%	85.2%	89.2%

Source: Mao 2005: 14

the MSA models were of marginal use for social security due to their limited amount of funding, their low level of social pooling and their usage restrictions. As noted in Chapter 4, the evaluation of the NRCMS pilot counties recommended a departure from MSAs, and the central government ultimately heeded this recommendation.

In 2009, the MoH began to set quotas for the gradual abolition of the MSAs (Weibannongweifa 2009, 108). By then, the usage rate had already decreased to 47 percent; 41 percent used broad outpatient pooling, and only 12 percent still used models focused on catastrophic expenditures (Barber and Yao 2011). By 2010, all field counties had already abolished the MSA system, although the accounts continued to exist in the computer systems of some localities for not yet having been fully depleted. By 2011, 93.5 percent of the NRCMS counties used an outpatient pooling model: 94.5 percent in Eastern China, 96.3 percent in Central China, and 90.1 percent in Western China (Chen and Zhang 2013: 68).

The counties in the first cohort often served as policy models in their prefectural jurisdictions. They set up the basic administrative system and drafted a regulatory framework, which later was studied by the other localities before they launched their own projects. Local governments from the second and third cohort applied similar if not the same regulations on administration, pooling and reimbursement; the systems differed mainly with regard to the specific levels of premiums and reimbursement. In the context of a prefectural jurisdiction, the tendency to copy from established approaches often led to striking similarities in administrative practices and models of administration, pooling and reimbursement. Sometimes, administrative documents were copied to the letter, and only the numbers were changed (Interviews 101125, 101129, 111205).[4]

Successful innovations, on the other hand, could receive a positive appraisal by higher levels of government, and subsequently be extended. These processes could differ from mainstream policy development. The Revolving Premium Collection model of A County in Jiangsu province was an example, which emerged in the context of the prevailing problems with household-by-household premium collection and the State Council's call in January 2004 to improve premium collection mechanisms. A County began to directly deduct the premiums of the following year from the reimbursements of households, and supported this method by outpatient pooling and a broad reimbursement catalog. More than 80 percent of the premiums could be collected this way, which reduced the administrative expenditures and conflict potential of the process (Müller 2016; Wang 2006).

Decision Mechanisms and Local Policy Output

Why did local governments make so strikingly similar choices regarding the policy design across so different socio-economic contexts? The answer becomes apparent with a closer analysis of the processes of decision-making and the stakeholders involved in it. Decisions on the original design of a local

NRCMS as well as its regular adaptations were usually negotiated between local governments and the healthcare facilities, rather than being made by the local government alone. A main reason for this is the asymmetries in information between the local government and the healthcare PSUs: local governments are dependent on specialist knowledge in order to effectively implement the NRCMS. Consequently, the results of those negotiations reflected the interests and preferences of those actors. In practice, local conditions and the preferences of the rural population indirectly influenced the decisions. The local population thus could have an indirect but significant influence.

In a basic and abstract version, the actor constellation for the policy design resembles a prisoner's dilemma between the local government and the healthcare facilities. Figure 5.2 illustrates this constellation, which focuses on the organizational interests of both actors in isolation. Both sides needed to simultaneously solve problems of production and distribution, and could maximize their common benefits via positive coordination and mutual cooperation (field A). As the healthcare facilities were formally subordinated to the local government, the latter could also turn to hierarchical coordination and unilaterally force the PSUs into cooperation (field C). The PSUs, on the other hand, could exploit the information asymmetries vis-à-vis the local government, which were inherent in the hierarchical relationship and the specialist knowledge of the medical profession, and turn to non-cooperation (field B and D). The sustainability of a unilateral defection of the healthcare facilities (field B) depended on their choice of a strategy and its respective risk of detection, which could cause the government to cease its cooperation (field D). These processes of decision-making are recurrent in nature; they apply to the original design of a local NRCMS as well as to its various adaptations in later years. The decision space strongly depended on administrative capacity, the level of socio-economic development, and the level of cohesion and coordination between local government bodies.

In the production dimension, the local government sought to minimize its administrative expenditures for the NRCMS to save scarce fiscal resources for politically and economically more lucrative projects. They could do so by either minimizing the administrative workload, or by delegating administrative tasks to the healthcare facilities. With regard to the reimbursement plan, the first strategy implied the selection of a reimbursement model focused on catastrophic diseases, to avoid the many small transactions connected to outpatient reimbursement. However, as Table 5.2 indicates, only a minority of the localities made such a choice. The second strategy often implied delegating expensive processes to the healthcare facilities, such as reimbursement or premium collection. Both strategies reduced some budgetary expenditures of the local government for the NRCMS under the respective reimbursement model. The second one was, however, clearly prevalent.

In the distributive dimension, additional administrative expenditures of the healthcare facilities—and the THCs in particular—could be compensated through the NRCMS funds. The PSUs were interested in maximizing their

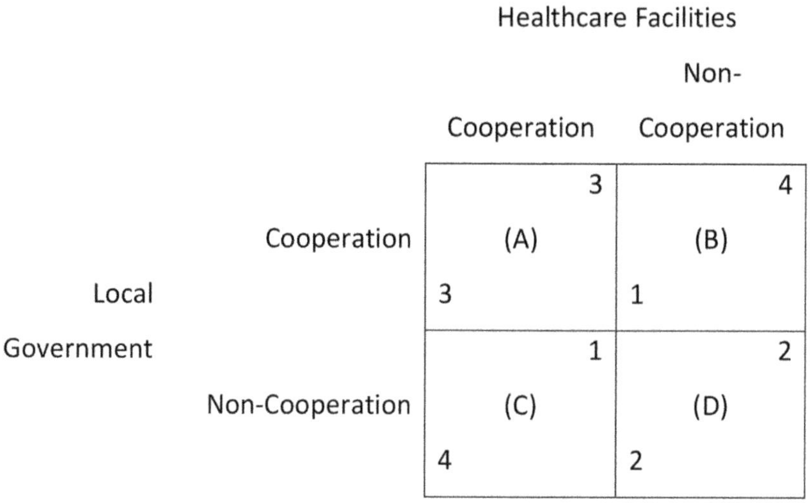

Healthcare Facilities

		Cooperation	Non-Cooperation
Local Government	Cooperation	(A) 3 / 3	(B) 4 / 1
	Non-Cooperation	(C) 1 / 4	(D) 2 / 2

Figure 5.2 Local Policy Design Constellation

benefits from the NRCMS, and one strategy to achieve this was to adapt the reimbursement regulations to the portfolio of the respective facilities. As catastrophic diseases tended to be treated at county facilities, the THCs were more interested in outpatient services and simple inpatient procedures, such as deliveries and appendicitis surgeries. Another strategy was to exclude potential competitors: for THCs, excluding village clinics from the reimbursement plans could create a local monopoly for reimbursable outpatient treatment. As of 2015, documents of the CHFP still call for extending the integration of village clinics into the NRCMS (Guoweijicengfa 2015, 4).

Field A pointed to a delegation of administrative tasks to the THCs and a broader reimbursement design, and to replacing administrative expenditures with the NRCMS funds. Field D, on the other hand, pointed to the absence of such cooperation: the government assumed and financed all administrative tasks and kept the reimbursement plan focused on catastrophic expenditures, while the healthcare facilities engaged in service provision only. When the local government turned to hierarchical direction, it could pressure the healthcare facilities to help with premium collection—a practice criticized by the State Council in 2004 (Guobanfa 2004, 3). Negotiations were, however, the dominant mode of interaction in designing the local policies, because both sides depended on each other, and the county hospitals and THCs were usually represented by facility directors in the negotiations (PEG 2006: 77f.).

Figure 5.2 describes an abstract model of the dynamics of the decision-making process, which is largely based on an aggregate analysis of the implementing counties in the pilot stage. These dynamics not only apply to the design of the general administrative and reimbursement systems, but also to the yearly adaptations of the NRCMS. The actual outcomes in the cases of particular counties can still display a considerable local variation regarding the details of the system. Most notably, the reimbursement rates for different kinds of treatment, providers at different levels or different kinds of illnesses are frequently adjusted according to the "local situation." This may point to the needs of the population—that is, the prevalence of certain diseases—as well as to the needs of the providers, such as the service portfolios of local THCs. The important point is that those decisions are usually reached in negotiations between local governments and healthcare providers, and primarily reflect the preferences of those actors.

The Role of the Health Providers in the NRCMS Administration

The healthcare facilities at the county, township and village levels came to play an important role for the NRCMS: the generalist THCs could assume the broadest set of functions in reimbursement procedures for inpatient and outpatient services, in the provision of medical check-ups and public health services, in the collection of premiums, and in the financial administration of outpatient funds—most notably MSAs. The functional spectrum of the county hospitals was by and large limited to reimbursement procedures. The role of village clinics could vary. Village clinics vertically integrated with the THCs could assume important tasks in reimbursement procedures and premium collection. Where the village clinics were independent, local authorities were often reluctant to integrate them in the NRCMS or delegate tasks to them. Still, however, village doctors could be drafted by village committees for premium collection (PEG 2006: 77ff.).

The administration of the NRCMS was a local task, to be financed via local budgets. For setting up the operative offices for the NRCMS, the bureaus of health were not to increase the number of established posts, but to reorganize the existing pool of human resources. Operations on the township level could be delegated to the THCs or other organs on the township level. Personnel and working expenses were theoretically to be covered by the budgets of the respective level of government, but THCs covered the costs of the delegated tasks themselves (Guobanfa 2004, 3; MoH 2009: 245).

The amount of administrative costs differed between localities and regions. This section presents the example of a hypothetical county with 1 million rural residents and 20 townships. A report of the MoH estimated the administrative expenditures for a county-level NRCMS office in 2005 to amount to RMB 1.6 million, RMB 1.14 million in Central and Western China, and RMB 1.94 million in Eastern China. Other estimates see the national average at RMB 1.32 million in 2008 (Gao 2008: 124). An average township-level NRCMS office caused expenditures of about RMB 18,000 per year, which would amount to RMB 360,000 for 20 townships. The expenditures for premium collection in the early years could amount to 20 to 30 percent of the premiums collected, but might have been higher in localities with difficult geographic conditions. In this example, the costs would amount to RMB 2 million to RMB 3 million. The example shows that premium collection could, despite substantial local variation, easily cause higher costs than the administration of the funds and the reimbursement procedures (MoH 2009: 238–52; Wang 2006: 141f.).

THCs generally played a crucial administrative role for the NRCMS. This generally strengthened their administrative capacity: many THCs only started using patient files and systematic statistical data when the NRCMS was implemented, and the computerization of management gradually spread. This increased the capacity for hierarchical steering between THCs and the county government. Where the regulations were executed to the letter, they could effectively direct and restrain the providers' behavior (MoH 2007: 112; PEG 2006: 96f.; Wang 2008: 165).

Direct reimbursement (*dangchang baoxiao, xianchang baoxiao*) means an administrative process in which reimbursements are handled directly between the NRCMS office and the healthcare facility, and do not involve the patients. Only patients' copayments are paid out-of-pocket. With *ex post* reimbursement, the entire amount is paid out-of-pocket first, and a part is reimbursed later. Direct reimbursement was a task that could be assumed by county hospitals, THCs and village clinics. It required the delegation of the reimbursement procedures to the healthcare facilities. The NRCMS offices compensated the healthcare facilities directly, after a review of the case. Compensation of the provider could be suspended if any irregularities were revealed. Direct reimbursement increased the restraints on health providers and lowered the administrative workload of the county NRCMS office.

Direct reimbursement and *ex post* reimbursement were often combined. As Table 5.3 illustrates, direct reimbursement in 2005 was the most common form of outpatient reimbursement in the first cohort, and 67.4 percent of the counties delegated reimbursement procedures to the healthcare facilities. It was much less common for inpatient services, which most counties reimbursed at a fixed organ other than the health provider—usually the county NRCMS office. Direct reimbursement was usually limited to facilities within the county, and reimbursement at out-of-town facilities continued to be conducted *ex post*, if it was allowed at all. In addition, the administrative tasks related to outpatient reimbursement were much more likely to be delegated to the THCs and village clinics, whereas inpatient reimbursement either remained with the bureau of health or was only conducted *ex post*. Outpatient reimbursement was characterized by a high administrative workload and a low financial risk. Inpatient reimbursement in turn was connected to a greater risk of overspending, which had affected 109 counties by the end of 2006 (Gao 2008; Wang 2006: 150–3, 2008: 257; Zong et al. 2010: 137).

There were a number of preconditions for the direct reimbursement of inpatient services, most notably with regard to administrative capacity: the NRCMS offices needed to be able to accurately forecast the demand for reimbursement and set the reimbursement rates accordingly. In practice, the NRCMS reimbursement catalogs often promised more than its financial

Table 5.3 Reimbursement Methods in 257 Counties of the First Cohort in 2005

	Direct reimbursement	*Ex post reimbursement at the provider*	*Ex post reimbursement at a "fixed organ"*
Inpatient services	19.3%	26.9%	48.7%
Outpatient services	50.9%	16.5%	26.4%

Source: PEG 2006: 35

capacity could keep (Yi et al. 2009). Furthermore, the timely arrival of NRCMS financial transfers was often not guaranteed, which could considerably delay the reimbursement processes or lead to higher effective reimbursement rates in the second half of a year (China News 2006).

Direct reimbursement for inpatient services was arguably even less common in the later cohorts, who faced a greater risk of overspending due to the lack of administrative capacity, and were more reluctant to conduct baseline surveys to generate data for the adaptation of their reimbursement designs. Instead, they tended to keep the reimbursement rates low and conduct rounds of second reimbursement (*erci buchang*) at year's end in order to reduce the fund's surplus. Second rounds of reimbursement could also be used to target special support for households with extremely high health expenditures or poverty households. The first variant constituted a strategy to cope with financial risk and a lack of administrative capacity (Gao 2008: 139–40; MoH 2007: 120f.).

The interviews with the cadres in the field indicated that direct reimbursement gradually spread. From early on, wealthy C District had used direct reimbursement for inpatient and outpatient services at contracted providers within the district and on the city level (Interview 111010). B County had started with *ex post* reimbursement for inpatient services in 2006, and introduced direct reimbursement for inpatient services in 2008 (B-zhengbanfa 2008, 88). A computerized and network-based administration system could enhance the speed of administrative processes between the NRCMS office and the health providers, and was described as a crucial asset in shifting from *ex post* and second reimbursement to direct reimbursement of inpatient services in B County and the surrounding areas (Interview 110901). By 2005, among 215 counties of the first cohort, 19.1 percent still had no computerized administration system; 36.7 percent had computers, but no integrated network; 42.3 percent had a computerized administration with an integrated network (PEG 2006: 41f.). However, even model counties such as A County were reluctant to introduce direct reimbursement for catastrophic health expenditures (Wang 2006: 150–3).

Fund Structure and Reimbursement Regulations

The local healthcare facilities played a crucial role in decreasing the administrative expenditures of local governments, but they also had a strategic interest in maximizing their revenues. The THCs in particular had very specific interests regarding the reimbursement regulations of the NRCMS, and rural patients were the crucial source of their revenues. For the county hospitals, the NRCMS was less important as their revenue basis consisted of patients in both the urban and rural areas. Furthermore, the THCs' position in the rural health service markets was structurally disadvantaged: in outpatient services, village clinics were often a more convenient choice for rural households. In inpatient services, the county hospitals usually had a strategic advantage due to superior equipment, more educated staff and a better reputation. Public health and administration—the THCs' other fields of activity—tended to generate costs rather than revenues.

The main beneficiaries of the NRCMS in the early years were the county hospitals and THCs with high service standards. In the pilot counties, the NRCMS channeled a comparatively large amount of new financial resources into the rural healthcare system. For county hospitals and THCs, this brought an increase in operational revenues and bed occupancy rates—the latter serving as an indicator of efficiency. In absolute numbers, the impact on the county hospitals was much higher than on the THCs—about 50 percent of the NRCMS funds were spent reimbursing services on the county level and above (MoH 2007: 104). The relative effects on the THCs, however, were much stronger than on county hospitals due to their smaller scale and worse economic situation. Their service volume, service income and efficiency rose more quickly than in counties without the NRCMS during the pilot stage (MoH 2007: 94f.). Due to the focus on inpatient reimbursement, county hospitals profited almost automatically from the NRCMS, whereas the situation for THCs depended on their own service capacity, on local patients' health-seeking behavior and on the choice of a reimbursement model.

Different healthcare facilities' shares in NRCMS patients and inpatient reimbursements changed over the years. Between 2005 and 2008, THCs could expand their share in inpatient treatments of NRCMS patients from about 45 percent to about 50 percent, but then it dropped to about 40 percent by 2011. THCs' share in inpatient reimbursements displayed a similar trend, from about 20 percent in 2005 to over 25 percent in 2008, and to below 20 percent in 2011. This indicates that the THCs mainly profited from the NRCMS in the early years, and that since the beginning of the New Health Reform in 2009 they have lost ground again. Between 2009 and 2011, the county hospitals and healthcare facilities outside the county attracted more patients and reimbursements: the increase of patients was relatively stronger for the county hospitals, whereas the increase in reimbursements was relatively higher for out-of-town facilities (Chen and Zhang 2013: 79–82).

The choice among the reimbursement models presented in Table 5.2 had important effects on the allocation of resources in the rural healthcare system. The models focusing on catastrophic diseases mainly channeled resources to county hospitals and to central THCs with high standards in service provision. The models with broad coverage—outpatient reimbursement and

MSAs—channeled more resources to central and general THCs (MoH 2007: 84; PEG 2006: 84f.). In many of the pilot counties, village clinics were excluded from NRCMS reimbursement, whereas county hospitals hardly provided any outpatient services. In such cases, a fixed part of the funds was predestined to be spent on THC services (MoH 2007: 81–95, 104).

The amount of funds channeled into outpatient reimbursement differed substantially between localities. The State Council in 2004 ordered that MSAs should contain a certain percentage of the individual premiums, which was to be defined locally (Guobanfa 2004, 3). In the 2006 evaluation's field counties in Henan and Shaanxi, RMB 8 of the RMB 10 premium were put in the MSAs; in Chongqing it was the full RMB 10 premium plus RMB 5 of the governmental contributions (PEG 2006: 49f.). According to B County's regulations, the MSAs should contain 20 percent of the overall funds in 2006 and 80 percent of the villagers' premiums in 2008 (B-zhengbanfa 2006, 98; B-zhengbanfa 2008, 88). In A County in Jiangsu, 65 percent of the NRCMS funds were channeled into a basic health service fund (*jiben yiliao zijin*), 10 percent were deposited in a risk fund, and only 25 percent went into the pooling of catastrophic diseases (*dabing tongchou zijin*) (Wang et al. 2005). All these regulations allocated money away from the pooling of catastrophic inpatient expenditures.

The specific reimbursement regulations influenced the effectiveness of the NRCMS and the allocation of funds to different healthcare facilities. The same basic set of tools as in the CMS was applied: deductibles, reimbursement rates (*buchang bili*) and maximum reimbursement ceilings. Setting different reimbursement rates for healthcare facilities at different levels (*fenji buchang*) could steer the flow of patients towards the THCs, which typically had lower deductibles and higher reimbursement rates (PEG 2006: 36ff.; Zou 2008: 187). Furthermore, including public health items such as medical check-ups (*tijian*) in the NRCMS channeled additional financial resources to the THCs, which were usually in charge of conducting those tests and received a compensation for them (MoH 2007: 59–67; PEG 2006: 51). A County, for example, allocated 80 percent of its NRCMS spending to THCs and village clinics. Its NRCMS provided coverage of inpatient and outpatient services without a deductible, which arguably facilitated its capacity for combating illness-induced poverty due to chronic diseases (Wang 2006: 403–12; Yip and Hsiao 2009).

Premium Collection and the Political Influence of the Rural Population

The strong preference for outpatient reimbursement models and MSAs in particular cannot be explained by analyzing the interaction of healthcare providers and local governments in isolation. Rather, the rural households should be taken into account as a third group of actors with more diverse preferences. While they are not present in the policy negotiations, their preferences influence the costs and risks of premium collection for the NRCMS, and thus can alter the preferences of the local government to some extent. I have presented a detailed analysis of the interactions of local governments and villagers elsewhere, so the following two paragraphs will briefly summarize the outcomes of that analysis and its effects on local policy design negotiations (cf. Klotzbücher and Laessig 2009; Müller 2016).

The preferences of rural households regarding the NRCMS depend on a large variety of factors. As a rule of thumb, however, wealthy households are more inclined to accept insurance plans focusing on catastrophic expenditures and inpatient treatment, as they can more easily afford the treatment of smaller ailments and outpatient care. Poorer households, on the other hand, struggle even to pay for outpatient care and regular health needs. They have limited benefits from hospital insurance with copayments they cannot afford, as is the case with the NRCMS. Thus, populations in wealthy localities in East China or urban regions can be expected to have a higher preference for NRCMS models focused on catastrophic expenditures.

Why would this have an effect on governmental decision-making? Earlier accounts attributed such effects to the "voluntary nature" of the NRCMS. However, the NRCMS was characterized by a contradiction between universal coverage and voluntary enrollment. In accordance with the suggestions of international policy experts, local cadres often had to achieve high enrollment targets, which contradicted the norm of voluntariness. However, coercion without an explicit political mandate was risky, especially during the early years of the NRCMS implementation, when the conflicts between the pro-government and pro-market forces were not yet fully settled. Trying to convince them without coercion often required repeated visits, which increased the costs in terms of time, transportation, etc. for the cadres. Local governments conceived of various ways to avoid the costs and risks of premium collection, and this way the preferences of the villagers came to influence the NRCMS policy design negotiations.

Premium collection potentially constitutes the most costly administrative task of the NRCMS operations. The regular method was for village and township cadres to go from house to house and collect the premiums. A County calculated the costs of premium collection via the household-by-household method in 2003: the administrative costs in the first round accumulated to almost RMB 1.5 million, or 20 percent of the amount of premiums collected. They included personnel expenditures—the largest part—as well as expenses for conferences and training, propaganda and transport. Of the overall costs, 73.8 percent were incurred at the village level, 22.5 percent at the township level, and 3.7 percent at the county level. The local variation of the costs depends on various factors, among which the natural terrain and infrastructure played a crucial role. In the more rugged terrains of Central and Western China, the administrative costs might amount to 30 percent, 50 percent or even 70 percent of the collected amount, based on a per capita premium of RMB 10 (Wang 2006: 141f.).

Local governments and grassroots cadres had a vital interest in lowering the expenditure for premium collection and developed different strategies in order to do so. A very common approach was to draft village doctors and THC staff to join the squads for premium collection and propaganda. Wang noted that the presence of village doctors and health staff could facilitate the villagers' trust and readiness to pay premiums, and was thus an important asset in the squads (Wang 2006: 134–7). The drafting of doctors also affected the THCs' operations and led to revenue losses, and the State Council criticized coercive drafting in 2004. Nevertheless, the cooperation of the health-care providers could facilitate effective premium collection (Guobanfa 2004, 3; PEG 2006: 77ff.).

There were alternative methods of premium collection that required lower levels of effort. Table 5.4 presents the use of four major premium collection methods in a number of counties from the first cohort: first, collection at the doorstep (*shangmen shoufei*); second, payment by villagers on their own initiative (*zhudong qujiao*), which means a genuinely voluntary enrollment process in which the villagers come to the village committee at a specified time to pay; third, different modes of delegation (*daikou daijiao*)—for example, to local enterprises or local banks; and, fourth, remitted or deducted payments (*jianmian*)—for example, a deduction from agricultural subsidy payments to rural households.

Comparing the cases of Gong'an and Zhenlai with that of Menghai shows that local governments had a vital interest in facilitating genuinely voluntary enrollment, because the mix of collection methods is an important factor for the overall costs. All other things being equal, premium collection was a greater burden in Gong'an and Zhenlai than in Menghai. This could be achieved by adapting the NRCMS to the villagers' interest. In middle- and lower-income localities, the most straightforward way to do this was to reimburse outpatient services. Direct reimbursement could be a crucial step, but was often too demanding in terms of administrative capacity. Localities with high shares of migrant workers could decide to reimburse health services

Table 5.4 Premium Collection Methods in Different Counties of the First Cohort in 2005

	Doorstep collection	*Villagers' initiative*	*Delegation*	*Deduction*
Kaihua County (Zhejiang)	44.9%	20.9%	33.9%	0.2%
Zhaoyuan City (Shandong)	1.9%	20.4 %		77.7%
Zhenlai County (Jilin)	84.4%	10.8%	4.8%	
Gong'an County (Hubei)	61.6%	29.0%	9.0%	0.2%
Menghai County (Yunnan)	31.5%	68.1%	0.4%	
Luochuan County (Shaanxi)	36.5%	8.9%	54.2%	0.3%
Sample of 29 counties	46.9%	32.4%	13.9%	6.5%

Source: MoH 2007: 157

consumed out of town. Finally, in localities where households were opposed to social pooling, MSAs could allocate their premiums back to them. However, such measures have their limitations and did not suffice in all localities (Klotzbücher and Laessig 2009; Müller 2016).

Some local governments could use the institutions of the local economy for premium collection, as the examples in Table 5.4 show. Kaihua was a NRCMS model county known for its innovation of delegating premium collection to local banks, but apparently it only managed to collect about one-third this way (Zong et al. 2010: 88–91). Luochuan, a former revolutionary area in Shaanxi, relied on agricultural "collectives" in the villages for premium collection (*cun jiti tongyi jiaona*), and managed to collect more than half the amount this way (Xiao 2010: 190–6). Such methods were, however, restricted to economically prosperous areas.

Finally, the government could use other payments to households as premiums. As Table 5.4 shows, the local government in Zhaoyuan managed to deduct most of the premiums from other payments, such as agricultural subsidies. A County developed an innovative method by having THCs and village clinics deduct the household premium from the NRCMS reimbursement when a member of the household was seeking treatment. Supported by computerized management of THCs and the vertical integration of the village clinics, as well as a rather large share of the NRCMS funds dedicated to the reimbursement of outpatient expenditure and basic health services, the model achieved similar rates as the approach in Zhaoyuan. A collusive version of this approach used MSAs instead of reimbursements for this purpose. In many areas, MSA funds had low usage rates due to complicated reimbursement procedures, the exclusion of village clinics and other factors. Household premiums were often deducted from the accumulated funds, a practice that was criticized by the center in 2007 and explains some of the high popularity of MSAs among local governments (Weinongweifa 2007: 253).

Figure 5.3 illustrates the effect of high costs of premium collection on the preferences of the local government regarding the cooperation of healthcare providers. THCs and township and village health staff played crucial roles in many of the premium collection models. They either joined the squads and collected premiums with the cadres, or deducted the premiums from the NRCMS reimbursements paid out in the healthcare facilities, or they managed the MSAs at the local level and organized for the collusive substitution of premiums with MSA funds. The option of cooperation (field A) became more attractive for the local government due to the high costs and the political risks of premium collection, compared with the original constellation. Even with the option of hierarchical steering at hand, the local government would prefer field A due to the lower risks and costs in their interaction with the rural households. The political influence of the rural population manifests itself in the more widespread integration of outpatient reimbursement, the prevalence of the MSA model, and innovative and collusive forms of premium collection that avoid the collection of cash at the doorstep.

Healthcare Facilities

Non-

Cooperation   Cooperation

		Cooperation	Non-Cooperation
Local Government	Cooperation	3 (A) 4	4 (B) 1
	Non-Cooperation	1 (C) 3	2 (D) 2

Figure 5.3 Policy Design with High Costs of Premium Collection

Summary

The first part of Chapter 5 provided an overview of the actors and structures of the local policy arenas—that is, the nexus between the local state and the three-tier healthcare system. This is the basis of the analysis of the local policy processes in Chapters 5 and 6. The local healthcare system is strongly affected by the institutional misfits between the public finance system and health sector regulation. Local governments prioritize family planning and public health, and tend to disregard curative care, health insurance and provider financing. Healthcare providers, on the other hand, struggle with contradictory business models. The institutional misfits largely determine the preferences of these actors, and therefore strongly influence the local policy output, which is generated in negotiations between the two.

The first cohorts of pilot counties largely determined the course of the NRCMS in terms of policy design. Pilot counties were usually selected for displaying above-average conditions—that is, having good fiscal and administrative capacity, previous CMS experience and a population with a comparatively positive attitude to health insurance. These counties made astonishingly similar decisions regarding the policy design, with the vast majority including outpatient services in the reimbursement plans. Most chose the MSA model, which was rather ineffective in terms of risk protection.

These decisions constitute the outcome of negotiations between the local governments and the healthcare providers, and represent their respective policy preferences. Local governments sought to decrease their administrative expenditures by delegating administrative tasks such as premium collection or reimbursement partially to the THCs, and compensated them by integrating outpatient services into the reimbursement plans. At the same time, outpatient reimbursement and MSAs in particular increased the readiness of the rural population to enroll, and provided a basis for informal enrollment practices. Therefore, the limited political influence that the rural population had on the implementation process often worked towards decreasing the effectiveness of the system in the early years.

A lack of administrative capacity could often undermine the effectiveness of the NRCMS as an insurance mechanism. Under conditions of scarce fiscal and human resources, the NRCMS offices often had difficulties in adequately forecasting the insurance expenditure. Local policy designs therefore often were overly optimistic about the level of reimbursements they could pay. This facilitated a low coverage of direct reimbursement, and thus patients often had to pay the full amount of costs out-of-pocket after treatment. Reimbursement payments were often affected by imbalances or delayed payments. These factors contribute to the NRCMS not being able to realize its full potential in terms of transparency, reliability and effectiveness.

List of Interviews

Interview 101105: Interview with a cadre in A County, November 5, 2010
Interview 101125: Interview with a city-level NRCMS administrator in Shandong Province, November 25, 2010
Interview 101126: Interview with a THC administrator in E district, November 26, 2010
Interview 101129: Interview with a city-level NRCMS administrator in Shandong Province, November 29, 2010
Interview 101202: Interview with two county-level NRCMS administrators in G County, December 2, 2010
Interview 101203: Interview with a student about his native village in Shandong Province, December 3, 2010
Interview 110901: Interview with a city-level NRCMS administrator in Inner Mongolia, September 1, 2011
Interview 110905–1: Interview with a county hospital director in B County, September 5, 2011
Interview 110906: Interview with a village doctor in B County, September 6, 2011
Interview 111010: Interview with a county-level NRCMS administrator in C District, October 10–11, 2011
Interview 111011: Interview with a county hospital administrator, C District, October 11, 2011
Interview 111012: Interview with a THC director in C District, October 12, 2011
Interview 111127: Informal interview with a villager in A county, November 27, 2011
Interview 111128: Telephone interview with a villager from Anhui, November 28, 2011

Interview 111205: Interview with a county-level NRCMS administrator in C District, December 5, 2011

Notes

1 This connection is by no means deterministic: it is guaranteed neither that wealthy local governments sufficiently allocate financial resources to the health sector, nor that poor counties necessarily have the worst financial conditions. Officially designated poverty counties often receive special fiscal support for healthcare, and their PSUs and social security systems may be better financed than those of slightly wealthier counterparts.
2 The medical profession in rural China is not a homogenous group: there are large differences in terms of income and training. It includes highly trained specialists in county facilities as well as former barefoot doctors who only underwent a few months of training.
3 There are three important exceptions to this rule. First, the birth-planning facilities are subordinated to an independent bureaucracy. In many areas, the PSUs in both networks were integrated to a certain extent, and since 2013 there is an increasing integration of the ministerial line bureaucracies. Second, the village doctors and many urban doctors are in fact private practitioners not administratively subordinated to the bureau of health. Third, especially in the urban county seats, a part of the hospitals may belong to other administrative or economic organizations, or may be formally private.
4 The local variation in the Medical Assistance system has received much less attention by Chinese scholars than that of the NRCMS. For an overview of the main patterns of system design in different provinces, see Zou 2008: 325ff.

Bibliography

Audibert, Martine *et al.* 2008, Activité et performance des hôpitaux municipaux en Chine rurale (Activities and Performance of Township Hospitals in Rural China), in: *Revue d'économie du developpement (Journal of Development Economics)*, 22, 1, 63–100.

Barber, Sarah L. and Lan Yao 2011, Development and Status of Health Insurance Systems in China, in: *The International Journal of Health Planning and Management*, 26, 4, 339–356.

B-zhengbanfa 2006, 98, B Xian Renmin Zhengfu Bangongshi guanyu yinfa B Xian 2007 nian xinxing nongcun hezuo yiliao shishi xize de tongzhi (Notification from the Office of the People's Government of B County about the Detailed Rules and Regulations on Implementing NRCMS in 2007).

B-zhengbanfa 2008, 88, B Xian Renmin Zhengfu Bangongshi guanyu yinfa B Xian 2009 nian xinxing nongcun hezuo yiliao shishi fang'an tongzhi (Notification from the Office of the People's Government of B County about the Detailed Rules and Regulations on Implementing NRCMS in 2009).

Caishe 2005, 2, Caizhengbu, Weishengbu guanyu jiang zhongxibu diqu bufen shixiaqu naru xinxing nongcun hezuo yiliao zhongyang caizheng buzhu fanwei de tongzhi (Notification from the MoF and the MoH about Entitling a Part of the Urban Districts in Central and Western China to Central Government NRCMS Subsidies).

Chen, Zhu and Mao Zhang (eds) 2013, *Zhongguo xinxing nongcun hezuo yiliao fazhan baogao 2002–2012 nian (The NRCMS Development Report 2002–2012)*, Beijing: Renmin Weisheng Chubanshe (People's Health Press).

China News 2006, Zhongguo xinxing nongcun hezuo yiliao shangwei jianli wending changxiao chouzi jizhi (NRCMS Still Lacks a Stable and Sustainable Financing Mechanism), online: http://news.qq.com/a/20060928/001241.htm (accessed July 4, 2014).

Edin, Maria 2003a, Remaking the Communist Party-State: The Cadre Responsibility System at the Local Level in China, in: *China: An International Journal*, 1, 1, 1–15.

Edin, Maria 2003b, State Capacity and Local Agent Control in China: CCP Cadre Management from a Township Perspective, in: *China Quarterly*, 173, 38–52.

Fang, Jing 2008, The Chinese Health Care Regulatory Institutions in an Era of Transition, in: *Social Science and Medicine*, 66, 4, 952–962.

Gao, Guangying 2008, Gonggu he fazhan juyou Zhongguo tese de xinxing nongcun hezuo yiliao baozhang zhidu (Stabilizing and Developing the NRCMS with Chinese Characteristics). In *Yiliao weisheng lüpishu—Zhongguo yiliao weisheng fazhan baogao No. 4 (Green Book of Health Care—Annual Report on China's Health Care No. 4)*, eds Lexun Du *et al.*, 118–142. Beijing: Shehui Kexue Wenxian Chubanshe (Social Sciences Academic Press).

Guobanfa 2001, 39, Guowuyuan Bangongting zhuanfa Guowuyuan Tigaiban deng bumen "Guanyu nongcun weisheng gaige yu fazhan zhidao yijian de tongzhi" (Notification from the General Office of the State Council about the Leading Opinion of the State Commission for Restructuring on Rural Health Reform and Development).

Guobanfa 2003, 3, Guowuyuan Bangongting zhuanfa Weishengbu deng bumen guanyu jianli xinxing nongcun hezuo yiliao zhidu yijian de tongzhi (Notification from the General Office of the State Council about the Opinion of the MoH and Other Departments on Establishing the NRCMS).

Guobanfa 2004, 3, Guowuyuan Bangongting zhuanfa Weishengbu deng bumen guanyu jinyibu zuohao xinxing nongcun hezuo yiliao shidian gongzuo zhidao yijian de tongzhi (Notification from the General Office of the State Council about the Leading Opinion of the MoH and Other Departments on Further Improving the NRCMS Pilot Work).

Guoweijicengfa 2015, 4, Guanyu zuohao 2015 nian xinxing nongcun hezuo yiliao gongzuo de tongzhi (About Accomplishing the NRCMS-Related Work in 2015).

Heberer, Thomas and Gunter Schubert 2012, County and Township Cadres as a Strategic Group. A New Approach to Political Agency in China's Local State, in: *Journal of Chinese Political Science*, 17, 3, 221–249.

Heberer, Thomas and René Trappel 2013, Evaluation Processes, Local Cadres' Behavior and Local Development Processes, in: *Journal of Contemporary China*, 22, 84, 1048–1066.

Hsiao, William C. 2008, When Incentives and Professionalism Collide, in: *Health Affairs*, 27, 4, 949–951.

Klotzbücher, Sascha 2006, *Das ländliche Gesundheitswesen der VR China: Strukturen, Akteure, Dynamik (The Rural Health Sector of the People's Republic of China: Actors, Structures, Dynamic)*, Frankfurt: Peter Lang.

Klotzbücher, Sascha and Peter Laessig 2009, Transformative State Capacity in Post-Collective China: The Introduction of the New Rural Cooperative Medical Scheme in Two Counties of Western China, 2006–2008, in: *European Journal of East Asian Studies*, 8, 1, 61–89.

Lam, Tao C. 2010, The County System and County Governance. In *China's Local Administration: Traditions and Changes in the Sub-National Hierarchy*, eds Jae H. Chung and Tao C. Lam, 149–173. London: Routledge.

Liu, Guoyan and Junfeng Zhang 2010, Xin yigai beijing xia xiangcun yisheng de shengcun yu fazhan wenti—Zhejiang, Guangxi liang shengqu diaoyan baogao (Subsistence and Development Problems of Rural Doctors in the New Health Reform—An Investigative Research Report from Zhejiang and Guangxi Province), in: *Zhongguo Jingmao Daobao (China Economic and Trade Herald)*, 4.

Liu, Yuanli, Keqin Rao and Shanlian Hu 2002, *People's Republic of China: Towards Establishing a Rural Health Protection System*, Manila: Asian Development Bank.

Mao, Zhengzhong 2005, Pilot Program of NCMS in China - System Design and Progress, Background Paper of the World Bank Rural Health Study.

MoH 2004, *Di san ci weisheng fuwu diaocha fenxi baogao (The Third National Health Service Survey Analysis Report)*, online: www.nhfpc.gov.cn/cmsresources/m ohwsbwstjxxzx/cmsrsdocument/doc9908.pdf (accessed July 18, 2016).

MoH 2006, *Zhongguo weisheng tongji nianjian (China Statistical Yearbook of Health)*, Beijing: Zhongguo Xiehe Yike Daxue Chubanshe (China Harmony and Medicine University Press).

MoH (ed.) 2007, *Zhongguo xinxing nongcun hezuo yiliao jinzhan ji xiaoguo yanjiu (Research on the Progress and Outcomes of the NRCMS)*, Beijing: Zhongguo Xiehe Yike Daxue Chubanshe (China Harmony and Medicine University Press).

MoH (ed.) 2009, *Weishengbu xinxing nongcun hezuo yiliao yanjiu zhongxin keti yanjiu baogao huibian, 2006–2008 (Compilation of Research Reports of the NRCMS Research Center of the MoH, 2006–2008)*, Beijing.

Müller, Armin 2016, Premium Collection and the Problem of Voluntary Enrollment in China's New Rural Cooperative Medical System (NRCMS), in: *Journal of Current Chinese Affairs*, 45, 1, 11–41.

PEG (ed.) 2006, *Fazhan zhong de Zhongguo xinxing nongcun hezuo yiliao—Xinxing nongcun hezuo yiliao shidian gongzuo pinggu baogao (China's NRCMS in Development—The NRCMS Pilot Evaluation Report)*, Beijing: Renmin Weisheng Chubanshe (People's Health Press).

Qu, Jiangbin *et al.* 2006, Shandong Sheng nongcun weishengshi zhuangkuang diaocha—2 (An Assessment of the Current Situation of Village Health Stations in Shandong—Two), Cun weishengshi guifanhua fuwu yu fuwu zhiliang fenxi (Analysis of the Standardisation and Quality of Care), in: *Zhongguo Weisheng Jingji (China Health Economics)*, 25, 2, 29–31.

Saich, Tony 2008, *Providing Public Goods in Transitional China*, New York: Palgrave Macmillan.

Tam, Waikeung 2011, Organizational Corruption by Public Hospitals in China, in: *Crime, Law and Social Change*, 56, 3, 265–282.

Teng, Shizhu 2010, *Xiangzhen weishengyuan guanli shiyong shouceng (Practical Handbook of THC Administration)*, Beijing: Renmin Weisheng Chubanshe (People's Health Press).

Wang, Jingyuan *et al.* 2005, Lun xinxing nongcun hezuo yiliao zijin fenge jizhi yu buchang bili (Mechanisms of Parting the Funds and Reimbursement Rates in the NRCMS), in: *Zhongguo Weisheng Jingji (China Health Economics)*, 24, 10, 29–30.

Wang, Jingyuan 2006, *Xinxing nongcun hezuo yiliao—Gundong chouzi lilun yu shijian (NRCMS—Theory and Practice of Revolving Premium Collection)*, Beijing: Beijing Daxue Chubanshe (Peking University Press).

Wang, Jingyuan 2008, *Xinxing nongcun hezuo yiliao zhishi wenda (Questions and Answers on the NRCMS)*, Beijing: Beijing Daxue Yixue Chubanshe (Peking University Medical Press).

Weibannongweifa 2009, 108, Weishengbu Bangongting guanyu zuohao 2009 nian xia ban nian xinnonghe gongzuo de tongzhi (Notification from the General Office of the MoH about Accomplishing the NRCMS Work in the Second Half of 2009).

Weiguicaifa 2006, 340, Guanyu yinfa "Nongcun weisheng fuwu tixi jianshe yu fazhan guihua" de tongzhi (Notification about the "Plan for the Construction and Development of the Rural Healthcare System").

Weinongweifa 2006, 13, Weishengbu deng qi buwei lianhe xiafa "Guanyu jiakuai tuijin xinxing nongcun hezuo yiliao shidian gongzuo de tongzhi" (The MoH and Seven Other Ministries and Commissions Jointly Transmit the "Notification about Accelerating the NRCMS Pilot Work").

Weinongweifa 2007, 253, Guanyu wanshan xinxing nongcun hezuo yiliao tongchou buchang fang'an de zhidao yijian (Leading Opinion on Improving the NRCMS Pooling and Reimbursement Regulations).

Weinongweifa 2007, 82, Weishengbu, Caizhengbu guanyu zuohao 2007 nian xinxing nongcun hezuo yiliao gongzuo de tongzhi (Notification from the MoH and the MoF about Completing NRCMS-Related Work in 2007).

Whiting, Susan 2004, The Cadre Evaluation System at the Grass Roots: The Paradox of Party Rule. In *Holding China Together: Diversity and National Integration in the Post-Deng Era*, eds Barry J. Naughton and Dali L. Yang, 101–119. Cambridge: Cambridge University Press.

World Bank 2007a, *China—Improving Rural Public Finance for the Harmonious Society*, online: www-wds.worldbank.org/external/default/WDSContentServer/WDSP/IB/2007/12/21/000020953_20071221113708/Rendered/PDF/415790CN.pdf (accessed April 25, 2012).

World Bank 2007b, *China—Public Services for Building the New Socialist Countryside*, online: www-wds.worldbank.org/external/default/WDSContentServer/WDSP/IB/2008/01/16/000020953_20080116091210/Rendered/PDF/402210CN.pdf (accessed November 10, 2012).

Wu, Ming 2004, *Nongcun hezuo yiliao zhidu de zhengce fenxi (A Policy Analysis of the Rural CMS)*, Beijing: Zhongguo Xiehe Yike Daxue Chubanshe (China Harmony and Medicine University Press).

Xiao, Xiangxiong 2010, *Pinkun shanqu xinxing nongcun hezuo yiliao changxiao chouzi moshi yanjiu (Sustainable Models of Financing NRCMS in Poor Mountain Districts)*, Xiangtan: Xiangtan Daxue Chubanshe (Xiangtan University Press).

Xu, Jie 2001, Xiangcun weisheng fuwu yitihua guanli ruogan wenti—Xia (Problems of the Integrated Management of Township and Village Health Services—Part Three), in: *Weisheng Jingji Yanjiu (Health Economics Research)*, 11, 5–7.

Yi, Hongmei *et al.* 2009, Health Insurance and Catastrophic Illness: A Report on the New Cooperative Medical System in Rural China, in: *Health Economics*, 18, 119–127.

Yip, Winnie and William C. Hsiao 2009, Non-Evidence-Based Policy: How Effective is China's New Cooperative Medical Scheme in Reducing Medical Impoverishment?, in: *Social Science and Medicine*, 68, 201–209.

Yuanfa 2011, 20, D Qu 202 Yiyuan yiwu renyuan zerenzhi kaohe jiangcheng banfa (Regulation about Rewards and Punishments in the Responsibility System for Medical Personnel in the 202 Hospital of D District).

Zheng, Xiaoying *et al.* 2010, *Zhongguo nongcun shengzhi jiankang weisheng ziyuan youhua he zhuanxing shizheng yanjiu (Optimal Health Resource Allocation and Evidence of the Transformation in China's Rural Reproductive Healthcare)*, Beijing: Beijing Daxue Chubanshe (Peking University Press).

Zhong, Yang 2003, *Local Government and Politics in China*, London: East Gate.

Zhongfa 2002, 13, Zhonggong Zhongyang, Guowuyuan guanyu jinyibu jiaqiang nongcun weisheng gongzuo de jueding (Decision of the Central Committee and the State Council on Further Strengthening Rural Health Work).

Zong, Yingsheng *et al.* 2010, *Xinxing nongcun hezuo yiliao—zhengce yu fuwu (NRCMS—Policies and Services)*, Beijing: Zhongguo Shehui Chubanshe (China Society Press).

Zou, Wenkai 2008, *Nongcun xinxing yiliao baozhang zhengce yanjiu (Research on the New Rural Health Protection Policies)*, Changsha: Hunan Renmin Chubanshe (Hunan People's Press).

6 Operating the NRCMS in a Context of Misfit Institutions

Chapter 6 continues the analysis of the NRCMS in the local arenas. Chapter 5 focused on the policy design in the implementation process, and how local governments and healthcare providers adjust the system in accordance with their preferences. Chapter 6 analyzes the impact of the institutional misfits described in Chapter 2 on the long-term operations of the NRCMS. It argues that the institutional misfits generate a deadlock in the governance and steering of the rural health sector, which affects not only the NRCMS but virtually all fields of local health policy. Chapter 6 focuses on the NRCMS and some of its complementary policies in the context of the institutional misfits, and reconstructs causal processes that explain some of the counter-intuitive effects of the NRCMS, such as accelerating rises in health costs.

The effects of the institutional misfits work as follows. As a rule of thumb, local governments are unable or unwilling to finance the local healthcare providers properly due to the incentive structures and fiscal capacity that the dysfunctional public finance system creates. The leading cadre evaluation system further modifies their preferences by emphasizing the importance of family planning and public health. Health sector regulation specifies business models for rural healthcare providers that implicitly assume a level of state funding which the public finance system can no longer provide. As a result, they often find themselves unable to make ends meet economically without violating their institutional roles, usually by overcharging and systematically inducing demand for drugs and diagnostic tests. Local governments, on the other hand, have little incentive to supervise and sanction these activities, as they are a structural component of healthcare financing.

For the NRCMS and its complementary policies, this deadlock has a number of important effects. With regard to budgetary financing, it contributes to frequent shortfalls in local governments' contributions to the NRCMS and Medical Assistance funds, a situation to which the central government reacted by raising the central and provincial shares in NRCMS funding. Furthermore, the NRCMS administrative bodies are chronically underfunded, most notably in comparison with urban health insurance administration. This renders the NRCMS less effective as insurance. Finally, some local governments tend to decrease their own budgetary funding for the health sector as the inflow of NRCMS subsidies from the higher levels increases.

For the rural healthcare providers, and the THCs in particular, the NRCMS means a new input of funding that substantially improves their financial situation. As this funding is largely connected to curative care provision, they intensify their efforts of inducing demand to maximize their financial revenues. This is particularly the case in localities that actually decrease their budgetary funding for the health sector when the NRCMS is implemented. The subsidies from the higher levels come to replace local budgetary expenditures. Appropriation of the NRCMS funds by the healthcare providers contributes to quickly rising health costs, which decrease the effects of the insurance for the rural population.

The different administrative and supervisory organs often lack the administrative capacity and, more importantly, the political mandate to effectively supervise and sanction the healthcare providers. Furthermore, measures of cost containment tend not to be effectively implemented by local governments and healthcare providers, as both directly benefit from rising health costs. This inherent reciprocity in non-compliance, the dynamics of which are illustrated in the deadlock constellation, is of particular importance for the prospects of cost containment measures, such as bidding and bulk purchasing for drugs, and provider payment reforms. Trying to change incentive structures without altering the financial and institutional foundations for health providers' business models is likely to produce systemic effects in contradiction to the intended effects of such reforms.

The Deadlock in Curative Care and NRCMS Administration

This chapter will analyze how the systemically interdependent yet misfit institutional structures in health sector regulation and public finances affect governance and steering in curative care provisions, and the maintenance and regulatory enforcement of the NRCMS in particular. The core of their effects manifests itself in a particular pattern of interactions between local governments and healthcare providers, which is framed as a deadlock constellation (see Figure 6.1). In such a situation, neither the local government nor the healthcare providers have an interest in living up to their formal responsibilities. There is a potential variation across space and time regarding the intensity of the institutional misfits, most notably the intensity of fiscal imbalances and the financial pressure on THCs. If both factors are sufficiently modest or absent, and higher levels of government emphasize and monitor rural health work seriously, the deadlock can turn towards a regular implementation dilemma. In such a prisoner's dilemma or similar constellation, both sides ultimately prefer conforming to their formal institutional role. Furthermore, some urban hospitals are in fact profitable enough to serve as cash cows for local governments. Exceptions to the rule exist on the level of localities and organizations, but they are exceptions that prove the rule (Tam 2008, 2011).

The mode of interaction is usually negotiation: the local government can consult the providers, and the latter have a certain leeway in cooperating on

Health Facilities

		Compliance	Non-compliance
Local Government	Financing, supervision, cost control	2 (A) 2	4 (B) 1
	Financial shortfalls, lax supervision, collusion	1 (C) 4	3 (D) 3

Figure 6.1 The Deadlock in Curative Care and NRCMS Administration

priority issues with the local government. The local government can, however, also resort to hierarchical steering and directly enforce its preferences on the providers, which is more common in public health work. This chapter will focus on curative care and NRCMS administration, where negotiations dominate due to the low political priority of the issues.

Generally speaking, three causal effects determine the interaction between local governments and healthcare facilities. First, local governments and healthcare facilities in the local arenas are facing an environment of contra-dictory institutional regulations. Local governments have a large array of expenditure assignments, most notably in public service provision. However, the public finance system fails to support those assignments with adequate fiscal capacity at the local level (Wong 2009). Usually, they are only willing and able to take care of tasks with political priority; in health policy, that is primarily birth planning and achieving public health goals such as infant mortality rates. In the evaluation system, these are usually subject either to the one-item veto rule (*yipiao foujue*) or to hard targets. Budgetary financing for healthcare facilities, on the other hand, is secondary, and a frequently neglected (field C and D).

Healthcare facilities are officially supposed to focus on the provision of public services with positive economic externalities: effective public health services and cheap basic curative care. As noted in Chapter 2, basic health services are often priced below the costs of production, and profits from drug sales and high-tech diagnostic services are meant to cross-subsidize them and compensate for the losses. These business models are, however, based on the assumption that local governments support the providers financially, most notably with regard to salaries and construction expenditures. As local governments frequently fail to do so, healthcare facilities cannot but violate some of the regulations if they want to survive economically (field B and D). While compliance to the pricing system can be monitored by local governments, compliance to normative role-orientations and medical ethics—acting in the best interest of the patient, and refraining from inducing demand or decreasing service quality for profit—is much harder to enforce.

Third, if local governments fail to finance their healthcare providers properly, but manage to integrate the interests of their administrative organs, they will usually refrain from tight regulatory enforcement. If they were to enforce regulations strictly, they would risk a financial collapse of the healthcare facilities in the long run (field C). Given the monopolistic structures of healthcare provision in the rural areas, the collapse of a THC or a county hospital could be interpreted as a rupture to social stability and cost points in the leading cadre evaluation (Tam 2011). On the village level, the lack of facilities can sometimes be hidden from higher levels (Zhou et al. 2012: 98). As a rule of thumb, rural health providers cannot live in accordance with their formal role, but they can also not be allowed to perish. Therefore, local governments avoid enforcing formal rules too strictly (field D).

The negotiations take a collusive form of positive coordination. In the production dimension, the deadlock is characterized by unilateral and cooperative strategies of the actors to raise their welfare. The local government unilaterally decreases its budgetary expenditures, and the healthcare facilities engage unilaterally in inducing demand and/or overpricing. Both parties maximize their welfare, ultimately at the expense of the patients who are not represented in the constellation.

In the distributive dimension, the government integrates the interests of its administrative organs and coordinates their conduct, so that they refrain from tight supervision and charging fees from the healthcare facilities. Various administrative departments have a mandate to monitor certain aspects of the health providers' operations, and they often have a monetary interest in fining them to generate extra-budgetary funds. Fang describes such an integration of interests in a county in Yunnan Province:

> [T]he heads of the Price Bureau, Auditing Bureau and FDA all mentioned their difficulties in implementing sanctions, because the person or institution being punished would use their *Guanxi* to bargain and negotiate a reduction in or exemption of sanction. Sometimes even the County Governors or Party Secretaries have been used in negotiation, which is expressed in "*Xietiao Guanxi*" (English: coordination of relationships).
>
> (Fang 2008: 961)

Zou emphasized the reciprocity in this mutual coordination: "In situations where the government's fiscal capacity does not match its ambitions (*li bu cong xin*), it cannot but tacitly consent to the profit-oriented pricing behavior of the public hospitals, or even give it a 'green light'" (Zou 2008: 235). The problems of supervision and control thus go beyond the lack of monitoring capacity and the fragmentation of supervision mandates and information flows, which previous studies have highlighted (see, for example, Ramesh et al. 2014).

For local governments in more abundant areas, the situation is more complicated. On the one hand, their ability to allocate budgetary resources to the health sector is greater. On the other hand, such expenditures compete with politically and economically more lucrative investments, and the motivation and capacity of higher levels of government to enforce compliance also depends on factors other than fiscal capacity, most notably the political priority of healthcare and the likelihood of sanctions by higher administrative levels in case of non-compliance. There are thus two conditions under which the effects of the deadlock are expected to be minimal or absent in a locality: sufficient fiscal capacity of the local government and strong mechanisms of accountability and monitoring in the health sector reinforced by the higher levels of government. But even if local governments choose compliant behaviors, the health facilities can still exploit the information asymmetry to induce demand or decrease service quality to raise their revenues with a low risk of detection (field B).

The Impact of the Institutional Misfits on the NRCMS

The following sections will focus on the effects of the deadlock on NRCMS administration. With regard to financing, there are substantial risks of shortfalls in local budgetary funding (field C and D). Those shortfalls affect payments for the NRCMS funds, for the NRCMS administrative organs, for the Medical Assistance program and for health-related capital investment in the extensive construction programs of the tenth and eleventh five-year plan period. The NRCMS-related shortfalls contributed to the problems of low risk-pooling capacity, low effective reimbursement rates and low coverage of direct inpatient reimbursement discussed above. For Medical Assistance, it decreased the capacity to reimburse the health costs of the poor. With capital investment programs, it increased the burden of debt for local healthcare facilities and thus the costs of healthcare.

Local governments and the healthcare facilities engaged in positive coordination: when the healthcare facilities provided services to the patients, they could decide whether or not to comply with the NRCMS regulations and medical ethics. They often choose to induce demand or other forms of non-compliance to increase their revenues from the NRCMS (field B and D). The local government usually chose not to supervise and sanction such practices too tightly (field D).

The NRCMS funds thus came to compensate for the shortfalls in local budgetary financing. Furthermore, the institutional misfits created incentives for local governments to replace their budgetary expenditures on healthcare by the NRCMS transfers from the higher levels, which increases health costs for the local population. This resulted in rising health costs for the patients, which could decrease or even neutralize the effects of the insurance. The central government has therefore called for a series of cost control mechanisms to be implemented by the local governments. As the implementation is, however, a negotiated process between local governments and healthcare facilities, cost control policies will be implemented in a way that does not harm the interests of both parties, and thus often does not significantly decrease the costs. This is part of the more general danger of central transfers to rural areas replacing budgetary expenditures, rather than adding new resources (World Bank 2007: 31).

Local Budgetary Funding for the NRCMS and Medical Assistance

The budgets of local governments were especially overburdened in poor and agricultural areas, which had a small tax base and were weakened by rural tax reforms. The amount of fiscal resources available for spending items such as NRCMS contributions and administrative expenditures was low and often tended to gradually decrease. Local cadres tended to attach only subordinate priority to budgetary spending on the NRCMS:

> Leading cadres in some localities think that the NRCMS is only one small aspect of their work, far less significant than economic development. Furthermore, in terms of career achievements, the significance of the results in the NRCMS is far less important than the results in economic development. Therefore, they do not attach enough importance to the NRCMS. When they plan the local copayments, they let the NRCMS fall back in the hierarchy of spending items time and again.
>
> (Wang 2008: 166)

Budgetary shortfalls in the NRCMS, Medical Assistance and capital investment were prevalent in areas under fiscal stress, but occurred also in healthier areas due to the strategic agency of local cadres (Wang 2008: 165).

NRCMS Funds

Figures 6.2 and 6.3 illustrate the changes in governmental regulations regarding the minimum per capita financing standards of the NRCMS in 2004 and 2013. Overall, the government's share in financing has risen from two-thirds to 80 percent, and the nominal level of funding has increased more than tenfold. In order to increase the sustainability of funding, the central government has developed differentiated standards for Central and Western China, and the provinces are taking on larger shares of the subnational contributions. Some funding is not regulated by specific figures, such as the central support in Eastern China or the so-called collective support. Per capita

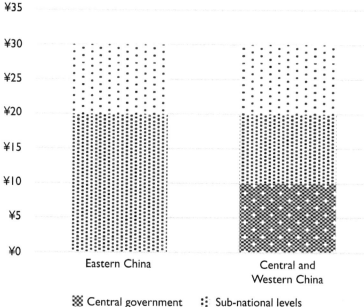

Figure 6.2 NRCMS Financing Standard 2004
Source: Guobanfa 2003: 3.

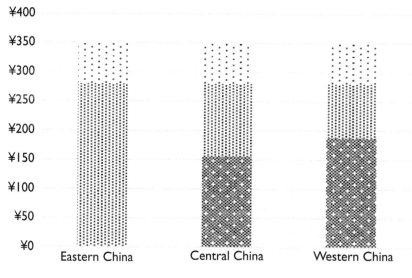

Figure 6.3 NRCMS Financing Standard 2013
Source: Guoweijicengfa 2013: 17.

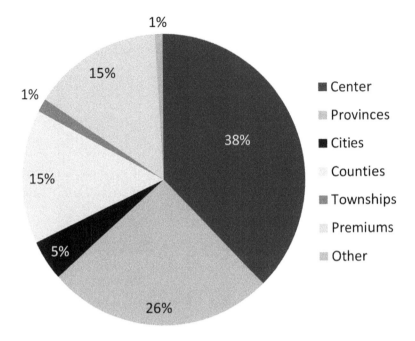

Figure 6.4 Sources of the Aggregated NRCMS Funds in 2011
Source: Chen and Zhang 2013: 61–6.

premiums increased seven-fold, and thus grew more slowly than the overall level of funding. The sub-national levels of government have the authority to increase their own contributions and the premiums in their jurisdictions, which allows for a considerable local variation in funding standards.

The aggregated NRCMS funds in 2011 were financed as illustrated in Figure 6.4. The center financed the largest share with 37.7 percent, followed by the provinces with 25.8 percent. The shares of the counties' contributions were largely equivalent to the premiums, with almost 15 percent each. The center financed only about 10 percent in Eastern China, but more than 45 percent in Central China and more than 50 percent in Western China. The townships only made significant contributions in Eastern China, and the cities also shouldered a larger share of the subnational contributions there (Chen and Zhang 2013: 61–6).

The distribution of the financial burden between the sub-national levels of government is primarily under the jurisdiction of the provinces. The situation in each province differs regarding the general vertical and horizontal distribution of fiscal resources on the one hand, and the distribution of the financial responsibility for NRCMS contributions on the other. Where local governments failed to come up with their budgetary contributions to the NRCMS funds, it was often the result of inflexible rules or cost-shifting by the provincial government. Wang noted in 2008: "If average county-level contributions are RMB 10 per capita, this clearly exceeds the fiscal capacity of the great majority of counties" (Wang 2008: 166). The increases in NRCMS funding gradually raised the pressure on local governments. The center reacted to the contribution problems by ordering the provinces to shoulder the main burden of additional contributions in 2008. Local governments' relative share in subnational contributions gradually declined in Central and Western China, but this occurred mainly before 2008 (Chen and Zhang 2013: 61–6). Based on the 2011 figures, budgetary shortfalls of local government contributions could decrease the financial capacity of the NRCMS by about 15 percent. The capacity could even decrease by up to 30 percent when adding a "fake contributions" strategy—that is, using local contributions or accumulated surpluses instead of premiums. In such cases, the NRCMS would be almost exclusively financed by central and provincial transfers.

Administrative Expenditures

Administrative expenditures usually were to be covered by local budgets, but there was a lack of clear regulatory standards regarding the administrative status and the number of established posts of the NRCMS offices. Even in the first cohort, many local governments guaranteed only for the startup costs. On average, administrative expenditure for personnel and material remained insufficient: for county-level NRCMS offices, it amounted to RMB 1.32 per insured villager by 2007—about 20 percent of the standard of the urban insurance systems. The number of insured per NRCMS administrator, on the other hand, was more than 20 times that of the urban insurance. Regional and local differences were very pronounced—among 244 counties of the first cohort, the average annual expenditures on county NRCMS offices were RMB 996,100 in Eastern China, RMB 238,400 in Central China and RMB 201,700 in Western China (PEG 2006: 41). The administrative capacity of the NRCMS was thus limited by a lack of funding and staff in general, and of qualified staff in particular. This was especially pronounced in Central and Western China, and exerted pressure on the county bureaus of health to delegate administrative tasks to the township level (Gao 2008: 124f.; Wang 2008: 166f.).

Administrative capacity at the township level was an even greater problem due to the regulatory ambiguity of THCs and their NRCMS offices, and the widespread lack of fiscal resources and qualified staff. The delegation of administrative tasks was particularly problematic where neither county nor township governments guaranteed salary payments or financial compensation for the additional workload. It compromised the effectiveness of supervision and sanctioning mechanisms vis-à-vis THCs, and undermined the motivation of the administrative staff, rendering it more prone to corruption (Wang 2008: 166f.; Zou 2008: 266f.).

A lack of administrative capacity decreases the effectiveness of the NRCMS and keeps the system from unfolding its full potential. The lack of financial resources and professional staff constitutes a common problem in the rural areas, most notably against the background of the double structures in health administration (Müller 2016; China News 2006). A lack of administrative funding contributes to understaffed administrative bodies, and over-ambitious reimbursement plans that promise more than the NRCMS funds can keep. Consequently, the administration is afraid of overspending and thus delays reimbursements to the end of the year. Especially for the more expensive inpatient services, this inhibits direct reimbursements, which greatly increase the benefits of the NRCMS for middle- and lower-income households. Direct reimbursement is also the basis for many provider payment methods, which are an important foundation of cost containment. The application of such methods is thus limited by administrative capacity.

Medical Assistance

The financial policy design of the Medical Assistance program, which relied primarily on local budgets, arguably contributed to the delays in its implementation. The documents of the 2002 reform had limited eligibility for intergovernmental transfers in support of Medical Assistance funds to poverty counties and poor areas, while the bulk of funding was to come from local budgets (Caishe 2004, 1). However, intergovernmental transfers accounted for 41.3 percent of the Medical Assistance funds in the first cohort of NRCMS pilots, whereas only 42 percent came from county and township budgets (PEG 2006: 155). According to a 2005 World Bank report, Medical Assistance budgets were:

> inversely related to per capita county income until the upper county quintile, which had the largest budget per capita. Township contributions, lottery contributions, and donations were largest in the richest fifth of counties. Central government funding varied relatively little with county income.
>
> (Wagstaff et al. 2009: 39)

By 2007, only some of the eastern provinces, as well as Tibet and Xinjiang, had formalized the financial responsibilities of the different levels of government. This ambiguity facilitated the instability of the financial input and dependence on local fiscal capacity (Zou 2008: 375f.). The official statistics point to large differences between the provinces regarding the priority of the reimbursement of health costs vis-à-vis the use for NRCMS premiums, and the overall levels of financing. The differences between the Medical Assistance programs were strongly but not exclusively influenced by local economic development. In some cases, poor provinces in Western China appeared to have better financed and more effective programs than some coastal provinces. Chinese researchers generally saw the Medical Assistance program as underfunded, and its integration with the premium collection process for the NRCMS raised some doubts regarding its effectiveness (Interview 101022; Li and Feng 2009; MoH 2011; Zou 2008: 339ff.).

Zero Investment

After the implementation of the NRCMS, some counties arguably decreased their budgetary support for capital investment and salaries of the rural healthcare facilities, and THCs in particular. Zou referred to such strategies as Zero Investment (*ling touru*), most notably in connection to capital investment projects: the "investments" of the local governments were not really conducted, but they retained their budgetary resources for other purposes. The providers in turn were under substantial pressure to invest in and modernize their facilities in order to attract patients, most notably the THCs with their difficult strategic position in the rural healthcare markets (Zou 2008: 268f.).

For the eleventh five-year plan period, the central government initiated a comprehensive investment program of over RMB 20 billion with detailed standards to be reached by county hospitals, THCs, TCM hospitals and public health organs (Gao 2006; Liu 2007). The provinces launched complementary programs.[1] These projects arguably had higher public copayments than those of the 1990s discussed in Chapter 2, which were primarily funded from local resources. Nevertheless, the targeted facilities still had to come up with a substantial part of the funding themselves. The burden of the facilities increased in cases of shortfalls of local government contributions. As a consequence, the debt of THCs further accumulated during the tenth and eleventh five-year plan period. By July 2011, the State Council announced a national debt reduction for THCs: all debt that had accumulated until December 31, 2009, would be settled by the central government; debt that had accumulated after January 2010 was to be settled by the subnational levels of government. The further accumulation of new debt was to be prevented (Guobanfa 2011, 32; Wu and Chen 2011).

Service Provision, Supervision and Regulatory Enforcement

As noted above, there is a close interdependence between the lack of budgetary spending on the one hand, and the lack of effective supervision and regulatory enforcement on the other. This interdependence and the positive coordination between local governments and healthcare facilities also affect the NRCMS. Where local governments avoided spending on THCs or decreased their health spending altogether, the NRCMS funds could help to compensate for the lack of budgetary funding. Health providers systematically induced demand, overcharged or colluded with patients to increase their revenues from the NRCMS. These strategies are best documented for THCs, but village clinics also tended to use them where they were integrated with the NRCMS. Controlling village clinics was often more difficult than controlling the THCs (Sun et al. 2009).

Increases in health costs following the implementation of the NRCMS had been frequently reported by villagers in the first cohort. To some extent, they were outcomes of the differing channels of pharmaceutical supply and different pricing systems between the THCs and independent pharmacies or private, for-profit practitioners. The latter two had greater leeway in choosing their suppliers and in setting their prices, and thus often offered cheaper drugs than THCs. Doctors in the public, non-profit facilities could, however, also strategically provide drugs and services with comparatively high prices and profit margins. An interviewee described such a perceived price increase after the vertical integration of formerly private clinics in his village: before the change, the doctors—then private practitioners—had been perceived to be responsive to patients' demands of finding the cheapest possible cure. Afterwards, they were perceived to behave differently in the framework of the new, public village clinic. Even the NRCMS reimbursements would not cover the full scope of the cost increase.[2] Apart from the different types of drugs and the pricing system, revenue targets and incentives the THC now set for the village doctors may have been a cause for the rising costs. Furthermore, overcharging remained a feasible strategy for village doctors: the pricing system could be circumvented by charging informal prices higher than those listed on the formal prescriptions. Effective supervision at the village level is particularly difficult due to multiple agency relations characterized by the deadlock (Bunkenborg 2012; Interview 101021, 111010; PEG 2006: 97–100; Sun et al. 2009).

Induced demand—that is, manipulating the types and volume of services provided to a patient to increase revenue—was a common strategy before and after the implementation of the NRCMS. Providers on all levels could strategically manipulate their diagnoses or issue large prescriptions (*da chufang*). The NRCMS increased the purchasing power of the rural households, which allowed for a general increase in service provision. Some forms of induced demand were also directly related to the NRCMS reimbursement regulations. As the 2006 evaluation notes, in one case, low deductibles for inpatient reimbursement incentivized THCs to pay kickbacks to village doctors for referring patients with a common cold to the THC, where they were reclassified as patients with a "serious cold" (*zhong ganmao*) and hospitalized. In another case, a THC systematically diagnosed appendicitis because the NRCMS reimbursed the respective operation, which led to a distinct rise in the appendicitis rate of the locality. Even serious cases of induced demand would hardly be sanctioned by the health administrations or the NRCMS offices (PEG 2006: 97–106).

The NRCMS also gave rise to various fraudulent strategies, and doctors have been reported as colluding with their patients in some cases. Such practices typically involved non-insured villagers using the NRCMS card of someone else (*maoming dingti*), doctors issuing false prescriptions (*jia chufang*) or prescribing and reimbursing drugs from the NRCMS positive list, while actually selling non-reimbursable drugs. THCs and county hospitals could forge inpatient episodes (*jia zhuyuan, guachuang zhuyuan*) and patients' files (*jia bingli*) in order to claim reimbursements (Bunkenborg 2012; PEG 2006: 100; Zou 2008: 240–3).

The 2006 evaluation report describes the supervision of the healthcare facilities as rather difficult. The NRCMS offices at the county level were the main organs of supervision, but largely lacked the administrative capacity to tightly monitor the rural healthcare facilities. Furthermore:

> [E]ven if [the NRCMS offices] had "sufficient" monitoring capacity, under the current administrative system, even the NRCMS supervision committees with the leaders of the People's Congress and the Consultative Conference are either not allowed or not willing to deal with certain issues ... What could the "powerless" NRCMS offices possibly hope for?
>
> (PEG 2006: 100)

A similar situation characterized the relationship between THCs and village clinics, as the supervisory role of the former also covered the NRCMS where the latter were integrated into it. In both cases, this is a manifestation of the reciprocal preference for non-compliance between the local government and the PSUs, and between the THC as the township representative of the health administration and the village clinics respectively (PEG 2006: 97–106).

Many pilot counties signed contracts (*xieyi shu*) with the NRCMS-approved healthcare providers, specifying requirements for service provision, drug use and health costs, and the sanctions of any violation. Despite its general potential, the method remained limited in its impact: it required administrative capacity, the involvement of the leadership of the bureau of health, and the political will to restrain the health facilities. It was further limited by the systematic creation of public provider monopolies on the township and village levels, which left little room for effective competition: with the exception of wealthy areas, most townships only had one THC, and revoking its contract had a potentially negative impact on service provision. In the villages, similar problems appeared where vertical integration was pursued; furthermore, as Bunkenborg reports from Hebei, the contract restrictions could be easily sidelined:

> In actual practice, the attempt to favour some doctors with the status of designated [NRCMS] clinic was bypassed quite easily as all doctors managed to get refunds through colleagues with access to the system, and fake prescriptions were quickly becoming the order of the day for doctors annoyed with the paper work and delayed reimbursements.
>
> (Bunkenborg 2012)

Direct reimbursement provided a more potent sanctioning mechanism for the NRCMS offices. They could withhold compensation for the providers, which those only received after an examination of the reimbursement cases. The NRCMS office could decrease the amount if it found irregularities, and thus help to enforce the NRCMS positive lists and the pricing system. The providers could, however, still induce demand or convince patients to purchase services or drugs not eligible for reimbursement (PEG 2006: 100ff.). The use of direct reimbursement for inpatient service was, however, restricted by problems of administrative capacity. In connection with outpatient pooling, it could provide an effective tool vis-à-vis the THCs.

Rising Health Costs and Cost Containment Strategies

In the course of the implementation of the NRCMS, the overall health expenditures of the rural population could rise very rapidly. Zou described the case of a county in the first cohort, where overall health costs increased by 368.5 percent within three years, due, among other things, to a strategy of Zero Investment by the local government (Zou 2008: 242f.). The 2006 evaluation notes that "although the villagers receive reimbursements after the implementation of the NRCMS, there is no notable decrease in their medical expenditures due to the increasing costs of treatment. Some villagers think that the health providers are the main beneficiaries of the NRCMS" (PEG 2006: 55).

It ultimately remains difficult to exactly draw the line between "legitimate" cost increases due to demand facilitated by the NRCMS on the one hand, and the appropriation of the financial resources of the NRCMS funds by the providers via induced demand and other strategic behavior on the other hand. But controlling rising health costs in the course of the NRCMS implementation quickly became one of the main concerns of the central government. Three types of instruments or mechanisms were crucial to its cost containment strategy: NRCMS positive lists for drugs and services, bidding and purchasing reforms, and provider payment reforms (Weibannongweifa 2005, 243; Weiguicaifa 2008, 6; Weinongweifa 2007, 82).

Positive Lists, Cost Containment and Decreased Coverage

Pricing and positive lists were crucial instruments in the attempt to control health costs. The lists had already been used in the CMS programs of the 1990s (Carrin et al. 1999). From 2004 on, the center had called on the provinces to draft catalogs of drugs and services reimbursable under the NRCMS (*xinxing nongcun hezuo yiliao jiben yaowu mulu, zhenliao mulu*), which should differ from the urban insurance catalogs. The basic logic was to maximize the effectiveness of the NRCMS funds by focusing reimbursement on cheap and effective services and drugs, and excluding expensive services and drugs from reimbursement. Services and drugs excluded from the positive lists would then have to be paid for directly by the patients. Ideally, the lists provide norms and incentives for treatment that ultimately decrease the healthcare expenditures of the villagers.

The NRCMS drug catalogs were typically smaller than the national Essential Medicines list, or the catalogs of the urban health insurance. Up to 2008, the provinces had full jurisdiction over drafting the catalogs, and there were substantial differences between them. Most had integrated provincial catalogs, some of which also differentiated the scope of drugs approved for village clinics, THCs and county hospitals; all of them included traditional as well as Western medicines, but they often lacked instructions for drug use.[3] For Western medicines, the degree of matching with the central government's Essential Medicines list before 2009 exceeded 50 percent only in a minority of provinces. This diversity between the catalogs was arguably facilitated by the orientation towards local treatment practices, which decreases the costs of adaptation in the local healthcare systems. Since 2009, the lists have undergone harmonization in the course of the New Health Reform (MoH 2009: 278–408; Tian et al. 2012).[4]

The use of positive lists raised various problems for medical practice. Before 2009, the drug lists were not considered very practicable: some mainly included commonly used drugs, the adaptation of the catalogs did not keep up with market development, and the scope of the lists was often perceived as too narrow. The wide range of pharmaceutical products and the lack of standardization in the product denominations were seen as problematic. Doctors in the field furthermore indicated that due to the parallel use of different catalogs, they had to learn two ways of treating a patient. The UEBMI and the NRCMS had different positive lists, and the course of treatment depended on the health insurance status and the types of drugs that were approved for reimbursement under the respective insurance (Interview 110905–1; MoH 2009: 295).

The inability of the lists to cover all services and drugs necessary for treatment was reflected in the usage rates, which hardly ever covered 100 percent of the drugs that doctors would prescribe. In some localities, less than 25 percent of the expenditure for drugs and diagnostic services in THCs, county hospitals and larger urban hospitals was approved for NRCMS reimbursement (MoH 2009: 513). A common strategy of local governments to try to close the gap between regulation and practice was to set minimum rates of 80 or 90 percent for the use of listed drugs, allowing for 10 to 20 percent of the reimbursed drugs to be unapproved. Wang argues that such rates could be achieved, provided a careful selection of the products, publicity of the list and strict controls were guaranteed. Overall, the variation of the usage rates of positive-listed drugs was substantial[5] (MoH 2009: 278–408; Wang 2008: 231–4).

Usage rates were, however, not only determined by medical necessity but also by the self-interest of the healthcare facility, and thus by the profit margins the respective products could offer. Before the implementation of the NRCMS, enforcement of positive lists for partially integrated village clinics hardly achieved usage rates above 50 percent (Xu 2001). The NRCMS positive lists typically excluded items with high profit margins, and thus incentivized healthcare providers to use additional or alternative services and drugs during treatment. According to the 2006 evaluation, the recourse to non-reimbursable drugs was widespread and systematic. In *ex post* reimbursement systems, patients were often unaware of the restrictions in reimbursement at the time of treatment. In direct reimbursement systems, doctors could talk patients into signing the statements of consent required for the use of unlisted drugs, or collude with the patients and manipulate medical records and prescriptions (PEG 2006: 99–106; Zou 2008: 209f.).

The positive lists were among the strongest tools of control the NRCMS administrators could use to restrain the healthcare facilities. In practice, however, they also increased the complexity of the NRCMS, which resulted in a lower transparency and predictability of the system for the villagers. The positive lists provided an institutional basis for a substantial gap between formal and effective reimbursement rates. The administrative documents of the NRCMS typically promised high reimbursement rates, which, however, only applied to listed drugs and service items. The lists often excluded cost drivers in order to set good incentives for the healthcare providers. As a result, the effective reimbursement rate—that is, the share of NRCMS reimbursements in the full amount of health costs—was much lower. This gap was further widened by budgetary shortfalls in NRCMS contributions and other administrative problems and informal practices.

Bulk Purchases and Bidding

Another central strategy for cost control in the NRCMS was the reliance on the purchasing reforms initiated since the late 1990s, which were discussed in Chapter 2. In document 13 on rural health reforms in 2002, the Central Committee and the State Council reiterated their commitment to the reforms. Bulk purchases and concentrated bidding were to guarantee value for money. NRCMS drugs were to be procured for entire counties via the established purchasing mechanisms at the city and provincial level. The approach was based on the larger system of bulk purchasing and competitive bidding for drugs, and the extension of organized purchasing, positive lists and wholesale structures into the rural areas. For drugs procured under this regime, retail prices were to be determined by the purchasing prices plus a 15 percent profit margin, rather than by the leading prices of the traditional governmental pricing regime. The decreases in purchasing prices achieved via bidding were thus to directly benefit the patients and decrease the costs of treatment (Guobanfa 2000: 16; Guobanfa 2001: 39; Guobanfa 2004: 3; Guoyaoguanshi 2000: 306; Weibannongweifa 2005: 243; Weiguicaifa 2000: 232; Weiguicaifa 2000: 148; Zhongfa 2002: 13).

The reform was affected by two important problems: first, the quality of the purchased drugs was difficult to guarantee due to problems of the regulatory regime of the pharmaceutical sector. China's drug markets lacked standardized and reliable quality indicators for drugs due to the failure of the FDA's endeavor to centralize regulatory competences, intense pharma-lobbying at the central and provincial level, and the over-competitive dynamics of China's pharmaceutical markets.[6] The lack of comparable standards greatly increased the complexity of the quality assessment process and rendered the bidding agencies dependent on the experience-based knowledge of the local doctors.

The price often became the only verifiable selection criteria, so the agencies purchased the cheapest merchandise rather than value for money (Gong et al. 2010; Liu 2011).

This issue greatly complicates the ethical assessment of the massive recourse to non-listed drugs under the NRCMS described above. The evaluation reports merely describe them as violations of the regulatory standards to be corrected by stricter enforcement and accountability mechanisms. It is, however, difficult to assess whether and to what degree collusion between doctors and patients may have been in the best medical interest of the latter. The same is true for localities that simply did not implement the bidding policies. Such practices may protect patients from cheap, low-quality or potentially harmful medicines. The dysfunctionality of the regulatory institutions may justify to some extent the culture of non-compliance prevalent in the NRCMS.

Second, bidding and purchasing reforms became affected by the interdependent forces of financial pressure and low accountability that characterize the deadlock described above. Most notably, hospitals and pharmaceutical firms as the main stakeholders and implementing agents had no interest in decreasing their own revenues with such reforms. Furthermore, local governments were expected to play a neutral role—that is, to oversee the organization, but not to interfere with the process. Bidding and purchasing reforms would have required a system of effective accountability mechanisms, which are, however, undermined by the institutional misfits in public finance and health sector regulation.

The drugs on the NRCMS positive lists therefore often tended to have profit margins substantially higher than 15 percent. Even before the introduction of the NRCMS, local governments systematically manipulated bidding and purchasing to appropriate the benefits of the reforms together with the healthcare providers (Klotzbücher 2006: 260f.). The bidding reforms achieved substantial decreases in wholesale prices, but this did not decrease the drug expenditures of the patients, as hospitals often kept selling according to the leading price system (Gong et al. 2010: 266). A cadre in A County explained this:

> If the fixed [i.e. formal] wholesale price for a drug was RMB 1, then hospitals were allowed to charge a markup of RMB 0.15 as their profit margin. But if you could decrease the wholesale price to RMB 0.5 [through bidding], you could still sell it for RMB 1.15. That increased the profit margin considerably.
>
> (Interview 111124–1)

Cadres in A county pointed out that the profit margins for individual drugs could be as high as 60 percent, and in C District it was reported that profits accounted for 40 percent of the overall drug revenue of THCs (Interview 111010, 111124–1).

The enhanced profit margins on drugs continued to be a crucial source of revenue for the rural health providers. In particular, the THCs, which had little or no profitable high-tech diagnostic services in their portfolio, and whose budgetary transfers were more insecure than those of the county-level PSUs, depended crucially on those revenues. One THC director, for example, reported that virtually all expenditures of the THCs, including salaries and construction, depended almost entirely on the profits from drug sales (Interview 111124–2). The NRCMS funds ended up financing the operations of the healthcare providers and the construction programs of the government. Avoiding an effective implementation of the bidding and purchasing reforms was crucial to achieve this.

Provider Payment Reforms

Chinese provider payment reforms are largely inspired by the practices of healthcare reform in OECD countries. They attempt to use health insurance systems such as the NRCMS as instruments of strategic purchasing. Their aim is to alter the problematic incentives of the fee-for-service system with its positive lists and state-led pricing for healthcare providers. The alternatives to fee-for-service payment largely depend on direct reimbursement mechanisms as an administrative foundation: the patients merely pay their copayments after treatment. The insurance reimburses according to its own rules and can withhold payment in case of any irregularities.

Table 6.1 provides an overview over the most common approaches to provider payment and their advantages and disadvantages, which is based on the works of Professor Yu Baorong. All other things being equal, fee-for-service payment guarantees doctoral autonomy, but it also facilitates induced demand and a neglect of preventive care. Catalogs of service items and price lists complicate the administration and cost control is weak. Alternative payment methods usually aim at decreasing costs, while maintaining the quality of treatment as much as possible. Global budgets (*zong'e yufu zhi*) allocate a fixed amount of funding to a facility, irrespective of the workload. This approach is easy to manage and creates strong incentives for cost control. However, it may decrease the volume and quality of medical services, especially if the budgets are too low. Per-capita payments (*an rentou zhifu*) facilitate the provision of preventive care and the control of service volume and costs, but may incentivize doctors to avoid treating serious and expensive cases. Payment by diagnosis-related groups (DRG—*an bingzhong zhifu*) compensates healthcare facilities with fixed sums for specific types of diseases and cases. Although it facilitates cost control, guaranteeing the quality of treatment and controlling induced demand is difficult under this system (Yu 2009: 86).

Provider payment reforms have been applied in both urban and rural China (Yu 2009: 85–92). In the rural areas, systematic experiments with alternative provider payment reforms have been conducted since the 1990s (Liu et al. 2002; Meng 2005). In the pilot stage of the NRCMS, several counties started

Table 6.1 Provider Payment Reforms, Their Advantages and their Disadvantages in a Chinese Context

	Payment method	Advantages	Disadvantages
Fee-for-service (*an xiangmu zhifu*)	Payment by service item (price and volume)	High autonomy of the doctor; quickly meets all types of medical demand; convenient accounting; facilitates medical innovation and technical development	Induced demand; neglect of basic and preventive care; high administrative costs, low cost control via health insurance
Global budget (*zong'e yufu zhi*)	Provider paid a fixed total sum for specified services	Simple accounting, low administrative costs; strong incentives for cost control	Inhibits technical innovation and development; volume and quality of services may decrease
Capitation (*an rentou zhifu*)	Provider paid by number of service population for specified services	High control of service volume and costs; facilitates preventive care; low administrative costs	Doctors may focus on simple cases and avoid serious cases
By case or bed-day (*an renci/ chuangri zhifu*)	Payment of a standard amount per treated patient or per bed-day	Incentives for provider to decrease costs per patient treatment or bed-day	Longer hospital stays, decomposition of prescriptions, repeated visits; serious cases may be avoided
Diagnosis-related groups (DRG, *an binzhong zhifu*)	Payment per patient based on group standard; groups based on diagnosis, age and type of disease	Prepayment system, effective cost control	Unable to guarantee quality of treatment; risk of induced demand by systematically over-estimating the severity of cases

Source: adapted from: Yu Baorong 2009: 86.

experimenting with alternative payment forms such as capitation, simple forms of DRGs called single-disease-type price-caps (*dan bingzhong xianjia*)[7] or global budgets for different types of services. Lufeng County in Yunnan Province is among the best known for its experiments with global budgets for outpatient services, and with payment by bed-days and DRGs for inpatient services (Wang 2010). The central government and the MoH have been continuously promoting the extension of provider payment reforms for the NRCMS, most notably of single-disease-type price-caps, which was the most common approach (Guoweijicengfa 2013: 17; Weibannongweifa 2005: 243; Weiguicaifa 2008: 6; Weinongweifa 2009: 68).

Although provider payment reforms may be a promising line of reform and experimentation for cost containment, their current impact in the NRCMS is limited due to two factors. First, the NRCMS only covers a limited amount of rural healthcare expenditure, and thus has only a limited impact on healthcare providers' incentives. By 2012, per capita funding for the NRCMS accounted for about 30 percent of overall per capita health costs. This share has been stable for several years and, as Chapter 7 will show, is only half as high as the respective figure for the UEBMI. Second, rural health insurance administration under the MoH tended to have lower administrative capacity than urban health insurance administration under the MoHRSS. This facilitated conservative fund management and high surpluses in the NRCMS funds (Zhang et al. 2010). Local governments were rather reluctant to engage in direct reimbursement for inpatient services and catastrophic health costs, which limited the application of most alternative payment forms to outpatient services. Thus, only a small share of the NRCMS funds was usually available for altering the incentives of the fee-for-service system. Recent research remains inconclusive regarding the potential of provider payment reforms to facilitate the effectiveness of outpatient care provision (see, for example, Powell-Jackson et al. 2015). Yu notes that even the UEBMI systems with their superior administrative and financial capacity continued to predominantly rely on fee-for-service payment, which indicates that provider payment reforms may still need some time until they can unfold their full potential in the NRCMS (Yu 2009: 87–92).

Summary

This chapter presented the various effects of the systemic interdependence and the institutional misfits between health sector regulations and the public finance system. Local governments and healthcare facilities were both exposed to substantial financial pressures, which facilitated them resorting to unilateral and cooperative forms of collusion. Their particular pattern of interactions resembles a deadlock constellation, in which neither side is interested in living up to its institutional role. Ultimately, the patients compensated the healthcare facilities for the shortfalls in public financial support, which were caused by the dysfunctional public finance system.

When the NRCMS was introduced to the local healthcare system, its financial transfers came to replace local budgetary funding for healthcare to some extent. The additional funds were appropriated by the underfinanced healthcare facilities and ended up paying for items such as salaries or copayments in governmental construction programs. This contributed to the rises in health costs, along with the additional demand for health services that the NRCMS created among the patients. These problems were prevalent among the counties of the first cohort of pilots with their above-average implementation conditions. They arguably intensified in the more average localities of the later cohorts, which have not been studied as thoroughly.

In a similar way, strategic manipulation and selective compliance with the misfit but interdependent institutions changed the outcome of complementary reforms, such as the bidding and purchasing of drugs. In theory, these reforms should enhance competition in the pharmaceutical sector and decrease public hospitals' purchasing prices for drugs. These decreases should be passed on to the consumers in the form of lower retail prices. The reform should decrease health costs while maintaining the quality of care. In practice, local governments often colluded with hospitals to retain and share the benefits by selling according to the higher prices indicated by the pricing system. Furthermore, in the absence of a functional system of quality indicators, the price was often the only feasible criterion of judging a product, which enhanced a tendency to simply buy cheaper merchandise. The rationale of the reform was to decrease costs and enhance value for money. Due to the systemic interdependence and institutional misfits, health costs remained largely unaffected, while the quality of care probably decreased.

With regard to the NRCMS as an insurance mechanism, the institutional misfits contributed to the lack of transparency and decreased its effectiveness. They widened the gap between the high nominal reimbursement rates presented in administrative documents on the one hand, and the low effective reimbursement rates that patients actually received on the other. Beyond the limited coverage of services and drugs specified by the positive lists, this gap was widened by a variety of factors: they include over-optimistic assessments of the insurance capacity discussed in Chapter 5, as well as shortfalls in governmental contributions to the funds, and the rises in health costs caused by providers' induced demand. As Chapter 7 will show, certain policies under the umbrella of the 2009 New Health Reform target some of these problems.

List of Interviews

Interview 101021: Interview with a health insurance expert in Beijing, October 21, 2010

Interview 101022: Interview with a rural health expert in Jinan, October 22, 2010

Interview 101126: Interview with THC administrators in E District, November 26, 2010

Interview 101203: Interview with a student about his native village in Shandong Province, December 3, 2010

Interview 110905–1: Interview with a county hospital director in B County, September 5, 2011

Interview 111010: Interview with a county-level NRCMS administrator in C District, October 10–11, 2011

Interview 111124–1: Interview with a local cadre in A County, November 24, 2011

Interview 111124–2: Interview with a THC director in A County, November 24, 2011

Interview 111127: Informal interview with a villager in A county, November 27, 2011

Notes

1 Shandong province, for example, launched two capital investment projects for THCs in 2006 and 2007, each with a volume of about RMB 400 million. Anhui launched a similar project in 2004 with a volume of RMB 290 million (CPC 2007; Zou 2008: 226).
2 The vertical integration may also have brought considerable improvements in the hygienic conditions and the safety of treatments, which the patients may have put less emphasis on. For example, the interviewee pointed out that, during the 1990s, independent practitioners would often reuse a single syringe for treating several patients. The practice disappeared when the patients gradually became aware of the health risks connected to it (Interview 101203).
3 According to an internal MoH study in 2007, among 26 provinces, only three had the positive lists drafted by the counties. Thirteen provinces would not differentiate between different levels of providers in the catalogs, nine would differentiate between providers on the village, township and county level, and the others would either add the city and provincial level, or merge the county and township level. Only 13 catalogs included instructions for drug use, and 17 included prescription limits for Western medicines. The drug catalogs in Central China were rated superior to those in Eastern and Western China (MoH 2009: 288f.).
4 In the 26 provinces analyzed, the degree of matching of Western medicines on the provincial lists with the 774 types of Western medicines on the central Essential Medicines list reached 81.2 percent in only five provinces, 53.8 percent in ten provinces, 36 percent in 15 provinces and only 10 percent in 20 provinces. Overall, the disparities between the lists were rather large (MoH 2009: 294f.).
5 An internal MoH study in 2007 pointed to considerable variations in the use of listed drugs in four different counties: the county-level facilities' rates were all above 60 percent, but the average rates for THCs could differ substantially—16.6 percent, 54.3 percent and 89.6 percent respectively (MoH 2009: 311).
6 For example, the provincial standards of drug registration were not public information, and provincial governments often deliberately lowered their standards as a means of local protectionism. In the introduction of national certification standards, the FDA remained largely dysfunctional due to a lack of administrative capacity and systematic corruption. The main authority over certifications of good manufacturing practices was delegated to the provinces in 2003, after a failed attempt of a top-down implementation of national standards, and thus failed to become a reliable standard as well. It was easy for companies to register old products as innovative brand drugs, or to attain the good manufacturing practices status with mere upgrades in equipment, but no changes to manufacturing processes. The privileged pricing status connected to such labels was therefore often arbitrarily assigned (Gong et al. 2010; Yang 2009).
7 The single-disease-type price-cap method is a simplified version of DRGs, which is easier to apply in the context of a fee-for-service system and low administrative capacity. Usually, the local bureau of health will analyze the past years' records of the costs of treatment of relatively common issues, such as appendix surgery, and define a maximum price-cap. This cap becomes mandatory for the health care facilities, and prices will often tend to converge towards this upper limit. The price-caps are usually determined in a negotiated process between the providers and the local government as described in Chapter 5. Local experimentation often starts only with a few diseases and one or several pilot hospitals.

Bibliography

Bunkenborg, Mikkel 2012, Organizing Rural Health Care. In *Organizing Rural China, Rural China Organizing*, ed. Ane Bislev and Stig Thøgersen, 141–156. Lanham, MD: Lexington Books.

Caishe 2004, 1, Caizhengbu, Minzhengbu guanyu yinfa "nongcun yiliao jiuzhu jijin guanli shixing banfa" de tongzhi (Notification from the MoF and the MoCA about the "Trial Measure for Financial Administration in Rural Medical Assistance").

Carrin, Guy *et al.* 1999, The Reform of the Rural Cooperative Medical System in the People's Republic of China: Interim Experience in 14 Pilot Counties, in: *Social Science and Medicine*, 48, 7, 961–972.

Chen, Zhu and Mao Zhang (eds) 2013, *Zhongguo xinxing nongcun hezuo yiliao fazhan baogao 2002–2012 nian (The NRCMS Development Report 2002–2012)*, Beijing: Renmin Weisheng Chubanshe (People's Health Press).

China News 2006, Zhongguo xinxing nongcun hezuo yiliao shangwei jianli wending changxiao chouzi jizhi (NRCMS Still Lacks a Stable and Sustainable Financing Mechanism), online: http://news.qq.com/a/20060928/001241.htm (accessed July 4, 2014).

CPC 2007, *Shandong shishi "360 gongcheng" gaishan nongcun yiliao tiaojian (Shandong Implements the 360 Project to Improve the Conditions in Rural Health Care)*, online: http://cpc.people.com.cn/GB/67481/94156/105719/105724/107203/6631932. html (accessed September 12, 2012).

Fang, Jing 2008, The Chinese Health Care Regulatory Institutions in an Era of Transition, in: *Social Science and Medicine*, 66, 4, 952–962.

Gao, Guangying 2008, Gonggu he fazhan juyou Zhongguo tese de xinxing nongcun hezuo yiliao baozhang zhidu (Stabilizing and Developing the NRCMS with Chinese Characteristics). In *Yiliao weisheng lüpishu—Zhongguo yiliao weisheng fazhan baogao No. 4 (Green Book of Health Care—Annual Report on China's Health Care No. 4)*, ed. Lexun Du *et al.*, 118–142. Beijing: Shehui Kexue Wenxian Chubanshe (Social Sciences Academic Press).

Gao, Qiang 2006, *Renzhen shishi "Nongcun weisheng fuwu tixi jianshe yu fazhan guihua" quanmian tigao nongcun weisheng fuwu nengli de shuiping (Seriously Implement the "Construction and Development Plan for the Rural Health Service System" to Comprehensively Increase Rural Health Service Capacity)*, online: http://www.moh.gov.cn/publicfiles/business/htmlfiles/mohbgt/s9635/200903/39461.htm (accessed September 11, 2012).

Gong, Sen, Wei Wang and Liejun Wang 2010, Gaige yu wanshan woguo yaopin jizhong caigou zhidu de zhengce yanjiu (Policy Study of the Reform and Improvement of the Centralized Bidding and Purchasing System for Medicines). In *Shipin yaopin anquan jianguan zhengce yanjiu baogao 2010 (The 2010 Research Report on Regulatory Policy in Food and Drug Safety)*. Shipin yaopin lanpishu (Blue Book of Food and Drug Security), ed. Minhao Tang, 262–279: Shehui Kexue Wenxian Chubanshe (Social Sciences Academic Press).

Guobanfa 2000, 16, Guowuyuan Bangongting zhuanfa Guowuyuan Tigaiban deng bumen guanyu chengzhen yiyao weisheng gaige de zhidao yijian de tongzhi (Notification from the General Office of the State Council about the Leading Opinion of the State Commission for Restructuring and other Departments on Urban Health Reform).

Guobanfa 2001, 39, Guowuyuan Bangongting zhuanfa Guowuyuan Tigaiban deng bumen "Guanyu nongcun weisheng gaige yu fazhan zhidao yijian de tongzhi" (Notification from the General Office of the State Council about the Leading Opinion of the State Commission for Restructuring on Rural Health Reform and Development).

Guobanfa 2003, 3, Guowuyuan Bangongting zhuanfa Weishengbu deng bumen guanyu jianli xinxing nongcun hezuo yiliao zhidu yijian de tongzhi (Notification from the General Office of the State Council about the Opinion of the MoH and Other Departments on Establishing the NRCMS).

Guobanfa 2004, 3, Guowuyuan Bangongting zhuanfa Weishengbu deng bumen guanyu jinyibu zuohao xinxing nongcun hezuo yiliao shidian gongzuo zhidao yijian de tongzhi (Notification from the General Office of the State Council about the Leading Opinion of the MoH and Other Departments on Further Improving the NRCMS Pilot Work).

Guobanfa 2011, 32, Guowuyuan Bangongting zhuanfa Fazhan Gaigewei, Caizhengbu, Weishengbu guanyu qingli huajie jiceng yiliao weisheng jigou zhaiwu yijian de tongzhi (Notification from the General Office of the State Council about the Opinion of the DRC, the MoF, and the MoH on Settling the Debt of Grassroots Healthcare Facilities).

Guoweijicengfa 2013, 17, Guanyu zuohao 2013 xinxing nongcun hezuo yiliao gongzuo de tongzhi (Notification about Accomplishing NRCMS-Related Work in 2013).

Guoyaoguanshi 2000, 306, Guanyu yinfa yaopin zhaobiao daili jigou zige rending ji jiandu guanli banfa de tongzhi (Notification about the Decree on the Necessary Qualifications and the Administrative Supervision of Medicines Bidding Agencies).

Klotzbücher, Sascha 2006, *Das ländliche Gesundheitswesen der VR China: Strukturen, Akteure, Dynamik (The Rural Health Sector of the People's Republic of China: Actors, Structures, Dynamic)*, Frankfurt: Peter Lang.

Li, Peilu and Xianwei Feng 2009, Woguo nongcun yiliao jiuzhu zhidu de xianzhuang, wenti yu duice (China's Rural Medical Assistance System—Current Situation, Problems and Solutions), in: *Zhongguo Weisheng Shiye Guanli (China Health Affairs Management)*, 8.

Liu, Kui 2007, "Shiyiwu" woguo nongcun weisheng fuwu tixi jianshe zhanwang (The Prospects of the Construction of the Rural Health Service Network in the Eleventh Five-Year Plan Period), in: *Zhongguo Yixue Zhuangbei (China Medical Equipment)*, 3, 7.

Liu, Peng 2011, *Zhuanxing zhong de jianguan xing guojia jianshe: jiyu dui Zhongguo yaopin guanli tizhi bianqian—1949–2008—de anli yanjiu (Building the Regulatory State in Transition: A Case-Based Study on the Change of China's System of Drug Administration—1949–2008)*, Beijing: Zhongguo Shehui Kexue Chubanshe (China Social Science Press).

Liu, Yuanli, Keqin Rao and Shanlian Hu 2002, *People's Republic of China: Towards Establishing a Rural Health Protection System*, online: www.sino.uni-heidelberg.de/a rchive/documents/health/liuyanli040825.pdf (accessed August 1, 2012).

Meng, Qingyue 2005, Review of Health Care Provider Payment Reforms in China, Background Paper for the World Bank Rural Health Report, Washington, DC: World Bank.

MoH (ed.) 2009, *Weishengbu xinxing nongcun hezuo yiliao yanjiu zhongxin keti yanjiu baogao huibian, 2006–2008 (Compilation of Research Reports of the NRCMS Research Center of the MoH, 2006–2008)*, Beijing.

MoH 2011, *Zhongguo weisheng tongji nianjian (China Statistical Yearbook of Health)*, Beijing: Zhongguo Xiehe Yike Daxue Chubanshe (China Harmony and Medicine University Press).

Müller, Armin 2016, Hukou and Health Insurance Coverage for Migrant Workers, in: *Journal of Current Chinese Affairs*, 45, 2, 53–82.

PEG (ed.) 2006, *Fazhan zhong de Zhongguo xinxing nongcun hezuo yiliao—Xinxing nongcun hezuo yiliao shidian gongzuo pinggu baogao (China's NRCMS in Development—The NRCMS Pilot Evaluation Report)*, Beijing: Renmin Weisheng Chubanshe (People's Health Press).

Powell-Jackson, Timothy, Winnie C.-M. Yip and Wei Han 2015, Realigning Demand and Supply Side Incentives to Improve Primary Health Care Seeking in Rural China, in: *Health Economics*, 24, 6, 755–772.

Ramesh, M., Xun Wu and Alex J. He 2014, Health Governance and Healthcare Reforms in China, in: *Health Policy and Planning*, 29, 6, 663–672.

Sun, Xiaoyun *et al.* 2009, Prescribing Behaviour of Village Doctors under China's New Cooperative Medical Scheme, in: *Social Science and Medicine*, 68, 10, 1775–1779.

Tam, Waikeung 2008, Failing to Treat: Why Public Hospitals in China Do Not Work, in: *The China Review*, 8, 2, 103–130.

Tam, Waikeung 2011, Organizational Corruption by Public Hospitals in China, in: *Crime, Law and Social Change*, 56, 3, 265–282.

Tian, Xin, Yaran Song and Xinping Zhang 2012, National Essential Medicines List and Policy Practice: A Case Study of China's Health Care Reform, in: *BMC Health Services Research*, 12, 1, 401.

Wagstaff, Adam *et al.* 2009, *Reforming China's Rural Health System*, Washington, DC: World Bank.

Wang, Jingyuan 2008, *Xinxing nongcun hezuo yiliao zhishi wenda (Questions and Answers on the NRCMS)*, Beijing: Beijing Daxue Yixue Chubanshe (Peking University Medical Press).

Wang, Lusheng (ed.) 2010, *Xinxing nongcun hezuo yiliao zhifu fangshi gaige shidian yanjiu baogao (Experimentation with Provider Payment Reform in NRCMS)*, Beijing: Beijing Daxue Yixue Chubanshe (Peking University Medical Press).

Weibannongweifa 2005, 243, Weishengbu Bangongting guanyu jiaqiang hezuo yiliao dingdian yiliao jigou yiyao feiyong guanli de ruogan yijian (Some Opinions from the General Office of the MoH on Controlling Health Costs at Approved NRCMS Healthcare Facilities).

Weiguicaifa 2000, 232, Guanyu yinfa yiliao jigou yaopin jizhong zhaobiao caigou shidian gongzuo ruogan guiding de tongzhi (Notification about Several Regulations Regarding the Piloting of the Concentrated Bidding and Purchasing of Drugs for Healthcare Facilities).

Weiguicaifa 2000, 148, Weishengbu guanyu jiaqiang yiliao jigou yaopin jizhong zhaobiao caigou shidian guanli gongzuo de tongzhi (Notification from the MoH about Strengthening the Administration of Bidding and Purchasing Pilots for Health Facilities' Medicines).

Weiguicaifa 2008, 6, Weishengbu, Guojia Zhongyiyao Guanliju guanyu jiaqiang yiliao jigou jiage guanli, kongzhi yiyao feiyong bu heli zengzhang de tongzhi (Notification from the MoH and the National Administrative Bureau for TCM about Strengthening Health Facilities' Price Administration and Controlling the Irrational Rise of Healthcare Costs).

Weinongweifa 2007, 82, Weishengbu Caizhengbu guanyu zuohao 2007 nian xinxing nongcun hezuo yiliao gongzuo de tongzhi (Notification from the MoH and the MoF about Completing NRCMS-Related Work in 2007).

Weinongweifa 2009, 68, Guanyu gongu he fazhan xinxing nongcun hezuo yiliao zhidu de yijian (Opinion on Consolidating and Developing NRCMS).

Wong, Christine 2009, Rebuilding Government for the 21st Century: Can China Incrementally Reform the Public Sector?, in: *The China Quarterly*, 200, 929–952.

World Bank 2007, *China—Public Services for Building the New Socialist Countryside*, online: www-wds.worldbank.org/external/default/WDSContentServer/WDSP/IB/ 2008/01/16/000020953_20080116091210/Rendered/PDF/402210CN.pdf   (accessed November 10, 2012).

Wu, Ting and Yingchun Chen 2011, Hubei Sheng xiangzhen weishengyuan jiben jianshexing zhaiwu yu caizheng touru tizhi tantao (Discussion of Capital Construction Debt and Budgetary Investment in THC in Hubei Province), in: *Yixue yu Shehui (Medicine and Society)*, 24, 1, 21–23.

Xu, Jie 2001, Xiangcun weisheng fuwu yitihua guanli ruogan wenti—Zhong (Problems of the Integrated Management of Township and Village Health Services—Part Two), in: *Weisheng Jingji Yanjiu (Health Economics Research)*, 10, 11–12.

Yang, Dali 2009, *Regulatory Learning and its Discontents in China: Promise and Tragedy at the State Food and Drug Administration*, online: https://daliyang.files.wordp ress.com/2013/09/sfda.pdf (accessed July 18, 2016).

Yu, Baorong 2009, *Yigai zhi lu—guoji jingyan yu zhifu fangshi (Health Sector Reform: International Experience and Provider Payment System)*, Shandong: Shandong Daxue Chubanshe (Shandong University Press).

Zhang, Luying *et al.* 2010, Balancing the Funds in the New Cooperative Medical Scheme in Rural China: Determinants and Influencing Factors in Two Provinces, in: *The International Journal of Health Planning and Management*, 25, 2, 96–118.

Zhongfa 2002, 13, Zhonggong Zhongyang, Guowuyuan guanyu jinyibu jiaqiang weisheng gongzuo de jueding (Decision of the Central Committee and the State Council on Further Strengthening Rural Health Work).

Zhou, Xueguang, Yun Ai and Hong Lian 2012, The Limit of Bureaucratic Power in Organizations: The Case of the Chinese Bureaucracy. In *Rethinking Power in Organizations, Institutions, and Markets*, eds David Courpasson, Damon Golsorkhi and Jeffrey J. Sallaz, 81–111. Bingley: Emerald.

Zou, Wenkai 2008, *Nongcun xinxing yiliao baozhang zhengce yanjiu (Research on the New Rural Health Protection Policies)*, Changsha: Hunan Renmin Chubanshe (Hunan People's Press).

7   Health Insurance and the New Health Reform

The New Health Reform in 2009 (Zhongfa 2009, 6) was enacted as a reaction to the SARS crisis in 2003, and the subsequent debate on the healthcare system in the PRC. As in the 1991 CMS initiative, fundamental criticisms on the "marketization" of healthcare were voiced, and the market-oriented reform model became only one of several options on the table. The opposing policy orientations, most notably of different ministerial bodies, were brought into public debate by intellectuals closely affiliated with those ministries, which constitutes an unprecedented level of transparency in the policy process (Huang 2013).

The New Health Reform aimed at a comprehensive transformation of the Chinese health system and a restoration of its public welfare orientation. Much like the earlier comprehensive health reforms of 1997 and 2002, it has become an umbrella of a vast array of policies, most of which had been experimented with before in some localities. Due to specific features in China's policy process, genuinely new policies are rarely tried on a national scale without *ex ante* policy experimentation (Heilmann 2008). Yip and Hsiao have provided a tentative assessment of the accomplishments of the various initiatives under the New Health Reform umbrella (Yip et al. 2012; Yip and Hsiao 2015).

This chapter reconnects to Chapter 2 in summarizing the ongoing institutional changes regarding health service providers, risk protection and health insurance, and market regulation under the New Health Reform. Furthermore, it connects to Chapters 5 and 6 with regard to the determinants of local provider behavior, and the potential of the New Health Reform to create a more coherent institutional setting. The New Health Reform is not analyzed in its entirety; the focus is on the areas of importance in the framework of this study.

The first part will analyze the field of risk protection and health insurance. Even though it was integrated into the New Health Reform, the decisive steps in NRCMS policy development and implementation had already been completed by 2009. The second part will analyze the field of market regulation, where there have been quite substantial changes. Most notably, the Essential Medicines policy has established the new national Essential Medicines list as a common frame of reference, and abolished drug profits for some healthcare providers. The third part will analyze the reform of healthcare providers, which is currently the most problematic field. Despite substantial efforts towards a rationalization of the business model of Chinese hospitals and grassroots healthcare providers, progress has been gradual and there are questions regarding the sustainability of the achievements.

Risk Protection and Health Insurance

Reshuffling Administrative Competences

The extension of health insurance and public risk protection was framed as one of the central fields of the New Health Reform, but the crucial advances had been made in the years before 2009. Three main public health insurance programs are operating in China: the UEBMI for urban employees, established in 1998; the NRCMS for rural residents, established in 2002; and the URBMI for urban residents, established in 2007. The three insurances are linked to different institutional foundations, which rendered the system fragmented along the lines of formal employment contracts and household registration. The main institutional basis for the UEBMI is the formal employment contract system, so it mainly covers urban citizens in the formal sector. The NRCMS and the URBMI, on the other hand, are mainly tied to the household registration system: as a rule of thumb, every household and citizen was to enroll in the locality of registration. The UEBMI is funded on the basis of parity between employers and employees, like a classic social insurance. The URBMI and the NRCMS are primarily tax-financed and funded via matching funds with contributions from all levels of government. This fragmented structure received a legal formalization and guarantee through the Chinese Social Insurance Law, which was enacted in 2010 (Renda 2010).

The NRCMS has been largely administered by the health bureaucracy, which is often seen as dominated by the interests of the medical profession. The UEBMI and the URBMI are under the jurisdiction of the MoHRSS, as are the different pension insurance programs, which renders the NRCMS an exception. The NRCMS is badly adjusted to urbanization and the mobility of the rural population due to its tight coupling to the *hukou* system in terms of enrollment, financing, administration, service provision and reimbursement (Müller 2016a). Under the New Health Reform, there has been increasing competition between the MoHRSS, the MoH and the insurance industry regarding administrative competences and jurisdictions in public health insurance programs. It has been accompanied by critical discussions of the MoH-dominated administrative model. Nevertheless, the newly founded CHFP remains a very strong player, and the county-level bureaus of health have a considerable leeway to obstruct a transfer of administrative jurisdiction over the NRCMS to another department in the course of urban–rural integration.

Urban social insurance bureaus emerged as competitors to the bureaus of health in the administration of the NRCMS during the pilot stage. In early 2004, the counties of Suichang and Tonglu in Zhejiang Province conducted preliminary evaluations of their NRCMS pilots and transferred the administrative responsibility from the bureau of health to the bureau of social insurance, which belonged to the line bureaucracy of the MoLSS. The change was motivated by a number of factors, including the relatively small rural populations in those counties and the comparatively high costs of dual administrative structures, the new administrative organs' greater administrative capacity and distance from the interests of the medical profession, as well as considerations of integrating the urban and rural healthcare systems. At the central level, this positioned the MoLSS as a competitor for the MoH regarding the competence for NRCMS administration (Shao 2007: 118–53).

Competition intensified in 2007, when the State Council enacted the URBMI policy. The URBMI was a health insurance system for the non-agricultural population not covered by the UEBMI system, enacted in 1998. The URBMI's mode of financing and administration, as well as the policy design strongly resembled the NRCMS, but it was placed under the jurisdiction of the MoLSS and administrated by the local social insurance bureaus. The provinces were to select two to three cities to pilot the system in 2007, and roll it out fully by 2010. The introduction of the URBMI intensified the competition between the MoH and the MoLSS in the field of health insurance: the MoH was now in charge of only one out of three public health insurance systems (Guofa 2007, 20).

In the following years, competences in social security were concentrated at the MoLSS. In 2008, it was merged with the Ministry of Personnel to form the MoHRSS. The new body was subsequently integrated into the NRCMS inter-ministerial conference. In 2009, a new rural pension insurance program was enacted, which was financed in a similar way to the NRCMS (Guofa 2009, 32). In 2011, a parallel pension program for urban residents not covered by social pension insurance followed (Guofa 2011, 18). In the course of administrative restructuring at the central level, the MoH was integrated with the NPFP to form the CHFP. In the course of this shift, it officially lost the jurisdiction over the NRCMS to the MoHRSS (Guobanfa 2013, 22). The implementation was scheduled to take six months, but was delayed. Although some provinces arguably organized the transfer swiftly, others delayed the process and/or installed cooperative arrangements between the two line bureaucracies.

For the NRCMS, a transfer from the CHFP to the MoHRSS has various potential benefits. First, it allows local governments to concentrate administrative and human resources for insurance management in one single organ. Second, it allows for a better coordination between the NRCMS and the other health insurance systems in a local context. This way, both systems can be better adapted to processes of urbanization and *hukou* transfer. However, due to the monopolistic structures of healthcare provision, the local bureaus of health have powerful instruments to defend their interests. This can pose substantial difficulties to such a transfer, and the local branches of the MoHRSS remain dependent on the bureaus of health (Müller 2016a; Shao 2007: 150ff.).

Furthermore, the insurance industry continued to lobby for an improvement of its position in the new policy regime after its integration into the NRCMS inter-ministerial conference in 2005. In 2010, the central government launched a program to enhance the health protection of children against serious illness (*ertong zhongda jibing yiliao baozhang*), which was to cover several severe child illnesses connected to high costs (Weinongweifa 2010, 53). Some insurance companies demonstrated their "public welfare orientation" by providing their services to local governments in poverty counties to aid the initiative (Caijing 2014). Survey research for the National Health Service Survey in 2011 found that catastrophic health expenditures were still a very common phenomenon in China, despite the extension of health insurance to the vast majority of the population (Meng et al. 2012). The finding arguably helped open a window of opportunity to increase the role of the insurance industry (Nanfang Zhoumo, September 5, 2012). In August, six ministerial organs, including the DRC, the MoH and the CIRC, announced the creation of a Catastrophic Disease Insurance: the program would use a certain share of the funding for the NRCMS and the URBMI to purchase insurance from commercial insurance companies for a specified selection of illnesses (Fagaishehui 2012, 2605). Interestingly, much like the NRCMS program, this policy was enacted before the Eighteenth Party Congress and the takeover of the Xi Jinping administration, and thus cannot simply be interpreted as a pro-market initiative of the new government (cf. Liu and Rao 2006).

The Catastrophic Disease Insurance funds were largely pooled at the city level, and the contracting model of administration shows some resemblance to the previous Ningbo model of NRCMS administration. The details of the new initiative were to be clarified by the provincial governments. By 2014, nine insurance companies, including China Life and Ping An, were arguably operating the Catastrophic Disease Insurance in more than 130 pilot cities in 27 provinces, covering 290 million urban and rural citizens. Most cities arguably only allocated between RMB 15 and RMB 50 per capita to Catastrophic Disease Insurance, which equaled 4.3 to 14.3 percent of the overall minimum NRCMS per capita funding of RMB 350 in 2013. Despite the relatively small amounts, the efforts of the insurance industry begin to materialize in a stronger role in China's emerging welfare regime (Caijing 2014).

In April 2012, another document that specified the regulatory guidelines for the participation of insurance companies in the NRCMS administration was issued by the MoH, the CIRC, the MoF and the Small Leadership Group for Deepening Health System Reform. The focus continued to be on the non-profit delegation model. In 2014, the CHFP's annual document on the focus of NRCMS work emphasized the role of commercial insurance companies in the cross-provincial extension of NRCMS coverage. Due to the tight linkup and systemic interdependence between the NRCMS and the *hukou* system, migrant workers were usually covered by the NRCMS, but could not use it in the cities where they worked (Müller 2016a). Commercial insurance companies' incentive structures are potentially more suitable for such cross-border insurance than those of local governments, and thus could constitute a comparative advantage (CHFP 2014, 39; Weinongweifa 2012, 27).

The Extension of Health Insurance Coverage

By 2010, the vast majority of Chinese citizens were covered by one of the three public health insurance programs. However, in terms of the types of medical services and the share of health costs covered, there were vast differences between the programs. Figure 7.1 illustrates the extension of health insurance coverage in the Chinese population in the 2000s. The most substantial rise was generated by the NRCMS program, whereas coverage of the UEBMI and the URBMI progressed more gradually and on a lower level. By 2013, the NRCMS covered about 59 percent of the Chinese population, and was thus the largest insurance program. The UEBMI and the URBMI covered about 20 and 22 percent respectively. NRCMS and URBMI coverage was primarily based on *hukou*, whereas the UEBMI was primarily based on labor contracts. Due to the different institutional foundations, there were gaps and overlaps between the systems. Overall coverage of public health insurance is therefore lower than the sum of the three systems.

Figure 7.2 illustrates the financial input and output of the three health insurance systems, and their share in overall per capita healthcare financing. The UEBMI is the most robust of the health insurance systems. It has the highest per capita revenues, and its per capita expenditures covered about 66 percent of overall per capita healthcare financing in 2013. The NRCMS and the URBMI had comparable absolute levels of funding; however, their coverage of health costs plays out very differently due to the different levels of per capita health costs in urban and rural China. In 2013, NRCMS per capita expenditures covered about 28 percent of rural per capita health costs,

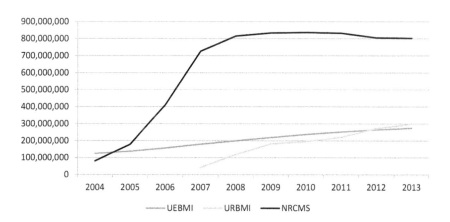

Figure 7.1 Extension of Health Insurance Coverage in the 2000s
Sources: CHFP 2014b; MoH 2009b.

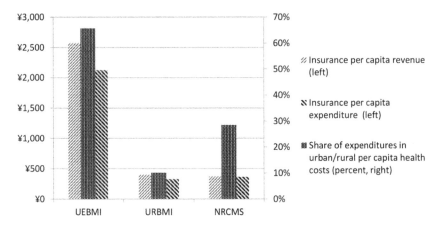

Figure 7.2 Insurance Revenues, Expenditures and Share in Per Capita Health Costs 2013
Sources: CHFP 2014b; MoHRSS 2014.

whereas the respective figure for the URBMI was only 10 percent. These figures are derived from official Chinese statistics and should be interpreted as a best-case scenario, in which the systems are fully funded and operating effectively. The implementation gaps described in Chapter 6 potentially decrease the financial capacity and cost coverage, most notably for the NRCMS.

The share of per capita insurance expenditures in per capita health costs points to the aggregate role of insurance in financing healthcare (Xu et al. 2010). It is a more accurate measure than the high levels of coverage indicated by local and central administrative documents. In 2011, for example, the center called for inpatient reimbursement rates to be raised to 70 percent (Weinongweifa 2011: 27). There was, however, a substantial gap between nominal and effective reimbursement rates for several reasons. First, on the regulatory level, the positive lists for services and drugs caused varying degrees of overlap between services and drugs approved for reimbursement on the one hand, and those actually used during treatment on the other. The degree of overlap depended on the quality of the positive lists and the incentive structures they created for the providers. As noted above, collusion between patients and doctors could under certain circumstances enlarge the overlap and thus improve insurance coverage. An internal MoH study of one city in 2007 found the overall share of health costs eligible for reimbursement to be 72.2 percent, with THCs having the highest rates (86.8 percent). Only 18.2 percent of drug costs and 9.8 percent of the costs for diagnostic services were eligible for reimbursement, which shows that the revenue-generating service items were largely excluded by the positive lists. The effective reimbursement rate in the city was only 21.5 percent on average (MoH 2009a: 513).

Second, low administrative capacity was also an important factor, most notably the inadequate ability to forecast the amount of reimbursements accurately. Quite often, the reimbursement catalogs did not fit the nominal amount of funding of the NRCMS, and thus promised higher benefits than the system could deliver. Yi et al. (2009), for example, report from a study of 25 counties in rural China that formal reimbursement rates for catastrophic health costs over 4,000 RMB in 2007 were 59 to 60 percent at a THC and 48 to 49 percent at a county hospital. The effective reimbursement rate for all facilities, however, was only 8 to 11 percent, and even if the entire NRCMS funds had been used for inpatient reimbursement, the effective reimbursement rate would not have risen above 20 percent. The prevalence of conservative fund management is closely related to this: most local governments shied away from direct reimbursement for inpatient services to avoid the risks of overspending (Zhang et al. 2010). An internal report of the MoH on Central China indicates that, in 2006, on average only 71 percent of the NRCMS funds were actually spent (MoH 2009a: 64f.). In many areas, the NRCMS funds retained high surpluses until the end of the year, when the adminis-trators had a clearer picture of the overall amount of reimbursements. The central government therefore issued upper limits for the funds surplus and called for the use of second rounds of reimbursement at year's end to spend the additional surplus (Weinongweifa 2008, 65). The low ability to forecast was also rooted in the low administrative expenditures for the NRCMS administration, and may improve when local health insurance administration is integrated under the social insurance bureaus.

Third, the actual amount of financial resources in the NRCMS funds was often smaller than the nominal amount. Two crucial mechanisms causing this phenomenon have been described in previous chapters: shortfalls in local governments' NRCMS contributions, and innovations and informal practices in the premium collection process. Shortfalls in local contributions could be caused by a lack of fiscal resources at the local level, or a lack of incentives to allocate fiscal resources to the NRCMS funds. Premium collection was affec-ted by the contradiction between universal coverage and voluntary enroll-ment, and furthermore it was a burdensome and costly activity of local cadres that they tried to avoid if possible (Müller 2016b). The premiums and local contributions by 2011 still constituted 20 percent of the overall NRCMS funding.

Fourth, the NRCMS facilitated rising health costs, as it came to compen-sate for the structural gaps in budgetary funding of the healthcare providers, which appropriated parts of the NRCMS funds by inducing demand and other strategies. Both the capacity and the incentives of local governments to supervise and sanction the providers' behavior are limited. There are local differences regarding the intensity of such effects, both within and between county-level jurisdictions. More research is needed to determine the cost-driving impact of the systemic interdependence and misfit institutions com-pared with other factors such as the demographic transition. This complexity also makes it difficult to determine the level of effective benefits that the NRCMS actually provides, and which is arguably also subject to substantial local variation despite the uniform standards of funding.

The burden of medical expenditures on the rural population has continued to grow since the introduction of the NRCMS. Figure 7.3 illustrates health expenditures as a share of consumer expenditures (*yiliao baojian zhichu zhan xiaofeixing zhichu* %) of urban and rural citizens over the past decade, as indicated in the *Statistical Yearbook of Health*. The financial pressure of health costs on urban citizens has been gradually decreasing, whereas it has been increasing continuously for rural citizens. Between 2008 and 2013, ill-ness-induced poverty has thus arguably been stagnating or decreasing in the urban areas, but increasing in the rural areas. Neither the financial upgrading of the NRCMS nor the New Health Reform so far has been able to slow down or reverse this trend. Even though these results depend on several fac-tors, including the development of rural incomes and the demographic tran-sition, they nevertheless cast serious doubts on the effectiveness of the NRCMS and the New Health Reform regarding some of their core goals in rural China.

Market Regulation: Realigning Provider Incentives

Market regulation is one of the central targets of the New Health Reform. Overall, its initiatives aim at rationalizing the pricing system and improving the incentives of doctors. Drug markets have seen very thorough changes with

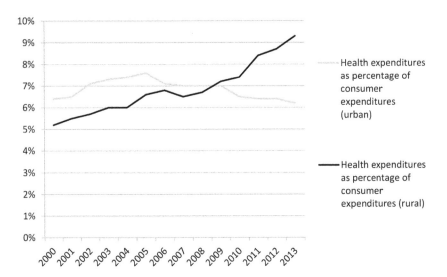

Figure 7.3 The Financial Burden of Households' Medical Expenditures in Urban and Rural China

the implementation of the Essential Medicines system, which aims at increasing the use of cost-effective generics and gradually abolishing the profit margins for such drugs. Furthermore, it regulates the drug supply channels for the Essential Medicines. Under Xi Jinping, the scope of the state pricing system for drugs has been significantly reduced to increase the role of bidding and insurance funds for cost control. In service pricing, higher cost-recovery rates are to be achieved via general price reforms or provider payment reforms.

The combination of policy instruments of the Essential Medicines program is not a genuinely new measure. There have been local experiments that preceded the enactment and implementation. For example, Klotzbücher (2006: 241–68) described health reform projects in North-Western China initiated in the late 1990s that also aimed at decreasing profit margins for drugs, increasing cost-recovery rates for services and regulating drug purchasing. These projects relied on substantial external funding, which allowed county governments in those poor areas to pay salaries for the local doctors and thus provide a basis for the reform. Nevertheless, some elements such as raising cost-recovery rates of services were not well accepted among the rural population. Ultimately, project funding was discontinued and the projects proved financially unsustainable.

At first, the Essential Medicines program came only with limited central compensations for the financial losses it inflicted on grassroots healthcare providers. This raised doubts about its effectiveness and financial sustainability (Müller 2015). Subsequently, financial support has been gradually increased, which arguably contributed to a partial consolidation. More research is needed about the financial arrangements of the reform, most notably at the sub-provincial levels, and how they fit in with the changing patterns of fiscal resource allocation there. For the original goals of the program to be achieved, a further expansion of financial support and stronger supervision arrangements will be necessary

The New Essential Medicines Program and Drug Pricing

In 2009, the central government initiated the Essential Medicines program of the New Health Reform, which envisioned fundamental transformations in the circulation and use of medical drugs. Like the NRCMS, many of the components of the Essential Medicines program had been piloted and tested in different localities and provinces before. A central component of the policy was a list of Essential Medicines, which was not an innovation as such. Since 1982, China had followed the WHO's Essential Medicines program and drafted lists of Essential Medicines based on the WHO lists. The WHO's Essential Medicines program aims at providing guidelines for efficacious, safe and cost-effective drugs that satisfy the basic healthcare needs of the majority of the population and should be universally available. During the 1990s and 2000s, China's Essential Medicines lists included more than 2,000 medicines, of which less than 50 percent were Western medicines. Access to Essential

Medicines has often been limited and problematic: pharmaceutical companies lacked the incentives to produce them due to low profit margins, and the unnecessary high level of drug expenditures in China has partly been caused by this situation. Chen and colleagues summarize that "manufacturers, retail pharmacies, and hospital pharmacies paid limited attention to China's 2004 [Essential Medicines list] in their decisions to manufacture, purchase, and stock essential medicines ... prescribing of essential medicines was frequently inappropriate" (Chen et al. 2010; see also: Tian et al. 2012; Yang et al. 2010).

The 2009 Essential Medicines program promoted a more comprehensive approach to drug policy, which linked the Essential Medicines list to specific purchasing and pricing regulations. The 2009 list reduced the number of Essential Medicines to 307—205 Western types and 102 Chinese types. It was much more restrictive than previous lists, but provided a largely reasonable and adequate portfolio of pharmaceuticals. The provinces were allowed to issue complementary Essential Medicines catalogs. The provincial catalogs were to compensate for the lack of certain medicines in the central catalog, which were necessary for grassroots healthcare work or the treatment of chronic diseases, or whose usage was regionally specific. In fact, the provincial catalogs remained strongly oriented towards local medical practices. The selection of medicines thus remained somewhat arbitrary and inefficient, and the links between doctors and pharmaceutical producers were not severed as originally envisioned. The central Essential Medicines catalog was harmonized with the positive lists for the different health insurance programs, and Essential Medicines were to be reimbursed at higher rates than others (Tian et al. 2012; Weiyaozhengfa 2009: 78).

The competence of purchasing drugs in the Essential Medicines catalog was centralized at the provincial level: provincial governments were to organize auctions and bulk purchases for Essential Medicines, and to ensure their distribution to the local healthcare providers. Due to the absence of a reliable system of quality indicators, provincial purchasing organs potentially face similar problems as local purchasing organs in the 2000s: unable to determine the quality of a product in a reasonable amount of time, they relied on the experience of local doctors and/or purchasing the cheapest merchandise. This practice generates a risk of buying ineffective or low-quality medicines, and to some extent Essential Medicines suffered from such a reputation in China. More research is needed about how the quality of Essential Medicines is guaranteed in a dysfunctional regulatory environment (Weiyaozhengfa 2009: 78).

A crucial trend in the drug pricing system since 2009 is the abolition of public healthcare providers' profit margins for drug sales (Fagaijiage 2009: 2844). The Essential Medicines regulations introduced a zero-markup policy (*lingchalü*) for government-operated grassroots healthcare providers. This mainly affected THCs and Shequ service centers, which were required to sell Essential Medicines at the purchasing price; this in turn was determined by central auctions. Initially, local governments on the county or city level were in charge of compensating the affected providers for their losses, and the central government only gave partial financial support as a prize for good implementation (*yi jiang dai bu*) (Caishe 2010: 202). This support was converted into a permanent central fund of 9 billion RMB a year in 2012 (MoF 2014).

Under the New Health Reform, the scope and modes of government pricing changed substantially. Administrative documents of the DRC in 2009 defined the scope of public pricing to include medicines on the Essential Medicines catalogs and the positive lists of the basic medical insurances, as well as special medicines with a monopoly character. The center was in charge of defining the pricing policies, principles and methods, as well as directly setting the prices for the national Essential Medicines list and prescription and monopoly medicines on the basic health insurance list. Provincial governments were in charge of setting prices for over-the-counter drugs on the national Essential Medicines list and for the provincial supplementary Essential Medicines lists, as well as regulating medicines produced by public healthcare providers. Leading prices were reintroduced as the main instrument of public drug pricing, and the pharmaceutical companies were to set the retail prices in accordance with government regulation. The pharmaceutical sector was to focus on the production of generics, and the profit margins were to be set low for expensive drugs and high for cheap drugs to create incentives for cost control (Fagaijiage 2009: 2844).

In 2015, the central government decided to substantially reduce the scope of the public pricing system for drugs. The scope of market-based pricing (by the pharmaceutical companies) was to be substantially extended; bidding and health insurance were to replace leading prices as the primary tools of price control. The government would continue to apply fixed ex-factory and retail prices (*dingjia*) to anesthesia and class-A psychotropic drugs. For drugs listed on the positive lists of health insurance programs, new pricing mechanisms were to be created that rely on bidding and health insurance. This indicates that pricing will rely more strongly on bidding, bulk purchasing and negotiations with the health insurance administration, while the state-set maximum price caps fall away as a frame of reference. This may decrease the ambiguity of pricing regulations, which facilitated informal practices around bidding as described in Chapter 6. Further research will be needed in the coming years to assess the impact of these new reforms (Fagaijiage 2015: 904).

The research on the implementation of the Essential Medicines policy in recent years displays rather mixed results, which overall are in line with the argument presented in this book and the expectations it creates for the New Health Reform. Due to its political priority, the zero-markup policy has been widely implemented on the level of THCs, and some localities even extended the implementation to the village level. As a result, drug prices have decreased. This has, however, not always led to a more rational use of drugs, and practices such as overuse of antibiotics and parenteral routes of administration have often remained in place. Tang and colleagues (2013) see a direct connection between governmental financial support and doctors' tendency to overuse injections during treatment to generate profits. This points to the importance of institutional fit between public finances and health sector regulation emphasized in this study. Furthermore, various studies point to a low availability of Essential Medicines in some regions, which may be related to issues in local policy design or to low prices, leaving pharmaceutical companies without incentives to produce certain Essential Medicines (Fang et al. 2013; Jiang et al. 2013; Li et al. 2013; Yang et al. 2010; Yang et al. 2013a; Yang et al. 2013b).

For the NRCMS, the zero-markup policy can considerably reduce the gap between nominal and effective reimbursement rates. Where it is properly implemented, it restrains THCs' legitimate drug portfolio to Essential Medicines. On the level of formal regulation, the approved drug lists of the NRCMS are being standardized and harmonized. In medical practice, THCs should no longer have unlisted drugs in stock, which should prevent numerous informal practices, such as persuading patients to purchase cost-driving medicines or issuing false prescriptions. However, there are a number of issues potentially undermining the effectiveness of the Essential Medicines policies, even if implemented properly. It constitutes a fundamental intervention into providers' business models and needs to be accompanied by compensatory policies. Such compensatory policies should not just maintain the financial status quo, but provide formalized, viable and enforceable rules, and incentivize both local governments and providers to comply with those rules.

Service Pricing

While the New Health Reform brought substantial changes in the area of drug pricing, the institutional principles of service pricing initially remained the same. On the one hand, the administrative documents called for a rationalization of the service pricing system, which was to strengthen the value of labor in TCM and technical services as a calculation basis for the costs. Prices for diagnostic services and treatment involving technical equipment were to be decreased, and prices for basic medical services were to be raised. On the other hand, however, the "public goods" quality of basic medical service pricing was to be maintained, and the financial burden of the patients was not to be raised. The conflict between achieving structural reforms and maintaining the status quo constituted a substantial restraint for the reform of service prices. In administrative terms, the DRC, the MoH and the MoHRSS, as well as their provincial and local counterparts, were defined as the main stakeholders of service pricing (Fagaijiage 2009, 2844).

A major modification of the service pricing system was the "recommended DRG catalog" (*an bingzhong shoufei tuijian mulu*), in which the DRC, the MoH and the MoHRSS proposed 104 types of diseases with specific treatments connected to them as a basis for pricing. It was based on the previous experimentation with provider payment and clinical pathway reforms, and meant to serve as a common frame of reference for old and new pilot projects. The provincial counterparts of the three ministerial organs were put in charge of determining the price levels for the aggregated disease- and treatment-categories. Following the logic of the general service pricing system, the catalog introduces an alternative to the national list of service items (Fagaijiage 2011: 674).

Other central initiatives of pricing reform were, as in drug pricing, targeted at specific types of healthcare providers. For grassroots providers, the general diagnosis and treatment fee (*yiban zhenliao fei*) integrates the former fees for registration, diagnosis, injections and pharmaceutical services. The fee should be 10 RMB as a national average, and the authority of setting the specific level of the fees was delegated to the provincial organs of pricing, health and human resources and social security. Payment for drugs remained separate. On the one hand, the general diagnosis and treatment fee was conceived as compensation for the zero-markup policy and should be integrated into the health insurance reimbursement catalogs accordingly. On the other hand, it should also not raise the overall financial burden of the rural population, which arguably restrains its compensatory effects (Guobanfa 2010: 62).

Under Xi Jinping's administration, a central adaptation to the pricing system was to rearrange the connection between provider status, service items and service pricing. Before, the national catalog of service items was the mandatory frame of reference for all healthcare providers, while all non-profit facilities were required to follow public service pricing—irrespective of ownership status (Jijiage 2000: 1751). According to new regulations of the State Council and the DRC, adherence to the service catalog and public pricing for county hospitals is now dependent on the ownership status. Non-public providers are allowed to use market pricing—that is, set their own service prices. Non-public providers are to be integrated into the public health insurance systems as approved providers, and service pricing and provider payment methods are to be negotiated between them and the insurance administrative organs. Service pricing is the key to a rational business model for healthcare providers, so modifications in this area potentially have a large impact (Fagaijiage 2014: 503; Guofa 2013: 40).

Service Providers—Towards a Rationalization of Business Models

The New Health Reform has initiated thorough reforms of China's healthcare providers, which all in all move towards a rationalization of their business models and may ultimately decrease the governance problems in the health sector. The reforms of market regulation described in the previous sections cannot be fully separated from the provider reforms. The introduction of the NRCMS and the gradual expansion of financial transfers for public health are milestones on the way towards the creation of viable and sustainable funding arrangements. However, there still remains a lot of ground to cross towards clearing out the institutional misfits and thus creating the foundations for effective supervision and more formal operations in the health sector.

The regulatory reforms aim to transform the business models of the different types of providers in the healthcare system. THCs have been a central target of the New Health Reform from early on. Their pharmaceutical port-folio has been limited to the Essential Medicines catalog, and and drug profits have been formally abolished for them, with the losses to be compensated from public funds. Furthermore, the central government has set up a matching-funds mechanisms to finance public health at the level of THCs and village clinics. The reforms for village clinics have been less comprehensive, and so far do not seem to have substantially altered their business models.

Public hospital reform has been another main field of the New Health Reform, but progress on this front has initially been gradual and piecemeal. In 2012, a separate reform of public county hospitals was enacted. It offers local governments the choice either to fund their facilities appropriately or to privatize them. Privatized facilities are granted the right to set their own service prices, and thus can work sustainably without government support.

Grassroots Providers

China's grassroots healthcare providers are a main target of reform. The category of grassroots providers includes THCs and village clinics in the rural areas, Shequ health centers and stations, and a variety of other small health-care facilities. Table 7.1 gives an overview of the grassroots healthcare sector, listing the most important variables for the classification of its providers. It shows that THCs and village clinics are exclusively rural, whereas all other providers exist in both the rural and urban areas. A large share of the provi-ders are classified as non-profit and expected to adhere to the public pricing system. The recent shift to ownership status—if implemented—would reduce the scope of public service pricing across all categories, with the most remarkable changes for Shequ service stations. The private, for-profit provi-ders are most prevalent in the primary care sector, and more dominant in the urban areas. In the rural areas, however, these formal categories may often have little impact on the practical operations: informally, public non-profit providers may behave like private for-profit providers.

The regulations of the 2009 Essential Medicines policy primarily targeted government-operated (*zhengfu ban*) facilities. As Table 7.1 shows, this affects virtually all THCs and Shequ service centers, as well as half of the Shequ service stations, but only a small minority of the village clinics and other organs. The Essential Medicines system required them to limit their phar-maceutical portfolio to the drugs indicated by the Essential Medicines cata-logs. It furthermore required them to implement the zero-markup policy. As these providers usually only have limited technological capacity to pro-vide profitable services, their primary source of profits formally vanished (Weiyaozhengfa 2009: 78).

The provider reforms aim at a new business model with multiple venues of compensation in the long run. An opinion by the State Council in 2010 recommended three channels of compensation. First, the government was to support and subsidize THCs and Shequ centers, most notably construction,

Table 7.1 Grassroots Healthcare Providers by Location and Status in 2012

	Number	Urban	Rural	Publicly owned	Govern-ment-operated	Non-profit (2009)
Shequ ser-vice center	8,182	75%	25%	94%	79%	99%
Shequ ser-vice station	25,380	67%	33%	72%	52%	95%
Township health center	37,707	0%	100%	99%	99%	100%
Village clinic	653,419	0%	100%	58%	9%	67%
Outpatient department	10,134	76%	24%	28%	7%	35%
Various other clinics	177,798	51%	49%	18%	2%	23%

Sources: CHFP 2014b; MoH 2010.

equipment purchases and service provision in public health. Second, the general diagnosis and treatment fee was to provide some compensation. Third, any remaining structural deficits were to be compensated by public funds. The local and intra-provincial compensation arrangements of the early years came to be backed up in 2012, when the central compensation fund was consolidated (Guobanfa 2010: 62; MoF 2014).

One important milestone towards funded social functions at the grassroots level is the program for basic public health service equalization, which created a new channel of matching funds from all levels of government, similar to the one financing the NRCMS. The program allocates a certain per capita amount of money to grassroots providers for a specified set of services. Per capita financing rose from 15 RMB in 2009 to 45 RMB in 2016 (Guofa 2012: 11; Guoweijicengfa 2016: 27). However, the THCs are supposed to share this funding with the village clinics, which may give rise to conflicts of distribution. Although the overall level of funding via public health service equalization was rather limited during the first years of the New Health Reform, this program could become a crucial pillar of THC funding if it is sufficiently extended.

Sun Zhigang, the deputy secretary of the DRC and director of the State Council Bureau for the New Health Reform, highlighted the contradiction between THCs' functional responsibilities and their institutional constitution in 2010, emphasizing the need for a "comprehensive reform" (*zonghe gaige*) of their systems of administration, human resources, evaluation and financing (Sun 2011). Human resources are an important source of costs for THCs, the funding of which should be guaranteed if THC reforms are to be effective and sustainable. First, local governments would have to extend the *bianzhi* system of established public sector posts to cover a larger part of the THC sector. Traditionally, this system covers central THCs, but not regular THCs (Klotzbücher 2006). Via this channel, local governments can support basic salary payments of the THC health staff. In May 2011, the State Commission of Public Sector Reform issued guidelines for the establishments of *bianzhi* posts in THCs, together with the MoH and the MoF (Zhongyangbianbanfa 2011: 28). Some provincial governments had already issued similar standards and begun an extension of the *bianzhi* system among THCs in 2010. Second, local governments would have to pay sufficiently high shares of the basic salaries of *bianzhi* staff at THCs. Increased salary payments were reported in various THCs in the field, but the field counties were an above-average sample and often piloted the Essential Medicines reforms (Müller 2015). Third, central policies called for performance evaluations and a performance-based salary to become an essential part of the governance and steering of grassroots healthcare providers (Weibannongweifa 2011: 34). Providing for both the fixed and the variable parts of the salaries of the health staff would allow local governments to regain control of their incentive structures. This would be in line with the focus on state provision that implicitly guides THC reforms. However, without fiscal reforms to support such measures, there is an inherent danger of financial shortfalls to negatively affect the reforms.

Further financial revenue can be generated when local health insurances shift from service items to disease-based standards for compensating healthcare providers. A sustainable mode of funding THCs and Shequ centers will also depend on the general reform of health service prices. Service pricing reforms have been discussed in the second part of this chapter, and recent developments in this area will be analyzed in the section on public hospital reforms. Higher cost-recovery rates for health services would be an essential part of a more coherent and sustainable business model for THCs.

At a speech in Boston in 2014, the new minister of health admitted that finding a "scientific compensation mechanism" for the zero-markup policy was one of the targets of the new government (Li 2014). Although this statement leaves considerable room for interpretation, it points to the problem that the general mode of financing of Chinese grassroots healthcare providers remains in flux. Official statistics indicate that public funding for THCs has increased considerably, but it primarily stems from local government budgets, while cost-recovery rates for services have actually decreased (CHFP 2014b). During fieldwork in 2011, THC staff in A County and B County described reforms largely in accordance with the central policies. However, both counties were above-average localities in terms of health policy and pilots for the zero-markup policy, and they received fiscal transfers from the provincial level that supported the implementation. More research is needed to illuminate the modes of funding the different provinces have selected and assess their financial sustainability (Müller 2015).

The reform approaches for the lowest level of healthcare service providers—that is, village clinics, Shequ health service stations, outpatient departments and other clinics—have been less coherent and energetic. Many of them are formally public, non-profit facilities, as Table 7.1 illustrates, but this is often not backed up by public financial commitment. The policies for village clinics illustrate the persistence of the regulatory misfits. The New Health Reform called for strengthening the direct administration of village clinics by THCs, and their vertical integration with THCs to ensure their commitment to public health work (Weibannongweifa 2010: 48). The central government issued common national guidelines for the performance evaluation of THCs and village clinics (Weibannongweifa 2011: 34). As central regulations mainly required government-operated grassroots providers to fully implement the Essential Medicines and zero-markup policies, only a small share of village clinics should be affected. Some provinces have, however, made moves towards covering the village level as well. A 2014 administrative guideline for village clinics described them as publicly built, privately run and subsidized by the government (*gongjian, minying, zhengfu buzhu*) (Guoweijicengfa 2014: 33). Village clinics are officially entitled to subsidies from public health service equalization, which could become a crucial pillar of funding their social functions if the program's funding is expanded and the THCs actually share the resources with the village clinics.

The experiences with village clinic reforms in recent decades provide warning examples of ineffective or unsustainable policy approaches that strongly resemble the rationale of the New Health Reform. Vertical integration policies for village clinics have been pursued since the 1990s, mainly in order to control their supply and portfolio of drugs (Weijifunongweifa 1999: 37). However, such policies tended to create informal drug supply channels and markets alongside the formal ones where they did not involve a full organizational integration of the village clinic into the local THC; incomplete integration gave the THCs incentives and opportunities for cost shifting to the village clinics, whereas complete integration required a substantial financial commitment (Xu 2001). Vertical Integration thus mainly spread in Eastern China (Liu and Zhang 2010). Klotzbücher (2006) described similar experiences with externally funded projects in Western China, which displayed some key similarities with the core policies of the New Health Reform. Maintaining centralized control over the drug supply and decreasing the role of drug profits depended strongly on continued public financial support. Furthermore, raising service prices to compensate for decreasing drug profits was not well accepted by the rural population. To some extent, the CMS was used to neutralize the increases in service prices. Under the New Health Reform, there has so far been little compensation for decreased drug revenues via higher service prices, which raises questions regarding the sustainability of the new reform approach (Müller 2015).

In order to be sustainable and effective, such initiatives require substantial financial commitment. According to the arguments presented in this study, a crucial weakness of the New Health Reform's approach to the business model of grassroots providers is its critical reliance on local government funding. Local governments and grassroots health providers resemble each other in having a large array of formal duties, which are not backed up by the necessary public funding. Although such funding requirements are now more specific with regard to THCs, they remain rather vague for village clinics.

Public Hospital Reform

The reform of public hospitals (*gongli yiyuan gaige*) is one of the core initiatives of the New Health Reform, and the initiative which encountered the most obvious setbacks. The overarching goal was communicated as being to restore and preserve their "public welfare" orientation (*gongyixing*) by comprehensively reforming their organization, mode of operations and regulatory environment. It called not only for an overhaul of the governance structures but also for important changes in hospital financing: the role of drug profits should be systematically decreased, and compensated for by increased financial support from local governments and increased revenues for technical and drug-related services. A certain share of public hospitals was to be privatized so that government expenditures could be focused on fewer PSUs, and public and private hospitals were to enjoy equal treatment as contracted providers for public insurance systems and in other areas. Implementation of the reform was supposed to start in 2009, with 16 pilot cities under the direct supervision of the central government. The extension was planned for 2011 (Weiyiguanfa 2010: 20),

The first cohort of public hospital reform pilots did not, however, live up to the expectations. As Yip and Hsiao note,

> [P]ilots for public hospital reforms in 17 cities have failed to yield useful lessons for guiding policy formulation, due to both cursory design and lack of scientific evaluation. Powerful stakeholders—the hospitals and their physician staff—also blocked any meaningful reform.
>
> (Yip and Hsiao 2015: 58)

Dong et al. (2014) argue that public financing is still insufficient for converting public hospitals back into a public service.

Facing these results, the central government decided to shift the focus to public county hospitals during the twelfth five-year plan period (Guofa 2012: 11). The reform followed similar basic principles as the reform of THCs—that is, severing the tie between drugs, medical equipment and profits by raising the support from public budgets and adapting the service pricing system. About 300 pilot counties were to initiate the reform in 2012, and summarize their experiences by mid-2013 (Guobanfa 2012: 33). In 2014, the reform was to be extended to 50 percent of China's counties, and in 2015 it was to be fully rolled out (Guoweitigaifa 2014: 12). The reform mobilized public budgetary support from all levels of government, which is an important step towards the feasibility and sustainability of comprehensive hospital reform.

In June 2013, the CHFP issued an evaluation report of the first cohort that briefly summarized the diverse local practices. In financial terms, it estimated that the costs of reform—mainly caused by the zero-markup policy—had so far amounted to 4.5 billion RMB. In compensation, county hospitals had received RMB 2.4 billion in increased service revenue and RMB 0.9 billion in governmental transfers, which covered about three-quarters of their losses. About RMB 1.2 billion in revenue losses was not compensated for. These figures indicate a considerable progress towards a sustainable rationalization of the institutional structures in the health sector (CHFP 2014a).

Public hospital reform remains, however, a highly problematic field. In 2014, the central government called for a second cohort of 17 pilot cities for the larger public hospital reform; a third cohort of 66 cities followed in 2015 (Guoweitigaifa 2014, 21; Guoweitigaifa 2015: 62). The City of Chongqing became a pilot city of the second cohort, and issued a comprehensive reform of service prices in early 2015. It adapted 7,886 of its 9,128 service items, by and large decreasing the prices for services involving technological equipment by 25 percent, and increasing prices for diagnosis and nursing by 30 percent, and for treatment and surgery by 13 percent. Furthermore, it created service price differentials between different levels of healthcare providers in order to steer patients towards the grassroots facilities. The price reform was aborted after only seven days. According to media reports, the Chongqing reform disproportionally increased the health costs of certain patients, most notably those in need of long-term dialysis due to kidney disease (China Economic Times 2015; Chongqing Government Network 2015).

According to some reports, service and drug income remain the most important sources of hospital financing in 2015: even though governmental budgetary support rose, it fails to fully compensate for the financial losses caused by the reforms (China Economic Times 2015). Service pricing reforms arguably run the risk of burdening people with chronic diseases, the coverage of which is often not well developed in China's public insurance. The prevalence of chronic diseases rises with age, and they thus especially affect the elderly.

Summary

The New Health Reform aims at a comprehensive overhaul of the Chinese health system, which is to be completed by 2020. Its institutional approach has considerable potential to improve the operations of China's health system. Public health insurance has been extended to the vast majority of the population, even though the crucial milestones in this respect have been accomplished before the new health reform. Most of China's citizens now have some form of health insurance, which supports rather than replaces the household and family as the primary institutional foundation of social security.

Nevertheless, when looking at the financial burden of healthcare, the results seem rather mixed. In urban China, the average share of health expenditures in consumer expenditures has decreased, whereas in the rural areas it increased.

With regard to market regulation, the New Health Reform aims at rationalizing the pricing system and decreasing the costs of healthcare by facilitating the use of cost-effective generics. It is gradually abolishing the drug profits for different kinds of healthcare facilities in order to decrease the incentives to over-prescribe, while at the same time trying to increase the cost-recovery rates of health services. In drug pricing, it has tightened the control of drug supply for healthcare providers, while at the same time strengthening bidding and insurance, and fading out government-set prices as mechanisms of cost control. Overall, the direction of these initiatives is promising.

However, substantial institutional misfits between public finances and health sector regulation remain. On the regulatory side, the reform aims at enhancing the role of the state in the provision of health services, and its overall regulatory authority. Crucial initiatives such as the zero-markup policy increased the fiscal burden on local governments by demanding local copayments or installing compensation arrangements only gradually in the process of reform. Within the central framework, provinces create different approaches to organizing and funding local healthcare, which may promote or hinder the implementation of central policies on the ground. The example of the NRCMS has illustrated how institutional misfits incentivize local governments and healthcare providers to exploit the complexity of the healthcare system to seek their own gains. This way, even comparatively well-designed and funded policies can produce distorted outcomes, and the role of the state fails to match the visions of the policy-makers (Zheng 2006).

These regulatory reforms have different effects on healthcare providers' business models. THCs are being transformed towards a government-funded public service with a focus on public health. County hospitals are either to be transformed into a public service, like THCs, or to be privatized. For village clinics, there are some regulatory guidelines, which arguably have so far not initiated a fundamental transformation of their operations. For county hospital and THC reforms, more research is needed to assess the public finance arrangements that support them and their fiscal sustainability. If implemented effectively, the New Health Reform's initiatives can enhance the effectiveness of health insurance by decreasing the gap between nominal and effective reimbursement rates. Furthermore, they can slow down the growth of health costs and decrease the share of medically unnecessary health expenditures.

However, the effectiveness of the New Health Reform crucially relies on the degree of institutional fit between health sector regulation on the one hand and the fiscal capacity and incentive structures of local government and administration on the other hand. Both local governments and healthcare providers are characterized by a mismatch between their formal functions on the one hand and financial endowment and incentive structures on the other.

A strategy of shifting the costs of reform to local governments with insufficient financial compensation and ineffective accountability mechanisms is unlikely to reduce health costs sustainably. Rather, it is likely to breed new informal practices and a shift from inducing demand for drugs to inducing demand for services. Some recent studies point in this direction (see, for example, Yi et al. 2015).

Bibliography

Caijing 2014, 27 sheng yi shidian dabing baoxian, chouzi biaozhun xiangcha 22 bei (27 Provinces already Pilot the Catastrophic Disease Insurance, the Funding Standards Differ by the Factor 22), online: http://money.163.com/14/0306/06/9MKPOTC300253B0H.html (accessed July 16, 2015).

Caishe 2010, 202, Weishengbu, Guowuyuan Yigaiban guanyu yinfa "2010–2011 nian jiceng yiliao weisheng jigou shishi guojia jiben yaowu zhidu he zonghe gaige yi jiang dai bu zhuanxiang zijin guanli banfa" de tongzhi (Notification from the MoH and the Health Reform Office of the State Council about the Administrative Decree on the 2010 to 2011 Earmarked "Awards for Compensations" Fund for the Implementation of the Essential Medicines System and Comprehensive Reform).

Chen, Wen *et al.* 2010, Availability and Use of Essential Medicines in China: Manufacturing, Supply, and Prescribing in Shandong and Gansu Provinces, in: *BMC Health Services Research*, 10, 1, 211.

CHFP 2013, *Zhongguo weisheng he jihua shengyu tongji nianjian (China Statistical Yearbook of Health and Family Planning)*, Beijing: Zhongguo Xiehe Yike Daxue Chubanshe (China Harmony and Medicine University Press).

CHFP 2014, 39, Guanyu zuohao xinxing nongcun hezuo yiliao ji xiang zhongdian gongzuo de tongzhi (Notification about Accomplishing Several Crucial Tasks Regarding the NRCMS).

CHFP 2014a, *Xianji gongli yiyuan gaige shidian pinggu baogao chulu (The Evaluation Report about the County Public Hospital Reform Pilots has Come Out)*, online: www.h-ceo.com/article/read/21/2541?page=1.html (accessed June 25, 2015).

CHFP 2014b, *Zhongguo weisheng he jihua shengyu tongji nianjian (China Statistical Yearbook of Health and Family Planning)*, Beijing: Zhongguo Xiehe Yike Daxue Chubanshe (China Harmony and Medicine University Press).

China Economic Times 2015, Chongqing yigai fengbo jingshi yiliao fuwu jiage gaige (Reforming Health Service Prices: Warnings and Inspirations from the Disturbance of Chongqing's Health Reforms), online: www.hkcd.com/content/2015-04/09/content_921692.html (accessed June 24, 2015).

Chongqing Government Network 2015, Chongqing guanfang jiedu yiliao fuwu xiangmu jiage tiaozheng (The Chongqing Authorities Decipher the Readjustment of Health Service Item Prices), online: http://news.sohu.com/20150401/n410660503.shtml (accessed June 24, 2015).

Dong, Lisheng, Tom Christensen and Martin Painter 2014, Health Care Reform in China: An Analysis of Development Trends and Lack of Implementation, in: *International Public Management Journal*, 17, 4, 493–514.

Fagaijiage 2009, 2844, Guanyu yinfa gaige yaopin he yiliao fuwu jiage xingcheng jizhi de yijian de tongzhi (Notification about the Opinion on the Emerging Pricing Mechanisms for Drugs and Health Services).

Fagaijiage 2011, 674, Guojia Fazhan Gaigewei, Weishengbu guanyu kaizhan an bingzhong shoufei fangshi gaige shidian youguan wenti de tongzhi (Notification from the DRC and the MoH about the Opinion on Problems of Initiating Pilots for the DRG Charging Method).

Fagaijiage 2014, 503, Guanyu fei gongli yiliao jigou yiliao fuwu shixing shichang tiaojiejia youguan wenti de tongzhi (Notification about Problems of Applying Market Pricing to the Health Services of Non-Public Healthcare Facilities).

Fagaijiage 2015, 904, Guanyu yinfa tuijin yaopin jiage gaige yijian de tongzhi (Notification about the Opinion on Drug Price Reforms).

Fagaishehui 2012, 2605, Guanyu kaizhan chengxiang jumin dabing baoxian gongzuo de zhidao yijian (Leading Opinion about Initiating the Work on the Urban-Rural Citizens' Catastrophic Disease Insurance).

Fang, Yu *et al.* 2013, Access to Affordable Medicines after Health Reform: Evidence from Two Cross-Sectional Surveys in Shaanxi Province, Western China, in: *The Lancet*, 1, 227–237.

Guobanfa 2010, 62, Guowuyuan Bangongting guanyu jianli jianquan jiceng yiliao weisheng jigou buchang jizhi de yijian (Opinion of the State Council's General Office on Strengthening the Compensation Mechanisms for Grassroots Healthcare Facilities).

Guobanfa 2012, 33, Guowuyuan Bangongting yinfa guanyu xianji gongli yiyuan zonghe gaige shidian yijian de tongzhi (Notification from the General Office of the State Council about the Opinion on Piloting the Comprehensive Reform of Public County Hospitals).

Guobanfa 2013, 22, Guowuyuan Bangongting guanyu shishi "Guowuyuan jigou gaige he zhineng zhuanbian fang'an" renwu fengong de tongzhi (Notification from the General Office of the State Council about the Task Assignments to Implement the "Program of the Reform and Functional Transformation of the State Council Organs").

Guofa 2007, 20, Guowuyuan guanyu kaizhan chengzhen jumin jiben yiliao baoxian shidian de zhidao yijian (Leading Opinion of the State Council on Piloting the Urban Residents Basic Health Insurance).

Guofa 2009, 32, Guowuyuan guanyu kaizhan xinxing nongcun shehui yanglao baoxian shidian de zhidao yijian (Leading Opinion of the State Council on Initiating Experimentation with the New Rural Social Pension Insurance).

Guofa 2011, 18, Guowuyuan guanyu kaizhan chengzhen jumin shehui yanglao baoxian shidian de zhidao yijian (Leading Opinion of the State Council about Initiating Experimentation with the Urban Residents Social Pension Insurance).

Guofa 2012, 11, Guowuyuan guanyu yinfa "shi'er wu" qijian shenhua yiyao weisheng tizhi gaige guihua ji shishi fang'an de tongzhi (Notification from the State Council about the Program and Implementation Plan for Deepening Health System Reform in the Twelfth Five-Year Plan Period).

Guofa 2013, 40, Guowuyuan guanyu cujin jiankang fuwuye fazhan de ruogan yijian (Opinions from the State Council on Developing the Health Service Industry).

Guoweijicengfa 2014, 33, Guanyu yinfa "Cun weishengshi guanli banfa—shixing" de tongzhi (Notification about the "Trial Administrative Decree for Village Clinics").

Guoweijicengfa 2016, 27, Guanyu zuohao 2016 nian guojia jiben gonggong weisheng fuwu xiangmu gongzuo de tongzhi (Notification about Accomplishing the State Public Health Service Item Work of 2016).

Guoweitigaifa 2014, 21, Guanyu queding di er pi gongli yiyuan gaige guojia lianxi shidian chengshi ji youguan gongzuo de tongzhi (Notification about Selecting the Second Cohort of Pilot Cities for Public Hospital Reforms and the Work Associated with It).

Guoweitigaifa 2014, 12, Guanyu yinfa tuijin xianji gongli yiyuan zonghe gaige yijian de tongzhi (Notification about the Opinion on Driving Ahead the Comprehensive Reform of Public County Hospitals).

Guoweitigaifa 2015, 62, Guanyu queding di san pi gongli yiyuan gaige guojia lianxi shidian chengshi ji youguan gongzuo de tongzhi (Notification about Selecting the Third Cohort of Pilot Cities for Public Hospital Reforms and the Work Associated with It).

Heilmann, Sebastian 2008, Policy Experimentation in China's Economic Rise, in: *Studies in Comparative International Development*, 43, 1, 1–26.

Huang, Yanzhong 2013, *Governing Health in Contemporary China*, New York: Routledge.

Jiang, Minghuan *et al.* 2013, Measuring Access to Medicines: A Survey of Prices, Availability and Affordability in Shaanxi Province of China, in: *PLoS Medicine*, 8, 8.

Jijiage 2000, 1751, Guanyu yinfa quanguo yiliao fuwu jiage xiangmu guifan—shixing—de tongzhi (Notification about the National Regulation of Health Service Items—Trial Version).

Klotzbücher, Sascha 2006, *Das ländliche Gesundheitswesen der VR China: Strukturen, Akteure, Dynamik (The Rural Health Sector of the People's Republic of China: Actors, Structures, Dynamic)*, Frankfurt: Peter Lang.

Li, Bin 2014, A Chinese Solution to the Global Problem: Progress and Prospect of China's Healthcare Reform, Dean's Distinguished Lecture, Harvard School of Public Health Office of the Dean, September 24, Boston, MA.

Li, Yang *et al.* 2013, Evaluation, in Three Provinces, of the Introduction and Impact of China's National Essential Medicines Scheme, in: *Bulletin of the World Health Organization*, 91, 3, 184–194.

Liu, Guoyan and Junfeng Zhang 2010, Xin yigai beijing xia xiangcun yisheng de shengcun yu fazhan wenti—Zhejiang, Guangxi liang shengqu diaoyan baogao (Subsistence and Development Problems of Rural Doctors in the New Health Reform—An Investigative Research Report from Zhejiang and Guangxi Province), in: *Zhongguo Jingmao Daobao (China Economic and Trade Herald)*, 4.

Liu, Yuanli and Keqin Rao 2006, Providing Health Insurance in Rural China: From Research to Policy, in: *Journal of Health Politics, Policy and Law*, 31, 1, 71–92.

Meng, Qun *et al.* 2012, Trends in Access to Health Services and Financial Protection in China between 2003 and 2011: A Cross-Sectional Study, in: *The Lancet*, 379, 9818, 805–814.

MoF 2014, *Zhongyang caizheng duofang buzhu wei jiceng yigai "huhang" (Central Budgets are Helping Out Grassroots Health Reform in Many Ways)*, online: http://sbs.mof.gov.cn/zhengwuxinxi/gongzuodongtai/201403/t20140304_1049711.html (accessed: October 18, 2016).

MoH 2005, *Zhongguo weisheng tongji nianjian (China Statistical Yearbook of Health)*, Beijing: Zhongguo Xiehe Yike Daxue Chubanshe (China Harmony and Medicine University Press).

MoH (ed.) 2009a, *Weishengbu xinxing nongcun hezuo yiliao yanjiu zhongxin keti yanjiu baogao huibian, 2006–2008 (Compilation of Research Reports of the NRCMS Research Center of the MoH, 2006–2008)*, Beijing.

MoH 2009b, *Zhongguo weisheng tongji nianjian (China Statistical Yearbook of Health)*, Beijing: Zhongguo Xiehe Yike Daxue Chubanshe (China Harmony and Medicine University Press).

MoH 2010, *Zhongguo weisheng tongji nianjian (China Statistical Yearbook of Health)*, Beijing: Zhongguo Xiehe Yike Daxue Chubanshe (China Harmony and Medicine University Press).

MoHRSS 2014, *Zhongguo laodong tongji nianjian (China Statistical Yearbook of Labor)*, Beijing: Zhongguo Tongji Chubanshe (China Statistics Press).

Müller, Armin 2015, Public Services and Private Financing, Paper presented at the 12th Annual Conference of the East Asian Social Policy Network, Singapore.

Müller, Armin 2016a, Hukou and Health Insurance Coverage for Migrant Workers, in: *Journal of Current Chinese Affairs*, 45, 2, 53–82.

Müller, Armin 2016b, Premium Collection and the Problem of Voluntary Enrollment in China's New Rural Cooperative Medical System (NRCMS), in: *Journal of Current Chinese Affairs*, 45, 1, 11–41.

Nanfang Zhoumo 2012, Liu buwei fabu dabing yibao zhidao yijian (Six Ministries and Commissions Issue the Leading Opinion about Catastrophic Disease Insurance), September 5, 2012, online: www.infzm.com/content/80433 (accessed September 7, 2015).

Renda 2010, Zhonghua Renmin Gongheguo Shehui baoxian fa (Social Insurance Law of the People's Republic of China).

Shao, Dexing 2007, *Xinxing nongcun hezuo yiliao gongji moshi yanjiu (Institutional Carrier Models of the NRCMS)*, Beijing: Zhonggong Zhongyang Dangxiao Chubanshe (The Central Party School Publishing House).

Sun, Zhigang 2011, Zhongguo jiceng de yiyao tizhi gaige (The Reform of the Grassroots Health and Medical System in China), in: *China Economist*, 2, 11f.

Tang, Yuqing *et al.* 2013, Application of Propensity Scores to Estimate the Association Between Government Subsidy and Injection Use in Primary Health Care Institutions in China, in: *BMC Health Services Research*, 13, 183.

Tian, Xin, Yaran Song and Xinping Zhang 2012, National Essential Medicines List and Policy Practice: A Case Study of China's Health Care Reform, in: *BMC Health Services Research*, 12, 1, 401.

Weibannongweifa 2010, 48, Weishengbu Bangongting guanyu tuijin xiangcun weisheng fuwu yitihua guanli de yijian (Opinion from the General Office of the MoH on Pushing Forward the Integrated Management of Township and Village Health Services).

Weibannongweifa 2011, 34, Weishengbu Bangongting guanyu yinfa "guanyu xiangzhen weishengyuan he cun weishengshi shishi jixiao kaohe gongzuo de yijian" de tongzhi (Notification from the General Office of the MoH on the "Opinion on Implementing Performance Evaluations in THCs and Village Health Stations").

Weijifunongweifa 1999, 37, Weishengbu Jifusi guanyu jinyibu guifan he jiji wentuo de tuixing xiangzhen cun weisheng zuzhi yitihua guanli de jidian yijian (Opinions of the Department of Basic and Women's Health of the MoH on Regulating and Actively and Reliably Carrying Out the Integrated Management of Township and Village Healthcare Organs).

Weinongweifa 2008, 65, Weishengbu guanyu guifan xinxing nongcun hezuo yiliao erci buchang de zhidao yijian (Leading Opinion of the MoH on Regulating Second Rounds of Reimbursements in the NRCMS).

Weinongweifa 2010, 53, Guanyu kaizhan tigao nongcun ertong zhongda jibing yiliao baozhang shuiping shidian gongzuo de yijian (Opinion on Initiating Experiments to Increase the Medical Protection of Rural Children against Catastrophic Diseases).

Weinongweifa 2011, 27, Guanyu zuohao 2011 nian xinxing nongcun hezuo yiliao youguan gongzuo de tongzhi (Notification about Accomplishing NRCMS-Related Work in 2011).

Weinongweifa 2012, 27, Weishengbu deng si bumen guanyu shangye baoxian jigou canyu xinxing nongcun hezuo yiliao jingban fuwu de zhidao yijian (Leading Opinion of the MoH and Three Other Departments about the Services of Commercial Insurance Companies Participating in the NRCMS Administration).

Weiyaozhengfa 2009, 78, Guanyu yinfa "Guanyu jianli guojia jiben yaowu zhidu de shishi yijian" (Notification about the "Opinion on Establishing the Basic Medical Drug System").

Weiyiguanfa 2010, 20, Guanyu yinfa gongli yiyuan gaige shidian zhidao yijian de tongzhi (Notification about the Leading Opinion on Public Hospital Reform).

Xu, Jie 2001, Xiangcun weisheng fuwu yitihua guanli ruogan wenti—Zhong (Problems of the Integrated Management of Township and Village Health Services—Part Two), in: *Weisheng Jingji Yanjiu (Health Economics Research)*, 10, 11–12.

Xu, Ke *et al.* 2010, Exploring the Thresholds of Health Expenditure for Protection Against Financial Risk, World Health Report, Background Paper, 19.

Yang, Hao *et al.* 2010, Prices, Availability and Affordability of Essential Medicines in Rural Areas of Hubei Province, China, in: *Health Policy and Planning*, 25, 3, 219–229.

Yang, Li *et al.* 2013a, Evaluation, in Three Provinces, of the Introduction and Impact of China's National Essential Medicines Scheme, in: *Bulletin of the World Health Organization*, 91, 184–194.

Yang, Lianping *et al.* 2013b, The Impact of the National Essential Medicines Policy on Prescribing Behaviours in Primary Care Facilities in Hubei Province of China, in: *Health Policy and Planning*, 28, 7, 750–760.

Yi, Hongmei *et al.* 2015, Intended and Unintended Consequences of China's Zero Markup Drug Policy, in: *Health Affairs*, 34, 8, 1391–1398.

Yi, Hongmei *et al.* 2009, Health Insurance and Catastrophic Illness: A Report on the New Cooperative Medical System in Rural China, in: *Health Economics*, 18, 119–127.

Yip, Winnie and William Hsiao 2015, What Drove the Cycles of Chinese Health System Reforms?, in: *Health Systems and Reform*, 1, 1, 52–61.

Yip, Winnie C.-M. *et al.* 2012, Early Appraisal of China's Huge and Complex Health-Care Reforms, in: *The Lancet*, 379, 9818, 833–842.

Zhang, Luying *et al.* 2010, Balancing the Funds in the New Cooperative Medical Scheme in Rural China: Determinants and Influencing Factors in Two Provinces, in: *The International Journal of Health Planning and Management*, 25, 2, 96–118.

Zhongfa 2009, 6, Zhonggong Zhongyang, Guowuyuan guanyu shenhua yiyao weisheng tizhi gaige de yijian (Opinion of the Central Committee and the State Council on Deepening Health System Reforms).

Zhongyangbianbanfa 2011, 28, Zhongyang Bianban, Weishengbu, Caizhengbu guanyu yinfa xiangzhen weishengyuan jigou bianzhi biaozhun zhidao yijian de tongzhi (Notification from the State Commission of Public Sector Reform, the MoH, and the MoF about the Leading Opinion on the Bianzhi Standard of THCs).

8 Conclusion

The Chinese healthcare system has been going through extremes since the middle of the twentieth century. During the planned economy era, its achievements were impressive given the limited resources the country had available. During the first two decades of the reform period, it was substantially weakened by a lack of public funding and political support, among other things. Since 2000, the central government has enacted a series of policies that aim at expanding public social security for the population, and at tightening the grip over the health sector and its dynamics. Despite these efforts, health costs have kept rising continuously, which casts doubts on the party-state's ability to steer the health sector in accordance with its stated goals.

Institutional misfits between the multi-level state (and the public finance system in particular) and health sector regulation are a crucial dimension of this development. In the reform period, the Chinese state experienced substantial decreases in its fiscal and steering capacity. Health sector regulation was only partially adapted to this change. Although public financial support for the healthcare providers decreased, they were still expected to perform their previous social functions, most notably the provision of basic health services below the costs of production. Relying on profits from drug sales and diagnostic tests as the primary mechanism of compensation created a regime of perverse incentives, which has substantially damaged the efficiency of the public and semi-public health sector, and the reputation of the medical profession in China.

This study challenges two larger paradigms that have been very influential in the research on health and social policy in the PRC, and the NRCMS in particular: the implicit notion of a united central government with an integrated hierarchy of preferences, and the dominance of practical constraints in restraining the implementation of health policy. I argue that the central government's contradictory decisions are largely generated by the coexistence of contradictory preferences between bureaucratic coalitions and factions on the one hand, and the prevalence of consensual modes of decision-making on the other. Although there is a strategic component to central–local relations as well, in this particular case, policy conflicts on the national level are a dominant explanatory variable. This study thus largely confirms Yip and Hsiao's (2015) conflict-centered view of Chinese health policy, though assigning explanatory power to organizational self-interest, rather than political ideology.

The second paradigm implies that practical constraints, such as the lack of fiscal capacity and control of local government agents, are the primary explanatory factors for problems and failures in implementing health policy. I argue that the state capacity perspective obliterates important structural dimensions. China's public finance system is in itself dysfunctional (Wong 2009) and not compatible with the regulatory system of the health sector. As Chapter 6 has shown, this is a primary cause for many of the governance and steering problems in local health policy. These structural institutional misfits are rooted in the transition from a planned economy to a market economy, and their continued prevalence is linked to the coexistence of opposing political interests and consensual modes of decision-making—that is, to the nature of the political system. The systemic interdependence between public finance and health sector regulation breeds complex problems of governance and steering, which are highly interdependent.

This perspective has far-reaching consequences for both research and policy. Several studies in the field of health economics have—in adherence to methodological individualism—argued for changes in the incentives of individual doctors to control induced demand. From the perspective of this study, the incentives of individual doctors are but symptoms of an illness, the causes of which lie in the structural institutional misfits between the multi-level state and health sector regulation. If significant changes in the remuneration practices of hospitals are to be sustainable, they have to come with changes in the funding of hospitals. These in turn will require structural reforms that provide a coherent formal institutional framework—either by increasing or by decreasing the role of the state.

Previous studies on the NRCMS have largely built upon the assumption that it is a genuinely voluntary program, in accordance with its official description in administrative documents (see, for example, Wang et al. 2008). Building on this idea, Klotzbücher and colleagues have interpreted the NRCMS as a market-based mechanism of governance: the center made the system voluntary to rely on the fluctuating enrollment rates as indicators of the quality of the local implementation (Klotzbücher et al. 2010; Klotzbücher and Laessig 2009). Recent research has questioned the degree to which the NRCMS is a truly voluntary system, given stable enrollment rates of almost 100 percent and a prevalence of informal practices connected to premium collection (Müller 2016). This study furthermore argues that the contradictory policy objectives of voluntary enrollment and fixed enrollment targets are an outcome of the interest conflict between the pro-government and pro-market actors: the former tried to implement a *de facto* mandatory system as advocated by international experts, whereas the latter sought to keep the door open for the insurance industry and retain well-tried vulnerable points of attack in the policy.

Another influential study has highlighted the role of advocacy coalitions in the policy process leading to the NRCMS reform, arguing that the central government had decided by the mid-1990s to implement a NRCMS-like policy, but lacked the fiscal capacity to do so until the early 2000s (Wang 2009). This study downplays the fact that there have been two initiatives to launch a CMS policy in the 1990s, both of which were largely aborted in the course of attacks defunding the policies and criticizing them as involuntary. A stable consensus in the leadership core only emerged after inside initiation in 2001 (Liu and Rao 2006), and even thereafter bureaucratic fighting continued until a consensual solution integrating the insurance industry had been found. While the advocacy-coalition perspective identifies some crucial policy dynamics, it does not fully recognize the opponents of the CMS and their counter-actions.

This book thus contributes to an ongoing paradigm shift in the research on health and social policy in the PRC. Previous studies have already criticized the idea of the collapse of the planned-economy CMS in the 1980s as being a mere by-product of economic reforms: although the reforms were a crucial factor, the sacrifice of rural health insurance was ultimately a political decision (Duckett 2011). My previous work has challenged the idea of universal voluntary enroll-ment. Building upon this, this book has come to challenge the assumption of a united central government with integrated preferences, which is held back in pursuing its beneficial policies merely by a lack of fiscal capacity and the ability to control its potentially deviant local agents. Rather, a variety of opposing social interests are represented at the central level. They manifest themselves in latent policy conflicts and contradictory policy decisions under the prevalence of con-sensus-oriented decision-making. Finally, my book challenges the prevailing state capacity perspective and the related focus on practical constraints, arguing that they fall short of grasping the fundamental institutional complexities that make health reforms more difficult and challenging than other fields of policy.

The benefits of the actor-centered-institutionalism perspective include the systematic linking of political dynamics at the central and local level, and the exploration of the interdependent nature of institutional structures and the synergies between different policy fields and policy processes regarding their political impacts. The lens of systemic interdependence creates important insights into the regulatory contradictions and how contradictory institutional structures neutralize one another in a local context. The case of the NRCMS bears important lessons about political decision-making in China's central government, and shows how even comparatively coherent policy designs with substantial political support at the central level can suffer from the distorting effects of the contradictory institutional context.

The National Policy Process Leading to the NRCMS Reform

1990s

The process that led to the drafting of the NRCMS policy was determined by the conflict between pro-government and pro-market actors and their oppos-ing visions of China's new welfare regime in the rural areas, rather than mere practical constraints and coordination problems. Most notably, the interest conflict between the insurance industry and the welfare bureaucracy previously has not received the academic attention it deserves. The process was largely driven by organizational self-interest, but was also affected by the ideological tides in the bureaucratic leadership core. The MoH, for example, has promoted the introduction of central subsidies to support the old CMS since the early 1980s, even though it abandoned the CMS program twice. At the same time, it engaged in marketization reforms of public hospitals and basic health service provision. Both primarily aimed at increasing funding for the health sector and at enhancing the health sector's control over this funding. Bureaucratic interest on the pro-market side was more diverse. The Chinese insurance industry sought to develop the rural markets and turn social security into a business, and the MoF sought to limit government spending on social security. Both sides formed coalitions of corporate actors that reached from the central level down to the county level, but central- and provincial-level actors were most influential in the national arena.

The preferences of the leadership core of the party-state have been of paramount importance for the balance of power between the bureaucratic actors on both sides, whose relationship and interactions have not been regulated by a stable institutional setup. These preferences are more difficult to systematize, as leaders' multiple organizational frames of reference, ideological orientations and situational factors all seem to play an important role. The leadership core determined the general framework of interaction by setting the priority of rural health insurance, and by supporting either the pro-market or the pro-government actors more. On the level of bureaucratic interaction, the political priority determined the two coalitions' viable strategies: when priority was low, they had more leeway and could ignore or contradict national policies; when the priority was high, they were more inclined to negotiate and cooperate. The relative support for either coalition determined which side momentarily had the upper hand and could enact policies according to its preferences.

By the mid-1980s, the central government had decided to establish a public social security system in the rural areas. In part, this was meant as compensation for the one-child policy, which undermined the traditional social security function of the family in rural China. During the seventh five-year plan period, various models of social security in healthcare and pensions were experimented with. There was a latent competition between China's insurance industry (at that time mainly the PICC) on the one hand, which sought to develop the rural insurance markets, and the MoH and the MoCA on the other, which sought to establish state-led social security systems. The competition between the two sides was primarily about policy jurisdiction and the control of financial resources, rather than ideological considerations regarding the welfare regime. Local experimentation unfolded under a status quo upheld by the balance of power in the leadership core. It included three main principles for rural social security and insurance in particular: the subsistence of local communities, the primary responsibility of the households and voluntary participation in insurance schemes. This status quo was biased towards the pro-market side and hindered the development of public insurance programs.

The events of 1989 changed the balance of power in the leadership core in favor of the pro-government side. This enabled the MoH to assemble a coalition of ministerial actors to launch a new CMS program that was massively supported by financial transfers from the central and provincial levels of government. The main policy document was openly critical of the commercialization reforms of the 1980s. The massive governmental financial support constituted a breach of the previous status quo. CMS coverage subsequently increased, but after the market reformers regained power in the course of the leadership change in 1992/93, they enforced the former status quo once more. Financial transfers from the center and the provincial governments had been discontinued by early 1993, a move arguably facilitated by China's looming fiscal crisis. After serious riots erupted in Renshou County in Sichuan province about irregular fees and charges, the farmers' burden became an issue of political priority. Subsequent burden-reduction policies forbade the use of village and township fees and charges for the CMS. They furthermore promoted strict requirements regarding the voluntariness of CMS enrollment, which were difficult to put into practice and increased the political risks for rural cadres promoting the policy. The CMS was effectively defunded, and coverage subsequently decreased. This first initiative to reanimate the CMS has not been sufficiently acknowledged in previous research.

In 1994, the MoH began to launch a pilot program for another CMS initiative. This time, it was primarily financed by household and community resources, and was thus more in line with the status quo. The pilot program and its evaluation were followed by a policy proposal, which was integrated into the 1997 national health reform. However, the 1997/98 leadership change strengthened the pro-market coalition again, and Zhu Rongji in particular. The expansion of the CMS in rural China began to stagnate in 1997, and coverage declined again in 1998. On the one hand, the central government renewed its emphasis on strictly voluntary enrollment, which exposed local cadres to political risks when they implemented the policy. On the other hand, Zhu Rongji's reform of the central government apparatus reshuffled the competences in rural social security and created confusion about the administrative jurisdiction over the CMS (see also Klotzbücher 2006: 201f.). Zhu also initiated structural reforms of the Chinese insurance industry, which subsequently expanded into the rural areas. Commercial insurance coverage rose quickly and surpassed CMS coverage in the middle-income areas by the early 2000s. The previous failure of the first initiative as a result of very similar causes and the subsequent expansion of the commercial insurance industry in rural China raise substantial doubts about the accidental nature that has been attributed to the failure of the second CMS initiative in previous studies.

The MoCA's rural pension program was exposed to similar challenges, yet its different mix of policy instruments facilitated different policy dynamics. Operating with savings accounts rather than social pooling funds, it could tolerate lower rates of enrollment and was less vulnerable to the issues of voluntariness and burdens. Both the CMS and the pension scheme saw major policy initiatives in the wake of 1989, and were dealt existential blows after the 1997/98 leadership change. Official reasoning emphasized practical constraints, problems with the policy design, and corruption and coercion at the local levels as limiting the effectiveness of these rural social security programs. The national policy process, however, was strongly determined by the political conflicts between the pro-market and pro-government coalitions. This finding also calls for a reinterpretation of the hypothesis that social policy experimentation in the 1990s failed primarily due to the lack of rent-seeking opportunities these experiments provided to local cadres (Heilmann 2008). Although the importance of this factor is hard to argue with, a united central government with an integrated hierarchy of policy preferences and substantial political support for rural social policy could have facilitated a broader extension of such policies, even if they were of limited effectiveness and financially unattractive to local cadres. Rural social policy is primarily of a distributive nature, and therefore its experimentation and diffusion are governed by different dynamics than those of economic policy.

2000s

It is an interesting coincidence that the preferences of the leadership core strongly shifted towards public social security at a time when commercial insurance companies were arguably thriving in the rural areas. China's WTO accession was crucial in raising the influence of more left-wing ideas in the leadership core (Fewsmith 2001; Zweig 2001). This provided a fertile ground for the inside initiation by the minister of health and several intellectuals, which turned Jiang Zemin into a supporter of a government-funded CMS program in the summer of 2001 (Liu and Rao 2006). In autumn, negotiations between the most important ministerial actors of both coalitions began under the imperative to achieve a consensus. At the same time, various provinces renewed their support for local CMS programs to prepare the implementation, and several insurance companies entered cooperative arrangements with local governments to manage CMS funds in order to get a foot in the door. The NRCMS policy was enacted in October 2002 by the Jiang and Zhu administration, only weeks before the Sixteenth Party Congress and several months before the SARS crisis hit China. As previous studies already noted, SARS was not the cause of the NRCMS policy, but it sparked a new policy process leading to the New Health Reform (Li 2010; Wang 2009). I argue that the SARS crisis furthermore provided an opportunity for the pro-market actors to have the previous minister of health replaced with a representative of their own networks, and thus to carry the previously inter-ministerial conflict into the MoH.

The NRCMS was piloted between 2003 and 2005, and bureaucratic con-flicts between pro-government and pro-market actors still characterized the policy process. While the MoF and the MoA had been integrated in the inter-ministerial conference that formed the central decision-making body, the CIRC had been left out and the status of the insurance industry was ambig-uous. Furthermore, the minister of health had been removed from office in the wake of the SARS crisis and replaced by a market reformer. The MoH now began to criticize non-voluntary enrollment practices in the pilot counties and halted the extension of piloting in early 2004. At the same time, the insurance industry increased its engagement in local pilot projects, which it wanted integrated into the NRCMS framework. In 2005, the status of the insurance industry was formalized, the pro-market minister of health stepped down, and the accusations of non-voluntary enrollment practices subsequently died down.

Between 2006 and 2008, the NRCMS program was extended in all of rural China, and it has been constantly adapted and developed ever since. Despite substantial nominal increases in government funding, however, the share of NRCMS funding in overall rural health costs stagnated around 30 percent in the early 2010s. Reimbursements usually remained below the levels indicated by the regulatory documents due to the use of positive lists for drugs and services, as well as budgetary shortfalls and other factors. The implementation of the Essential Medicines system and the zero-markup policy arguably narrow this gap at THCs and public county hospitals. Direct reimbursements were still beyond the administrative capacity of many local governments, which limited the benefits of the NRCMS for the poorer strata of rural society, and constrained the use of effective cost containment via provider payment reforms. Patients often only received their reimbursements towards the end of the year, which were often lower than expected.

The development of rural health insurance delivers important insights into national politics in China. Like health policy in general, the field of rural health insurance has been dominated by the political contradictions between pro-market and pro-government actors. Bureaucratic self-interest played a paramount role in actors' behavior. For example, through the 1980s and 1990s, the MoH liberalized healthcare provision and initiated marketization reforms in the hospital sector, while at the same time promoting a CMS pro-gram supported by financial transfers of the central and provincial govern-ments. The insurance industry, on the other hand, engaged in the commercial sale of insurance contracts as well as cooperative projects with local govern-ments, in which it would manage public insurance funds for a fixed fee. In both cases, the actors' self-interest in raising funds for themselves and their affiliated organs dominated ideological considerations regarding the sources of funding or the scope and characteristics of social pooling.

The NRCMS in a Local Context

Local Policy Design and Implementation

The central NRCMS policy provided a general framework that granted local governments considerable leeway regarding the design of the local systems. Previous studies of the NRCMS have often assumed the local government to be a solitary decision-maker, emphasized the substantial local variations in the NRCMS with regard to the types of services and drugs covered, and analyzed people's readiness to enroll with the system (see, for example, Brown et al. 2009; Brown and Huff 2011; Cai et al. 2007). A central contribution of this study is to frame local policy decisions as an outcome of negotiations, thus explaining and highlighting the substantial structural commonalities in local NRCMS design across China's diverse regions and localities, and con-textualizing it in the gradually declining decision-space that local governments are granted by the higher levels. Successive cohorts of counties implemented the policy, and, as a rule of thumb, the pilot counties of the first two cohorts developed systems that were imitated by the later cohorts. Inter-estingly, local governments made strikingly homogeneous decisions across very different socio-economic settings. Most notably, the vast majority chose to include outpatient reimbursement in the insurance plan, despite the addi-tional administrative workload and costs this step brought. The most popular model of outpatient reimbursements was MSAs, which, however, had little to no protective effect and thus decreased the effectiveness of the insurance system. These patterns of decision-making can be rationally explained when they are framed as the outcome of an interactive process of decision-making.

The implementation of the NRCMS in the local state is determined by the interactions of local governments and the healthcare providers, most notably county hospitals and THCs. Even though local governments are in a formal position of hierarchy vis-à-vis the healthcare providers, the latter are empow-ered by the information asymmetries inherent in medical specialist knowl-edge. In order to effectively design local NRCMS policies, local governments depend on the consultancy of the healthcare facilities. Furthermore, the local governments have strong incentives to delegate certain administrative tasks to the healthcare facilities in order to decrease the administrative costs of oper-ating the NRCMS. Therefore, they negotiated the policy designs with the healthcare providers.

Healthcare providers could perform a variety of tasks to ease the adminis-trative burden of the local government. County hospitals, THCs and village clinics could all conduct reimbursement processes, provided that the county introduced direct reimbursement. This was more common for outpatient ser-vices than for inpatient services, as the former included a smaller financial risk for the funds. Counties with limited administrative capacity were hesitant to introduce direct reimbursement for inpatient services, and village clinics were rarely integrated in the healthcare administration to a degree that would allow for it. THCs could furthermore perform administrative tasks in out-patient funds administration, most notably managing the MSAs. As this work consists of numerous small-scale transactions, it takes a considerable burden from the NRCMS administration at the bureau of health. Finally, THC and village clinic staff could be recruited to aid in the premium collection process, which was often described as the most expensive and burdensome task related to the NRCMS. The difficulties of premium collection usually decreased somewhat after a few years, when implementation was consolidated.

The structure of the local NRCMS funds included important distributive decisions. This is closely related to the service portfolios of the different types of healthcare providers. Village clinics provide only basic outpatient services, whereas THCs provide outpatient services and some basic inpatient services. County hospitals focus on the provision of inpatient services, but also provide some outpatient services. Designated outpatient reimbursement funds effectively allocated a certain share of the NRCMS funds to the THCs and village clinics, which could compensate them for the administrative tasks they performed. Other NRCMS regulations could further fine-tune the distributive effects. For example, county governments could exclude village clinic services from NRCMS reimbursement, and they could adapt the reimbursement plans to the service portfolios of the THCs. They used the NRCMS as both insurance for the rural population and a financing instrument for the health sector.

But why were reimbursement models restricted to catastrophic health expenditures so rare when local governments could also just coerce THC staff and village doctors into aiding premium collection? Even though the rural population was not included in the decision-making process, their preferences still had an indirect impact. The national policy featured a contradiction between universal coverage and voluntary enrollment, which created political risks for local governments that relied too strongly or openly on coercive enrollment measures. If a high share of the local population was reluctant to enroll or outright opposed enrollment, this raised the costs of the premium collection process. Outpatient reimbursement could improve the premium collection situation in several ways. It increased the scope of direct and visible benefits and thus made the NRCMS more attractive. MSAs furthermore suited the conservative attitudes of some villagers who regarded health as a family issue rather than a public issue and were opposed to social pooling. Finally, if the local cadres resorted to informal practices, they could use the money from the MSAs to replace the premiums, and thus skip the burdensome premium collection process altogether. Ironically, the political influence of the local population to some extent decreased the effectiveness of the NRCMS as an insurance mechanism.

Budgetary Funding and Regulatory Enforcement

Regulatory enforcement and the institutional maintenance of the NRCMS are strongly affected by the institutional misfits described in Chapter 2.

Generally, there is a mismatch between formal responsibilities and financial capacity for both the government and the healthcare providers. The latter are expected to provide basic health services below the costs of production and to engage in public health work. However, these social functions are largely unfunded, because local governments lack the fiscal capacity and/or the incentives to conduct the funding. With regard to budgetary funding and regulatory enforcement, this creates a deadlock in rural health governance: local governments are unwilling or unable to pay local health service providers appropriately, and local health service providers deviate from their institutional role in return. Finally, local governments have little to no incentive to enforce the regulations and strictly sanction the providers. This basic mechanism applies to virtually all areas of local health governance in one way or another.

With regard to the NRCMS, previous studies have already pointed out that the actual rates of reimbursement were far below the rates promised in administrative documents, and identified some of the crucial reasons for this (Klotzbücher et al. 2010; Yi et al. 2009). This study offers a more comprehensive grasp of the low effectiveness of the NRCMS by putting it into the context of regulatory institutions. Structural misfits facilitate distorted policy implementation and institutional malfunctioning, which undermine the effectiveness of the NRCMS policy as well as other initiatives central to the New Health Reform. It highlights the importance of structural reforms in China's multi-level state and the creation of an effective fiscal equalization system, which has been previously pointed out by several scholars and remains a central precondition for enhancing the effectiveness and formalization of governance in healthcare, social policy, and public service provision in general (Bohnet et al. 2003; Wong 2009).

The budgetary funding of the NRCMS is potentially affected by the deadlock dynamic. With regard to NRCMS funds, the contributions of the county-level governments cannot always be guaranteed, most notably in provinces that shifted large shares of the financial burden downwards. Over the years, however, the central and provincial levels have assumed growing shares of the financial burden. Furthermore, budgetary funding for other policies is a potential problem. Indirectly, the NRCMS can be affected by financial shortfalls in the Medical Assistance program, which is primarily funded from local sources and usually finances part of the NRCMS premiums. In capital investment programs, shortfalls in local funding increase the burden of debt for local providers, which then come under intensified pressure to increase their revenues. Some local governments even decreased their spending on healthcare after the introduction of the NRCMS.

Healthcare providers tend to violate their institutional roles. In curative care, overcharging and induced demand are important strategies to raise revenue and increase the profitability of the health business. This is particularly important when high levels of debt exert pressure on the healthcare providers. The local NRCMS administration usually lacks the administrative capacity—

partly due to underfunding—and the political mandate to effectively sanction the healthcare providers. As a result, a certain share of the NRCMS funds is appropriated by the local healthcare providers, rather than benefitting the rural population. To some extent, the financial transfers for the NRCMS thus replace local budgetary funding, and health costs rising at an increased speed is one consequence of this phenomenon.

There is a variety of strategies in the NRCMS program to control the rise of health costs. The classic tool is the use of positive lists for services and drugs eligible for reimbursement. Although they provide potentially powerful instruments of cost control, they can be avoided by collusive measures between doctors and patients, especially in counties with limited administrative capacity. Due to the dysfunctional nature of drug quality indicators in China, such collusion may sometimes be in the best interest of the patients. One problematic aspect of the positive lists is the exclusion of profitable service items from the reimbursement plans, and the degree of complexity the lists add to the NRCMS regulations. The formal reimbursement rates specified in the regulatory documents are often much higher than the effective reimbursement rates, as patients need to pay for some types of services and drugs entirely out-of-pocket. These uncovered services and drugs generate most revenues for the healthcare providers, so they have strong incentives to induce demand for them.

Bulk purchases and bidding have been part of the regulatory regime for drugs since the early 2000s, as described in Chapter 2. In theory, local healthcare providers were to engage in bulk purchasing and bidding in order to decrease the purchasing prices of drugs, and to pass these decreases on to the consumers. Local governments were to play a neutral, regulatory role. In practice, local governments and healthcare providers colluded very often: they managed to decrease the purchasing prices, but the benefits were shared between the local governments and the providers rather than passed on to consumers. This way, the profits did not decrease health costs, but greatly increased the providers' drug profit margins and thus relieved the financial pressure and the need to induce demand. As centralized bidding is also a crucial element of the New Health Reform, it is important to emphasize that experiences with such policies were made long before 2009, and that the little research that exists on this subject points to massive distortions in the implementation.

Finally, provider payment reforms have become a mainstay of local NRCMS reforms and are commonly recommended by Chinese and international specialists. Provider payment reforms aim to replace the common mode of fee-for-service payment by alternative modes that strategically modify providers' incentives, and health insurance plays an important role in those reforms. Payment by capitation or payment by type of disease, rather than service items, are among the most common forms. Such reforms have a certain potential to improve the incentive structures of the healthcare providers. However, provider payment reforms alone cannot compensate for budgetary shortfalls and gaps in public funding. Furthermore, alternative modes of payment tend to require direct reimbursement, which overburdens the administrative capacity of many local governments. If problems of fiscal and administrative capacity can be resolved, provider payment reforms may offer an opportunity to effectively contain costs.

The New Health Reform and its Comprehensive Approach

The New Health Reform, enacted in 2009 and scheduled to last until 2020, aimed to reverse the problematic tendencies of service provision and govern-ance in the health sector, and has brought on track important and promising initiatives. However, the central government appears to see itself primarily as a regulator, and only creates stable, long-term financial commitments in selected areas, such as the NRCMS or public health service equalization. In those fields, matching-funds mechanisms have been established that require each level of government to contribute to the financing of specific local programs and tasks. In other fields, such as capital investment, the central government provides project-based funding that requires substantial copayments by local governments and healthcare facilities. Yet in other areas, such as the zero-markup policy, it merely reluctantly provided some compensations and left many details to the provinces to specify.

The history of post-Mao health policy illustrates that funding arrangements are crucial for the success of policy initiatives. Unfunded mandates tend to provoke counter-measures by local governments, which are often under con-siderable fiscal stress and lack the fiscal capacity to bear the policy burden. Against the background of a dysfunctional public finance system, funded policy mandates too are at risk of producing distorted outcomes. Local governments and healthcare providers have incentives to exploit the complexity of the health sector's regulatory institutions to pursue their own gains. In the context of fiscal imbalances, the effectiveness of supervision mechanisms is easily compromised.

The New Health Reform comprises an array of policy initiatives targeting health service provision, social security and market regulation. In market regulation, the Essential Medicines program increasingly replaces the pre-vious drug policy regimes. At the center of the Essential Medicines regime is the respective central drug list and the complementary lists of the provincial governments. The list is intended to contain mainly cost-effective generics. It is being harmonized with the positive lists of China's health insurance pro-grams and grassroots health providers in order to decrease the costs of healthcare. Purchasing of Essential Medicines should be centralized at the provincial level, and was to be organized via bidding and provincial delivery systems. More research is needed regarding the local effects of centralized bidding, and the potential informal practices it may spark.

Furthermore, the profit margins of Essential Medicines are increasingly abolished. In 2009, the zero-markup policy (*lingchalü, lingchajia*) targeted government-operated grassroots healthcare providers—that is, large shares of the Shequ service centers and stations, virtually all THCs, but less than 10 percent of the village clinics. Since 2012, this regulation has also been increasingly applied to public hospitals at the county level. These initiatives aim to improve the incentive structures of healthcare providers and decrease induced demand and other informal practices. One mode of compensation for the costs of these reforms was to be rising service prices and increased cost-recovery rates for health services. The reforms towards DRG-based payment and the general diagnosis and treatment fee are central initiatives in this direction. At the level of THCs, the Essential Medicines and zero-markup policies have arguably narrowed the gap between nominal and effective reimbursement rates in the NRCMS. At the same time, the THCs seem to become less popular with customers.

Under the Xi Jinping administration, some important modifications to market regulation have been made. First, the right of market pricing for services—that is, to set prices autonomously—has been shifted from for-profit status to non-public ownership status in the county hospital reform. Second, the scope of the public pricing system for drugs has been greatly reduced, which implies a shift to bidding and health insurance as the main tools to influence prices. More research is needed to evaluate the effects of these most recent reforms.

With regard to health service providers, the New Health Reform aims at a rationalization of business models. THCs are in the process of transformation towards primarily state-funded providers with a focus on social functions. Where such reforms are backed up by appropriate public funding arrangements, the new institutional fit between the role of the state and the business model of the provider can enhance the capacity for steering and public service provision in the rural health sector. For village clinics, there seems to be no coherent model of reform so far. Whether the New Health Reform can partially or fully resolve the deadlock dynamics in rural health governance will crucially depend on its ability to increase the institutional fit between local state capacity and health sector regulations. More research is needed to assess the progress on this front.

Public hospital reforms are in the course of experimentation and piloting. The sub-branch of county hospital reforms displays a relatively coherent policy design: local governments should follow a similar model as in THC reforms—that is, raise government spending and cost-recovery rates for services. Some provinces established matching funds to ensure fiscal capacity to support the reforms locally, which indicates a greater fiscal sustainability. Alternatively, county hospitals can be partly or fully privatized, thus gaining the right to set their own service prices. This can ensure the sustainability of their operations in the absence of higher government funding, but might also decrease their social functions. The provider reforms are a legacy of the Hu and Wen administration, but under Xi Jingping there seems to be a somewhat greater emphasis on privatization as an alternative to state provision.

While the extension of health insurance coverage was listed as a central part of the New Health Reform, the crucial stages of policy development and implementation in this area actually preceded it. The NRCMS already covered all rural jurisdictions by 2008, and its coverage slowly rose towards 100 percent of the rural population after 2009. The URBMI program was enacted in 2007 and based on the model of the NRCMS. It covers a much smaller share of the population and is supported by the higher administrative capacity of the line administration of the MoHRSS. While the UEBMI expenditures covered about 66 percent of urban per capita health costs by 2013, the NRCMS and the URBMI only covered about 28 and 10 percent of rural and urban health costs respectively.

In recent years, the role of the former MoH in health insurance has somewhat decreased. The MoHRSS and its line bureaucracy have officially gained jurisdiction over the NRCMS. Nevertheless, the CHFP and its line bureaucracy will most likely continue to play an important role in the administration of the NRCMS, most notably at the county level. Also, the role of insurance companies has been further strengthened in recent years. Among other things, the Urban Rural Residents Catastrophic Disease Insurance program enacted in 2012 called on the provinces to use a certain share of NRCMS and URBMI funds to purchase insurance for a defined set of illnesses from insurance companies. This was to provide complementary insurance for a specified set of diseases that was to cover at least 50 percent of the out-of-pocket payments remaining after regular reimbursement. The initiative was enacted a few months before the Eighteenth Party Congress by the Hu and Wen administration, which is an interesting parallel to the original NRCMS initiative. By 2015, 16 provinces had arguably rolled out the program to all of their NRCMS and URBMI recipients. More research is needed to assess the added value of insurance companies managing new programs, such as catastrophic disease insurance or cross-border insurance for migrant workers.

Public Opinion on Healthcare and the NRCMS

With regard to public opinion, there are indicators that the NRCMS has gained considerable ground. In the early years of its implementation, rural citizens were often reluctant to enroll, even though the program was backed by financial transfers. The politicized character of the voluntariness debate and the goal conflict between voluntariness and universal coverage have undermined the reliability of official statistics on the readiness to enroll (Müller 2016).

In the informal interviews in 2011, the villagers by and large expressed a positive attitude towards the NRCMS, even though some were disillusioned with the narrow coverage it provided. Anecdotal evidence from other studies also reflects this observation, which stands in contrast to the often more pessimistic assessments of the NRCMS managers and policy experts (Zhou et al. 2014). These perceptions are arguably influenced by the amount of information the actors have about the system and by their direct stakes in it.

The villagers see that the NRCMS reimburses a share of their ever-increasing healthcare expenditures, and perceive this as positive. Many of them may not be aware of the complexity of health sector regulations and the complex dynamics of local health governance, by which the introduction of the NRCMS also contributes to rising health costs. Administrators, on the other hand, are more sensitized with regard to the complexities and problems.

Nevertheless, a health insurance system like the NRCMS can be a double-edged sword in terms of public opinion. Recent survey research indicates that critical attitudes towards inequality are usually most prevalent among the urban and well-educated citizens, and among those living in worsening economic conditions (Duckett et al. 2013). Health insurance coverage in general reduces critical attitudes regarding social inequality in the field of healthcare in China; however, negative experiences with the healthcare system or health insurance increase critical attitudes. Since the beginning of the New Health Reform in 2009, intolerance against inequality has been increasing, and the population's satisfaction with the government's performance in healthcare has been decreasing (Flatoe 2015).[1]

Hospitalization rates have increased substantially since the introduction of the NRCMS in rural China, and the prevalence of chronic diseases is on the rise. Many hospitalizations are due to relatively inexpensive procedures, such as giving birth, and a substantial share of hospitalizations is not medically necessary. Nevertheless, the share of rural households exposed to catastrophic health expenditures continues to rise. In cases of serious illness and catastrophic expenditures, a badly performing NRCMS can potentially undermine the patients' trust in the government's performance. For inpatient services, bad performance includes *ex post* reimbursement, if it is not expected by the patients. The full amount of costs needs to be paid up front and becomes a financial burden temporarily, and patients potentially need to go into debt to afford an intervention. Bad performance furthermore includes delays in the reimbursement process: patients may have to wait for months and travel to the county seat repeatedly in order to claim their reimbursements. Last but not least, bad performance includes the sometimes vast gap between the promised nominal reimbursement rates and the effective reimbursement rates, if it is not properly communicated by the local government. Patients may, for example, expect to receive 50–70 percent of the overall costs, but actually only receive 20–40 percent. Catastrophic outpatient expenditures, which are often connected to chronic diseases, have long been a blind spot of the NRCMS that is only slowly improving. In the process of consolidation, experience-based knowledge about the NRCMS and its operations can be expected to spread in the rural areas and generate realistic expectations among the insured. Nevertheless, in the context of the crisis type of situation often connected to catastrophic inpatient expenditures, people may feel let down by the government.

Policy Options and the Prospects of Chinese Health Reforms

This study has strongly focused on the issues of political contestation and systemic interdependence, and their effects on the policy process connected to the NRCMS. Against the background of the rising dissatisfaction of the Chinese population with the government's performance in health policy, the case of the NRCMS provides two important lessons for the ongoing New Health Reform. First, China needs a coherent reform approach which, at the same time, enjoys a stable consensus at the central level. Second, reforms need to establish a stronger institutional fit between the multi-level structure of the state and the public finance system on the one hand, and the regulatory regime of the health sector on the other. These are necessary, but not sufficient preconditions for an effective overhaul of China's health system. In the past, the political system has often produced incoherent policy designs, especially with regard to financial issues, which add to the imbalances in the public finance system. This reinforces the misfits between systemically interdependent institutions, which are an important source of informal practices and induced demand. In one way or another, structural reforms are needed to cope with this situation. Otherwise, even comparatively well-designed and funded policies risk not achieving their goals on the systemic level due to the distorting effects of the institutional misfits. The key to success in health reforms therefore lies, at least partly, beyond the realm of health policy.

In the policy debates preceding the enactment of the New Health Reform, three larger types of reform models have been open for discussion: a formally marketized system largely inspired by US practices, a state-dominated system largely inspired by the British National Health Service, and a regulated market largely inspired by health systems on the European continent (Huang 2013). Below the unitary rhetoric that characterizes the self-description of the political system, decision-making is characterized by permanent contestation between opposing political camps and highly consensus-oriented modes of decision-making based on extensive negotiations. The scope of policy options that the political system can realistically reach a consensus on is therefore rather limited, and a regulated market option is the most likely compromise in the long run. Policy negotiations for the New Health Reform were arguably very difficult, and the initial documents left many of the details open to be defined in the course of the implementation. Certain patterns of central-level decision-making appear to be changing under the Xi administration, but it is too early to assess their impact on national policy-making in China. So far, the consensual mode of decision-making largely favors a regulated market model as the middle way.

The current institutional misfits between the multi-level state and health sector regulation are to some extent rooted in the mix of consensual decision-making and political contestation. They can largely be interpreted as an accumulation of decisions aiming at maintaining or extending the role of the state, which are, however, often not backed up with adequate financial commitment. Some bureaucratic actors seek to maintain or extend their competences, whereas others deny them the allocation of funding. The result is an overstretched local state, which fails to live up to its formal role. It resembles local healthcare providers in being characterized by a mismatch between assigned tasks and financial resources. Therein lies the cause of the problematic dynamics of steering and governance, which have been reconstructed in the deadlock constellation.

The conceptual lens of systemic interdependence illuminates those institutional misfits, which need to be resolved if the problems of governance and steering are to be overcome. The reforms need to increase the institutional fit between the now overstretched local state and the underfunded healthcare system. Given the dysfunctional public finance system (Wong 2009), the multi-level state in its present shape is arguably better suited for a market-oriented approach to healthcare provision. Driving forward formal privatization and marketization in the Chinese health sector is a relatively feasible task, as the state has already largely withdrawn from public service provision. Its seemingly omnipresent role often remains a formality. Transforming the function of the local state organs towards an effective regulatory model will require a good deal of capacity-building and a severing of the links between party and state organs on the one hand, and a large share of healthcare providers on the other hand. Marketization is one way of achieving a greater institutional fit, and it appears to be the path of least resistance from the given point of departure.

Establishing a regulated market model with a greater institutional fit is a double challenge, as it requires thorough reforms of both the health sector and the multi-level state apparatus. Currently, a large number of local governments are unable and/or lack the incentives to adequately support public healthcare providers, so that they can adhere to the pricing system and medical ethics without compromising economic sustainability. Apart from the comprehensive New Health Reform, a comprehensive public finance reform would be required to realign the patterns of resource distribution and the incentive structures that condition local governments' actions. This is a potentially difficult and contentious endeavor with unclear chances of success, given the prevalent modes of decision-making. A regulated market model would, however, require less painful reforms in the healthcare system to strengthen the institutional fit.

On the basis of a stronger coherence between public finances and health sector regulation, accountability mechanisms would need to be created that reinforce the financial commitment of local governments. Leading cadre evaluations are a strong system of accountability, but it can handle only a limited number of priorities and may be insufficient to guarantee such commitment in the long run. Further research should explore the degree to which Chinese legal reforms can enhance the enforcement of the entitlements of healthcare facilities, and inflict meaningful restraints on governmental spending behavior. Structural reforms of such a nature will not be achieved overnight, and the question remains whether the Chinese political system is capable of producing the political consensus needed to initiate and effectively implement them.

If China's health reforms are to substantially increase the institutional fit between the multi-level state and health sector regulation, a crucial difficulty lies in realigning the political visions communicated at the central level with the realities of governing healthcare at the grassroots levels. On the one hand, there is a desire to expand the role of the state and provide social security and public services to a population growing increasingly intolerant of inequalities in health policy. On the other hand, the record of health policy measures in the past decades provides many examples illustrating how the institutional misfits, and the "culture of non-compliance" (White and Smoke 2005: 14) they create, can neutralize such efforts.

It is not uncommon for developing countries' political ambitions not to match their administrative and financial capabilities. A market model would encounter opposition from bureaucratic stakeholders in the status quo, but overcoming some of this resistance may be an easier task than an overhaul of the public finance system. For the multi-level state to adjust to a market or regulated market model, and to develop the administrative capacities to effectively steer and monitor a more independent health sector, is already a formidable challenge. Irrespective of the model being pursued, the key to success in health reform lies in the concentration of scarce public and administrative resources where they are needed most, in the adaptation of the administrative and service structures to a coherent and viable functional and institutional blueprint, and in the creation of institutional fit between the multi-level state and the health sector. In the absence of such developments, China's New Health Reform runs the risk of mainly producing new variations of informal practices, and thus reproducing the old status quo.

Note

1   The Survey of Inequality and Distributive Justice cited in this paragraph was conducted by Marty Whyte and his colleagues at Harvard University in 2004 and 2009, and by the Fafo Research Foundation in Norway in 2014. It was implemented by the Research Center for Contemporary China (RCCC) at Peking University.

Bibliography

Bohnet, Armin *et al.* 2003, *Theoretische Grundlagen und praktische Gestaltungsmöglichkeiten eines Finanzausgleichssystems für die VR China (The Theoretical Foundations and Options for the Practical Design of a Fiscal Equalization System for the PRC)*, Frankfurt am Main: Peter Lang.

Brown, Philip H., Alan de Brauw and Yang Du 2009, Understanding Variation in the Design of China's New Co-operative Medical System, in: *China Quarterly*, 198, 304–329.

Brown, Philip H. and Thomas Huff 2011, Willingness to Pay in China's New Cooperative Medical System, in: *Contemporary Economic Policy*, 29, 1, 88–100.

Cai, Min *et al.* 2007, Nongmin jiating canhe ji canhe yiyuan fenxi (Rural Households' NRCMS Enrollment and Willingness to Enroll). In *Zhongguo xinxing nongcun hezuo yiliao jinzhan ji xiaoguo yanjiu (Research on the Progress and Outcomes of the NRCMS)*, ed. MoH, 41–46. Beijing: Zhongguo Xiehe Yike Daxue Chubanshe (China Harmony and Medicine University Press).

Cao, Pu 2009, 20 shiji 90 niandai liang ci "Chongjian" nongcun hezuo yiliao de changshi he xiaoguo ("Rebuilding" CMS Twice in the 1990s—Attempts and Results), in: *Dangshi Yanjiu yu Jiaoxue (Party History Research and Education)*, 4, 18–26.

Duckett, Jane 2011, Challenging the Economic Reform Paradigm, Policy and Politics in the Early 1980s' Collapse of the Rural Co-operative Medical System, in: *The China Quarterly*, 205, 80–95.

Duckett, Jane *et al.* 2013, Public Attitudes toward Health Care Provision in China: Is There Demand for Equality? Paper presented at the Association for Asian Studies Annual Meeting, San Diego, March 20–24, online: www.gla.ac.uk/media/media_292424_en.pdf (accessed June 29, 2016).

Fewsmith, Joseph 2001, The Political and Social Implications of China's Accession to the WTO, in: *The China Quarterly*, 167, 573–591.

Flatoe, Hedda 2015, *What Do Chinese People Think about Fairness and Government Performance in Health?* Presentation at the 5th Congress of Asian and the Pacific Studies, Paris.

Heilmann, Sebastian 2008, Policy Experimentation in China's Economic Rise, in: *Studies in Comparative International Development*, 43, 1, 1–26.

Huang, Jing 2000, *Factionalism in Chinese Communist Politics*, Cambridge: Cambridge University Press.

Huang, Yanzhong 2013, *Governing Health in Contemporary China*, New York: Routledge.

Klotzbücher, Sascha 2006, *Das ländliche Gesundheitswesen der VR China: Strukturen, Akteure, Dynamik (The Rural Health Sector of the People's Republic of China: Actors, Structures, Dynamic)*, Frankfurt: Peter Lang.

Klotzbücher, Sascha *et al.* 2010, What is New in the "New Rural Co-operative Medical System"? An Assessment in One Kazak County of the Xinjiang Uyghur Autonomous Region, in: *The China Quarterly*, 201, 38–57.

Klotzbücher, Sascha and Peter Laessig 2009, Transformative State Capacity in Post-Collective China: The Introduction of the New Rural Cooperative Medical Scheme in Two Counties of Western China, 2006–2008, in: *European Journal of East Asian Studies*, 8, 1, 61–89.

Li, Ling 2010, *Jiankang qiangguo (A Strong State in Health)*, Beijing: Beijing Daxue Chubanshe (Peking University Press).

Liu, Yuanli and Keqin Rao 2006, Providing Health Insurance in Rural China: From Research to Policy, in: *Journal of Health Politics, Policy and Law*, 31, 1, 71–92.

Müller, Armin 2016, Premium Collection and the Problem of Voluntary Enrollment in China's New Rural Cooperative Medical System (NRCMS), in: *Journal of Current Chinese Affairs*, 45, 1, 11–41.

Wang, Hongman, Danan Gu and Matthew E. Dupre 2008, Factors Associated with Enrollment, Satisfaction, and Sustainability of the New Cooperative Medical Scheme Program in Six Study Areas in Rural Beijing, in: *Health Policy*, 85, 1, 32–44.

Wang, Shaoguang 2009, Adapting by Learning, The Evolution of China's Rural Health Care Financing, in: *Modern China*, 35, 4, 370–404.

White, Roland and Paul Smoke 2005, East Asia Decentralizes. In *East Asia Decentralizes*, ed. World Bank, 1–23, Washington, DC: World Bank.

Wong, Christine 2009, Rebuilding Government for the 21st Century: Can China Incrementally Reform the Public Sector?, in: *The China Quarterly*, 200, 929–952.

Yi, Hongmei *et al.* 2009, Health Insurance and Catastrophic Illness: A Report on the New Cooperative Medical System in Rural China, in: *Health Economics*, 18, 119–127.

Yip, Winnie and William C. Hsiao 2009, Non-Evidence-Based Policy: How Effective is China's New Cooperative Medical Scheme in Reducing Medical Impoverishment? in: *Social Science and Medicine*, 68, 201–209.

Yip, Winnie and William Hsiao 2015, What Drove the Cycles of Chinese Health System Reforms? in: *Health Systems and Reform*, 1, 1, 52–61.

Zhou, Xu D., Lu Li and Therese Hesketh 2014, Health System Reform in Rural China: Voices of Healthworkers and Service-Users, in: *Social Science and Medicine*, 117, 134–141.

Zweig, David 2001, China's Stalled "Fifth Wave": Zhu Rongji's Reform Package of 1998–2000, in: *Asian Survey*, 41, 2, 231–247.

Index

For Product Safety Concerns and Information please contact our EU
representative GPSR@taylorandfrancis.com
Taylor & Francis Verlag GmbH, Kaufingerstraße 24, 80331 München, Germany

www.ingramcontent.com/pod-product-compliance
Ingram Content Group UK Ltd.
Pitfield, Milton Keynes, MK11 3LW, UK
UKHW020956180425
457613UK00019B/705